William Vans Murray
Federalist Diplomat

William Vans Murray Federalist Diplomat

*The Shaping
of Peace with France
1797-1801*

Peter P. Hill

SYRACUSE UNIVERSITY PRESS

To
My Father
George Alfred Hill

Foreword

Had William Vans Murray kept a diary during the first thirty-five years of his life, he would long since have been the subject of a full-dress biography. But if nothing at all were known of those years, Murray's part in negotiating an end to the Quasi-War with France would, of itself alone, justify this biographical study. Happily, enough details of the man's youth and early manhood are preserved in the record to give some idea of the circumstances which molded the mature politician and diplomat.

Today the name of William Vans Murray is a familiar footnote to scholars of the Federalist era. Chiefly, he is remembered as the Maryland congressman who, as American minister to the Netherlands, became an important channel of communication between Paris and Philadelphia at a time when France and the United States seemed destined to plunge from a state of quasi-war into full-scale hostilities. It was Murray who listened carefully, though skeptically, when Paris spoke of peace, and Murray who faithfully served John Adams' wish that the peace be kept. Though not a mover, Murray was uniquely an instrumentality. His willingness to receive the first peace overtures from the French capital and his insistence on setting honorable conditions for a negotiation gave President Adams the confidence, as well as the opportunity, to send still another diplomatic mission to France.

Murray was a member of that three-man mission and served it well, keeping alive the options of diplomacy while insisting that his colleagues remain flexible. His diary entries for this period cast a new and welcome light on the whole dynamic of peacemaking. Inevitably, factors of domestic politics intruded on foreign policy and national interests; and the personalities of the French and American negotiators occasionally threatened the outcome. Peace came officially with the signing of the Franco-American Convention in the early fall of 1800. Peace had its price, however, especially in personal terms. For John Adams it meant the disruption of the Federalist party on the eve of his hopes for re-election. For Murray it brought an abrupt end to a promising diplomatic career.

Throughout his public life Murray identified himself closely with John Adams and John Quincy Adams. While still a law student in London in the 1780s, Murray was a frequent visitor at the Adams home. From the elder Adams, then minister to London, he received encouragement to expand his political consciousness. There in London he wrote a series of essays on American government which was mildly imitative of Adams' own *Defence of the Constitutions of the United States.* With the younger Adams he struck up a lifelong friendship which, during his later missions to The Hague and Paris, manifested itself in a copious and lively correspondence.

A personal friend of the Adamses, Murray may also be classified politically as one of that elusive breed, an "Adams Federalist." It is well known that when Adams became President, Alexander Hamilton continued to exert a direct influence in Federalist party leadership. Adams himself did not possess, and was never able to muster, a cohesive political following. Ultimately, Hamilton's challenge spelled disaster for the unity of the Federalist party. But even before the final break between President and party leader, it was apparent that many Federalists had never been wholly committed to Hamilton's leadership. These non-Hamiltonian Federalists tended to be agrarian in origin and moderate in outlook. Like Adams, they were prone to take an independent line which, in Congress, was marked by a certain disregard for party discipline during roll calls. To some extent Murray exhibited this maverick quality. The record shows, for example, that during his congressional years Murray voted with his fellow Federalists only 79 percent of the time. And while this figure may seem to suggest a high degree of party regularity, it contrasts sharply with the better than 97 percent record of party fidelity evinced by such Federalist stalwarts as Fisher Ames, Chauncey Goodrich, William Hindman, Theodore Sedgwick, or Peleg Wadsworth. For Murray this occasional straying from the "party line" explains, in part, why he was never fully accepted into the hierarchy of the Federalist leadership.

Also like Adams, Murray continually sought to take what he called the "great middle ground," to establish a distinctively American position between the pro-French biases of the Jeffersonians and the pro-British leanings of the Hamiltonians. In both word and deed Murray dwelt on the urgency of his country's need for a clear-cut national identity. He also lived with the belief that only a period of peace would allow Americans to develop those economic and political institutions by which that identity could be achieved.

In sum, this biographical study deals with the politics and diplomacy of the Adams era. William Vans Murray's career is the vehicle of the narrative, sustaining it and carrying it forward, just as he himself sustained and carried forward the politics and diplomacy of John Adams. That narrative begins where Murray was born—on the Maryland Eastern Shore.

Acknowledgments

To Professor James Morton Smith of Cornell University I am profoundly indebted not only for his keen criticism of this study but also for the personal encouragement and wide-ranging assistance he has given me. No less am I indebted to Professor Howard M. Merriman of the George Washington University who, in the first instance, urged me to undertake this study of Murray's career and kept a critical and sympathetic eye on its development. I also thank Professors Wood Gray and Richard C. Haskett, both of The George Washington University, who contributed much to the form and structure which this work took when it was still a sprawling doctoral dissertation. For more recent assistance I wish to express my gratitude to Stephen G. Kurtz and the staff of the Institute of Early American History and Culture, whose detailed suggestions for changes have helped to shape this book in its final form. For the same type of assistance I also owe a debt of gratitude to the Syracuse University Press. I can repay these debts only by the disclaimer that nothing of error contained herein can be laid at their inkstands.

The University Committee on Research of The George Washington University made funds available for subsidizing part of the original printing costs. For this grant I am most grateful.

Of the many staff members at the Library of Congress, the National Archives, and such repositories as the Maryland and Massachusetts Historical Societies, I would name two whose services went beyond the call of duty: Daniel T. Goggin, who many years ago helped me to find my way around the General Records of the Department of State; and Leonard Rapport, also of the National Archives, who in recent times has fed me bits of Murrayana as he finds them.

My debt to my wife Barbara cannot be measured. As Abigail was to John Adams, if I may presume to borrow that gentleman's characteristic mode of address, my own wife has been, throughout it all, "my dearest friend."

Peter P. Hill

Washington, D.C.
Summer, 1970

Contents

1

The Early Years

THE CHOPTANK is a small river that runs wide into a broad estuary on the Eastern Shore of Chesapeake Bay. On the south bank of the estuary, about halfway between its mouth and upper reaches, stands the old Maryland town of Cambridge, once a bustling seaport that did business with the world in grain and tobacco.

Here on February 9, 1760, was born one of America's lesser known statesmen. His family and the name of Murray had been known and respected on the Maryland Eastern Shore for three generations. His parents drew on old family names, both of Scots origin, when they christened him William Vans. The boy's grandfather, William Murray, had come to Cambridge in 1715, having fought under the flag of the Stuart Pretender and having fled Scotland when the rebellion failed. Family tradition holds that William Murray landed in Maryland with only fifty guineas in his pocket. The family fortunes, however, were well established by the time of his death. The elder Murray prospered, not only as a physician but also as the owner of a grain mill, a speculator in real estate, and possessor of several merchant ships which traded to the West Indies. Of these various enterprises the most profitable was doubtless his purchase of land on the Choptank estuary where, as the century progressed, the port of Cambridge came into being. More acres were added to the family holdings in the second generation when Henry Murray, father of William Vans, made a judicious marriage with one Rebecca Orrick. Although land ownership was an important base of the family's prosperity, the Murrays were not tempted to become planters. They leaned, rather, toward commerce and the professions. Henry Murray, like his father, was the town physician; his brother James was one of the port's leading merchants. And by the time William Vans Murray opened his law practice at Cambridge in 1788 the family's landholdings had dwindled to insignificance.[1]

As an adult, William Vans Murray seldom alluded to the circumstances of his boyhood. The records show that he was one of five children, of whom a brother and two sisters were still living at the turn of the century. But apart from the admiration which he felt for his father and a certain protectiveness toward his sister Rebecca, his familial relationships remain obscure.[2]

If the boy mirrored the man who was to be, the young Murray was an active, intelligent, insatiably curious, and sensitive person whose energies were sapped from time to time by bad health. He was fortunate, perhaps, that his father was a physician, although in later life his all too ready familiarity with mortal symptoms made Murray something of a hypochondriac. Still, nothing suggests that the boy was bedridden, and one can imagine him exploring the wharves and warehouses of the port, keeping an eye on the tall ships as they came and went, and doubtless being kept from mischief by his Uncle James, who still carried on the import-export business begun by the grandfather. Surely, too, he roamed the woods around Cambridge where remnants of the Nanticoke tribe still lived, and at some point was inspired to undertake a study of local Indian customs which he proudly published at the age of twenty-one.[3]

The war for independence probably did not disrupt the quiet serenity of the Murray household. The family supported the cause, however, and only Murray's weak health explains why he himself saw no active military service. From this period the only surviving record is a colorful vignette of the victory celebration. When news arrived in the spring of 1783 that England had signed a peace treaty which explicitly recognized American independence, Murray told of joining his fellow townsmen in a joyous orgy of cannonades and heavy drinking. "What with bawling—

1. Information about the Murray family has been gathered largely from Elias Jones, *Revised History of Dorchester County, Maryland* (Baltimore: Read-Taylor Press, 1925); J. Winfield Henry, ed., *Letters and Papers of Governor John Henry* (Baltimore: G.W. King Printing Company, 1904), 109–12, hereinafter cited as *Letters of John Henry;* and from the Murray diaries in the Library of Congress, especially that entitled "Commonplace, 1800," 138–39, 152–152v. This collection is hereinafter referred to as WVM MSS, LC.

2. WVM to JQA, The Hague, April 30, 1799, in "Letters of William Vans Murray to John Quincy Adams, 1797–1803," *Annual Report of the American Historical Association for the Year 1912* (Washington, D.C., 1914), 546, hereinafter referred to as *AHA Report of 1912.*

3. WVM to Henry Maynadier, Cambridge, 1781, WVM MSS, Maryland Historical Society.

making speeches when licentiously drunk to the goddess of Liberty—and singing songs all night—I am extremely hoarse," he wrote.[4]

What formal schooling Murray received during his early years is not discoverable. He may have attended a nearby private academy which, along with its records, has long since been destroyed by fire. Or he may have been tutored privately, as was often the custom among the Southern gentry. Whatever the formalities of his education, Murray early cultivated the reading habit and with it a witty and perceptive prose style. His boyhood correspondence with a friend named Henry Maynadier, though few pieces are extant, revealed him to be both precociously literate and much given to gentle irony. That his education also included putting in social appearances at Annapolis is likewise well documented. Complaining to Maynadier that young ladies were "confoundedly" scarce in Cambridge, Murray crossed the Bay to the state capital often enough so that on one occasion he drew unfavorable comment on the "republican" cut of his clothing. His anonymous critic attacked in the press. Murray, in a fulsome rejoinder, defended his wearing apparel with such verbosity that he was able to tell Maynadier laughingly that his attacker had been unable to "make head or tail" of his "cursed hard words," and had fled the field.

Murray never explained why he chose the law as a profession. A sense of obligation to his family's position in the community may have partly determined the choice. Whatever his motives, the year the war ended, 1783, found him reading law under the tutelage of a man named Milligan, writing to Maynadier that he was "chained" to his studies quite as fully as he had heard that English law students were, in fact, chained to their benches in the Temple. Before another year had elapsed Murray himself was a Templar, completing his law studies in a manner traditional to sons of the Southern aristocracy.

Murray was twenty-four years old when he sailed for London. During the passage he suffered in about equal proportions from both seasickness and homesickness. Although a landfall would cure the former, the loneliness never quite left him. Qualities that were later rubbed smooth by maturity must have been etched rawly in the youth. From the few letters of this period, as from later reminiscences, one can sense the finely-drawn melancholy, the quick, good-humored sallies, the unsureness that

4. WVM to Henry Maynadier, Cambridge, April 2, 1783, *ibid.* Other letters to Maynadier also are in the Maryland Historical Society collection.

made him a mocker, and above all, the sensitivity that could catch the whisper of an innuendo or the merest shade of another's mood. Physically, there was little to distinguish him. He was slightly built and of medium height. To the casual observer, only the reddish hair and the dark, alert eyes would have attracted notice. It would be in the projection of his personality that Murray would have made his impact, in that candor and openness of manner which was later to make him as much at ease among farmers, ostlers, and innkeepers as he was among Bonapartes and fallen aristocrats. And yet, beneath the free-spoken exterior lay a core of uncompromised self, a quiet patrician dignity that never lost sight of place and station.

Murray later described his three years at the Temple as "almost waste time." "Not but what London did me good," he explained, "but it was a sort of fever life." [5] Gregarious by nature and made lonely by circumstance, he found more solace in his friends than in his books. Some he befriended were Americans who, like himself, were being educated by exile. Others were native Britons like Benjamin Vaughan, the unofficial but effective agent of Anglo-American conciliation during the recent peace-making in Paris. Also among his London friends Murray counted an unlikely pair of biographers, Johnson's James Boswell and Washington's "Parson" Mason Weems.[6] Most lasting, however, was the friendship he struck with John Quincy Adams. The two men could never agree as to where they had first met. Murray recalled that it was at the home of Consul Joshua Johnson, a Maryland merchant whose daughter, Louisa, later became Mrs. John Quincy Adams. Adams, however, insisted that he had first been introduced to Murray at Vaughan's house where, after discussing the Christian and Moslem concepts of paradise, they had gone to listen to a debate in Coach-maker's Hall. "But whenever our friendship began," Adams later told him, "I hope and trust that no spot on this earth is destined to witness its end." [7] No spot ever did.

In dismissing his London years as "almost waste time," Murray uncharacteristically forgot that London was the scene of his successful courtship. When and where he met Charlotte Hughens, or what her family background was, he never disclosed. So little, in fact, is known of

5. To JQA, The Hague, February 3, 1801, *AHA Report of 1912*, 679.

6. Entry of August 7, 1795, in Murray's "Commonplace," 162–63, WVM MSS, Princeton University Library (hereinafter PUL); also entries of January 6, 1801, and February 1, 1801, in a manuscript diary which has been photocopied by the Library of Congress, hereinafter referred to as Photostat Diary, WVM MSS, LC.

7. WVM to JQA, The Hague, January 20 and February 3, 1801, *AHA Report of 1912*, 676, 679–80; JQA to WVM, Berlin, January 27, 1801, Microfilm reel (MR) 134, Adams MSS.

the delicate young woman who became Charlotte Murray that doubt remains even as to the correct spelling of her maiden name. The courtship matured slowly, however, and not until two years after he had left England did he arrange for Charlotte to follow him. They were married in Cambridge in 1789, at a time when his law practice had been established and his election to the state legislature confirmed. Although Charlotte bore him no children, or perhaps because of this lack, Murray displayed only the most devoted affection for the woman whom he invariably addressed as "my beloved Charlotte." After a decade of married life he wrote that their years together had brought "uninterrupted goodness on her part," so much so that he could look to the "shiftings of the future with complacency." [8]

Also from the wasteland of his London exile came Murray's first effort to express some of his ideas about the workings of American politics. In 1787 he published in London a booklet of six tightly written essays entitled *Political Sketches*. The avowed purpose of the *Sketches* was to correct certain misconceptions which French publicists, notably Mably and Montesquieu, had fallen into from a too theoretical study of American local governments. The publication also served, however, to bring Murray more closely to the attention of John Adams, the American minister at whose London home Murray was a frequent visitor and whose patronage he undoubtedly sought. In his title-page dedication to Adams, Murray made it quite clear that the minister had been his source of inspiration. The allusion was unmistakable. Adams himself was contemporaneously writing his own objections to another Frenchman's critique of American state governments (that of Robert Turgot) and would soon publish them in his *Defence of the Constitutions of the United States*. In all likelihood the elder Adams did indeed take a friendly interest in Murray's *Sketches* and doubtless gave him explicit encouragement. Murray's later remark that "from 1785 I have been, as it were, his pupil, always . . . enjoying a great freedom of argumentation with him on hundreds of questions," would seem to leave no doubt as to the closeness of this early relationship.[9]

The fascination of the *Sketches* lies in what they tell us about their author. They speak a mixture of political ideas as yet unsorted by the "mine" and "thine" of two-party politics. Echoes of Jeffersonian ideology

8. Entry of August 20, 1800, Photostat Diary, 141, WVM MSS, LC.
9. To JQA, April 16, 1799, *AHA Report of 1912*, 539. For speculation that Murray's essays may have had some influence on members to the federal convention, see DeConde's "William Vans Murray's *Political Sketches*: A Defense of the American Experiment," *Mississippi Valley Historical Review*, XLI, No. 4 (March 1955), 623–40.

mingle amiably with social and political attitudes later classifiable as Hamiltonian. On the side of Jefferson, Murray makes an awkward paraphrase of the "inalienable rights" doctrine and follows it with elaborate praise for the pure and correct democracy which the American states are practicing. Like Jefferson, Murray sets forth the safeguards necessary to democracy: that all men must be entitled to equal rights, and no quarter given to the pretensions of an aristocracy. It is in his doubts and misgivings that Murray becomes less Jeffersonian. He is not certain, for example, where democracy will find its leaders. He alludes vaguely to a leadership provided by "an ascendency of superior merit" which, though it sounds like Jefferson's "aristocracy of talent," is found in a Hamiltonian context. Like Hamilton, he expects government to protect the citizen's accumulation of property. He fails to foresee, however, that wealthy men may seek political office purposely to exploit that governmental function. The wealthy man, he concludes, may lay claim to political leadership, but unless that man also possesses "superior merit" his incumbency will be short. Rule by the rich may not be desirable, but is not so dangerous to democracy as would be the claims of a hereditary aristocracy.[10]

More visibly Hamiltonian is Murray's early abhorrence of political disorder. While Jefferson is contemporaneously suspecting that "the tree of liberty must be refreshed from time to time with the blood of patriots and tyrants," Murray is writing that people who govern themselves need never be turbulent. Nor even divided into factions. "Faction," he writes naively, is unknown to America because "the American democracies are governments of laws and not of parties." [11] John Adams must have smiled when he read this innocent passage. And yet, it was typical of later Federalists to cherish the notion that elected officials should be exempt from partisan attack; and John Adams himself would one day sign into law a Sedition Act designed to limit such attacks. In the view of these later Federalists, persons who disapproved the conduct of an elected official should take their complaint quietly to the polls. To carp at an incumbent officeholder was to shake the public trust, perhaps endanger the fabric of government. Like so many of his later Federalist contemporaries, the young Murray seemed to envision elections without parties and changes of policy without the articulation of political alternatives.[12]

10. See William Vans Murray, *Political Sketches* (London: C. Dilly in the Poultry, 1787), especially pages 12–14, 44–47, 56, and 59–63.
11. *Ibid.*, 13–14. The famous quotation from Jefferson comes from his letter to William Short, Paris, November 13, 1797, in *Works of Thomas Jefferson*, ed. Paul Leicester Ford (New York and London: G.P. Putnam's Sons, 1904), V, 362, hereinafter referred to as Jefferson's *Writings*.
12. James Morton Smith deals with this anomaly in his "The Sedition Law, Free Speech, and the American Political Process," *The William and Mary*

Murray's faith in democracy, as revealed in the *Sketches,* seemed to put him surefootedly on the road to a meeting with Jefferson. The road forked abruptly, however, when the French Revolution disclosed to Murray how violently destructive the democratic process might become. No other event in his early life so profoundly affected his political outlook as did the revolution in France. The more so because Murray shared with his generation the excited hope that France would carry forward the republican drama begun in 1776. When the French Revolution began, shortly after he had returned to Cambridge, Murray instinctively hailed it as "that most illustrious event . . . a crisis the most auspicious to the Freedom of man that ever happened." [13] Two years later he was not sure that "reason" had triumphed. The difficulty of making what is "into what ought to be," he wrote, was that rational men could seldom agree as to what changes in governmental forms "reason" might dictate.[14] As one excess followed another, Murray retreated unhappily to the conservative end of the political spectrum. "I love philosophy," he wrote, "and of course dislike the philosophers. These fellows cover with the name [of philosophy] every crime & hurtful opinion. . . . a robber thus puts on the coat of the very man he has plundered and murdered.[15] Between the outworn monarchies and France's riotous republicanism, he sadly concluded that mankind's hope for political advance had been "thrown back for an age." "A suspicion of ourselves will now restrain men." [16]

Murray's studies at the Inner Temple were cut short in the spring of 1787 by the news that his father had died. Years later he recalled to John Quincy Adams how starkly the news had come from a "cold-hearted" Cambridge lawyer who had written with a "Dutch mourning messenger's nonchalance" that his father had died "on such a day." For six weeks Murray lay in a state of collapse at the home of some friends named Harrison in Epping Forest. Out of this bereavement, however, came the more matured Murray who later confided to Adams that "from that time I have kept my heart and mind exceedingly on the poise; and cultivated in all—except Love! that tranquillity of mind of which I once spoke to you." [17]

An autumn passage from England brought Murray home to Cambridge in late 1787 where he began a law practice that was almost im-

Quarterly, IX, 3d Series (October 1952), 499–500. Murray later elaborates it in his entry of October 12, 1795, "Commonplace," 282–90, PUL.

13. Undated entry of 1789, *ibid.,* 107–108.
14. Entry of July 12, 1791, *ibid.,* 258.
15. Entry of August 29, 1800, Photostat Diary, 101, LC.
16. Entry of August 25, 1798, "Commonplace," 348, PUL.
17. To JQA, The Hague, February 9, 1801, *AHA Report of 1912,* 681; see also entries of August 7 and September 5, 1795, "Commonplace," 162–63, 264, PUL.

mediately interrupted by politics. Within a year of his return he was elected to the Maryland House of Delegates; here he served three terms from 1788 through 1790. How Murray arranged his debut to public office is not recorded. The publication of his *Sketches* undoubtedly helped to make him known. It is also possible that his uncle, James Murray, used his considerable influence to get him launched. At all events, Murray began a lively career in the state legislature that was to lead him three years later into the national arena.

2

The Federalist Emerges

MURRAY, like many another United States Representative, reached the nation's capital by first proving his mettle in his own state legislature. The lesser office gave him a well-heeded opportunity to assure his constituents that he would serve their local interests and to call to their attention the fact that he stood for certain principles of public policy.

At Annapolis Murray fought one of his first political battles to guarantee that, by law, at least one of the state's two United States Senators would always be an Eastern Shore man. A law was enacted that so specified. Next session he began a labor of even greater local import that was to last for two years before it succeeded. This was to bring out of committee a bill to allow persons whose land was threatened by flooding to cut drainage ditches through adjacent private property. This measure had strong support from Eastern Shore farmers whose low-lying lands were often inundated for lack of drainage facilities.[1]

Murray's attention to such local problems spelled good politics, but the record also shows that the young delegate from Dorchester County was developing important attitudes toward more general public policy: public spending, for example. Characteristic of later congressional Federalists, Murray gave vigorous support to state appropriations for courthouses, roadbeds, postal services, and for raising the salaries of public officials. Also characteristic was the fine line he drew between necessary expenditure and what he believed to be extravagance. He balked, for example, when Maryland was asked to contribute $72,000 toward the construction of public buildings in the new national capital. Although his opposition may have been partly grounded on a regional

1. Maryland General Assembly, House of Delegates, *Votes and Proceedings of the House of Delegates of the State of Maryland,* sessions of December 5, 1788; November 21, 23, and December 7, 1789, and November 8 and 13, 1790, hereinafter cited as *Votes and Proceedings;* also *Maryland Gazette,* December 10, 1789.

concern that the Bay would profit less than the Potomac from such an appropriation, his stated reason was the undue expense.[2]

Less readily classified but certainly smacking of a states' rights sensitivity was the position Murray took toward a piece of legislation aimed at requiring Charles Carroll of Carrollton to give up either his seat in the Maryland Senate or his seat in the United States Senate. Murray strongly objected to Carroll's dual officeholding, and took the lead in forcing the "Signer" to make his choice. As he explained to Charlotte, he felt that "the independence of the State Govt. depends on this—& I think the Liberties of America will one day rest on the independent unbiassed [sic] functions of the State Legislatures." Two years after he introduced the bill it passed both houses. Carroll, it appears, was not particularly eager to retain both seats, and gladly opted for Annapolis rather than Philadelphia.[3]

Quakers and blacks, whose problems have challenged the enlightened goodwill of nearly every generation, made no exception to Murray's. The delegate from Dorchester County voted repeatedly, though in vain, to relieve Quaker members of the House from the constitutional requirement that they take office under oath. Quaker scruple against oathtaking remained unsatisfied. He also voted for—and the House ultimately enacted—a bill to permit Maryland slaveowners to manumit their chattels by last will and testament.[4] On the slavery question as a whole, Murray's attitude was uncertain. Several years later, when the House was debating a naturalization bill, he and Henry Latimer of Delaware were the only slave-state congressmen to favor a motion that would require prospective citizens to renounce their slave property. The motion lost. While this incident suggests that Murray was definitely opposed to slavery, it is not conclusive. The antislavery motion had come from the Federalist side in the wake of a Republican motion to require would-be citizens to renounce foreign titles of nobility. The Federalists knew that if they opposed the titles amendment, they would be accused of wanting to introduce an aristocracy. The call for a divesting of slave property as well, therefore, was a partisan counter-thrust. Murray voted in favor of both forms of divestiture, but the sincerity of his commitment against

2. WVM to his wife, Annapolis, November 27, 1790, Misc. Letters, WVM MSS, LC; *Votes and Proceedings*, November 17, 1790; see also correspondence of Englehard Yeiser, Maryland Historical Society.

3. Letter to Charlotte Murray cited above. For Carroll's reaction see his letter to John Henry, Annapolis, December 3, 1793, *Letters of John Henry*, 45.

4. On the oath question see *Votes and Proceedings*, December 21, 1789; December 3, 1790. For the votes on manumission, the sessions of December 21, 1788, and November 19, 1790.

slavery was obviously clouded by partisan considerations.[5] He may well have been one of those curious Southern gentry, not altogether atypical, who professed to hate slavery but owned slaves. We know, for example, that an elderly Negro servant named Will was part of the Murray household, but whether "old Will" was slave or free cannot be determined.

In 1790, presumably having acquitted himself in the state legislature to the satisfaction of his constituents, Murray was ready to take the next step upward in his political career. Now lost to view is the nominating procedure, if any, by which he was selected to run for the Second Congress. Nor did any local newspaper publish either the names of candidates or the voting results which might have shown whether his first election to the House of Representatives was seriously contested. Two years later, however, when Murray ran for reelection, the *Maryland Gazette* of November 1, 1792, reported that he won 1,515 votes against six opponents whose total was only 102. The heavy margin suggests that his earlier election was easily accomplished and says much for the "safeness" of his district.

When Murray took his seat in the House on November 9, 1791, the political scene was momentarily quiet. The noisy opposition evoked by Hamilton's financial measures had faded to a faint echo. Madison and the Virginia Republicans, having battled in vain against funding, assumption, excise, and Bank, were now waiting to cry havoc at the consequences. Beneath the surface tranquility, however, the machinery of Republican opposition was being assembled to wrest the political initiative from Alexander Hamilton.

Thrust into the polarizing situation of Madisonians versus Hamiltonians, Murray seemed at first to settle somewhere in the middle. Efforts have been made to identify the factional leanings of various congressmen through their responses to roll-call votes. For example, the historian Noble Cunningham identified as "Madisonians" some seventeen members who voted with Madison on twenty-three or more roll calls in this first session of the Second Congress.[6] By this test Murray, who spoke up on Madison's side no fewer than twenty-one times, would seem to be very nearly a Republican. One finds, however, that eight of Murray's "Madisonian" votes were cast on a House reapportionment bill wherein his motives, as revealed in debate, were clearly sectional, not factional.

---

5. U.S. Congress, *The Debates and Proceedings in the Congress of the United States* (Washington, D.C.: Gales and Seaton, 1834–1856), IV, 1030–58, hereinafter referred to as *Annals*.

6. Noble Cunningham, *Jeffersonian Republicans: The Formation of Party Organization, 1789–1801* (Chapel Hill, N.C.: University of North Carolina Press, 1957), 21, 267–71.

These eight votes, therefore, must be subtracted from the coincidental total. To find the embryonic Federalist one must look to the issues themselves. When, for example, the federal bounty to cod fishermen came up for renewal, Murray uttered none of the constitutional objections raised by the Madison faction. And when the House combined the cod bounty with a tariff schedule that gave price protection to Northern manufactures, Middle States' iron, and Southern hemp and cotton, Murray commended the omnibus bill for its very "nationality." [7]

As the session wore on Murray identified himself still more closely with the Federalists. He defended Hamilton's right to suggest to the House how it might raise additional revenue. He supported the administration's sword and olive branch policy toward the whiskey-makers of Western Pennsylvania (a bill which authorized Washington to use the militia but also reduced the tax on certain types of stills).[8] And then, as if to show his independence, he joined the Virginia Republican William B. Giles in support of a bill to deny the franking privilege to members of Congress. The two men carried the day against a largely Federalist minority that would have liked to keep the privilege of free postage.[9]

As the House crowded toward adjournment Murray moved decisively toward the Federalist camp. The issue was Hamilton's stewardship of the Treasury Department. Giles brought forward nine resolutions charging Hamilton with overstepping his authority. Although the Secretary did not lack for defenders it was Murray and William L. Smith, a South Carolina Federalist, who argued Hamilton's innocence most cogently. Yet the two men differed so markedly in their defense strategies that one can only conclude that Murray was completely out of touch with the Federalist leadership. Smith, who bore Hamilton's personal imprimatur, moved to dismiss the first two resolutions without debate. Murray objected: the first two resolutions, though restrictive of Treasury operations, contained general principles that warranted debate. What Murray intended was to defeat the restrictions with positively worded assertions of the Secretary's discretionary powers. Should the House establish that Hamilton possessed such powers, there would be no need to examine the more explicit charges contained in the remaining resolutions. The Federalist leadership, however, preferred to vindicate the

7. *Annals*, III, 363–65, 396–401, 571–72.

8. *Ibid.*, 575–76, 588–89. For evidence that the whiskey-makers were not placated see Leland Baldwin, *Whiskey Rebels* (Pittsburgh: University of Pittsburgh Press, 1939), 69–72.

9. *Annals*, III, 296–98.

Secretary by resoundingly defeating the resolutions *a seriatum.* The strategy succeeded handsomely: all of the Giles resolutions were beaten down by large majorities.[10] Although Murray must have applauded the outcome, the incident revealed plainly that he did not belong to, or at least was not heeded by, the inner council of administration strategists. This was to be Murray's fate throughout his congressional career: to be *with* the Federalist leadership but not *of* it.

Hardly had Congress adjourned when Philadelphia was assailed by reports that France and England had gone to war. First came the news on March 27, 1793, that Louis XVI had been executed. Three days later the *National Gazette* published the rumor that France had declared war on Britain, Russia, and the Netherlands. Except that Russia was not yet involved, the rest of the rumor was true. The implications were ominous. The United States was now to be torn between the claims of its chief trade partner and its only ally.

Like thoughtful Americans everywhere, Murray watched uneasily as Washington and his cabinet began to grapple with the first serious threat to American neutrality. Rapidly the threat took on formidable dimensions. On April 22, the day Washington officially declared his government's neutrality, news arrived in the capital that Edmond Genêt, emissary of the French Republic, had landed at Charleston. Worse, reports followed shortly that Genêt was commissioning American privateers to make war on British commerce. Even if Genêt's unneutral activities did not bring war between the United States and England, they foretold that the course of American neutrality would not be smooth.

The Franco-American treaties of 1778, with the interpretation of which Murray was later to become so intimately concerned, required three things of the United States whenever France was at war with a third power. These requirements were contained in Articles 17 and 22 of the commercial treaty and in Article 11 of the alliance treaty. All three had a bearing on the ability of the United States to perform its duties as a neutral.[11]

10. *Ibid.,* 903–904, 955–63. Irving Brant finds the Federalist majority guilty of prolonging the debate in order to magnify the impact of their victory. See Irving Brant, *James Madison, Father of the Constitution, 1787–1800* (New York: The Bobbs-Merrill Company, Inc., 1950), 369.

11. Neutral duties rather than neutral rights were the major issue throughout the controversy that followed. This is an important distinction, first made by Charles Marion Thomas in *American Neutrality in 1793: A Study in Cabinet Government* (New York: Columbia University Press, 1931), 67.

Under Article 17, French warships and their prizes might enter and depart freely the ports of the United States, the like privilege to be withheld from France's enemies. Article 22 forbade the use of American ports for either the fitting out of warships hostile to France or, somewhat superfluously, the sale of French vessels, captured by an enemy of France. From those last two "negatives" Genêt perversely derived two "positives," by construing what was forbidden to Britain to be permitted to France. That is, because Article 22 clearly prohibited the fitting out of British warships in American ports, he presumed for France a positive right to fit out French-commissioned privateers. Similarly, the clause which forbade British prize-masters to sell vessels captured from France was read in such a way as to permit French consuls in the United States to act as prize-court judges with powers to condemn and dispose. Article 11 of the other treaty was, potentially, the most perilous of all. Herein was the insidious "guarantee," by which the two Revolutionary War allies had agreed to guarantee each other's possessions in the New World. Fortunately, the administration was spared the embarrassment of refusing a French request to join in the active defense of the French West Indies. Genêt did not invoke the "guarantee" for the most obvious of self-interested reasons: the United States was more valuable to France as a neutral carrier than she would have been as a co-belligerent.[12]

The reality of the crisis lay, therefore, in Genêt's misuse of American ports. On June 5, Jefferson informed him that if privateers sailing from Charleston brought back prizes they would not be allowed to reenter an American port.[13] Murray, it chanced, figured personally in one of the earliest attempts to prevent just this type of illicit reentry. In early May, before the policy was formulated, a "Genêt privateer" put into Cambridge, bringing with it a captured British merchantman. Murray and Port Collector Jeremiah Banning promptly went on board the privateer, the *Eagle,* where they confirmed their suspicion that her captain had accepted a French commission at Charleston. On Murray's advice, Banning took the *Eagle* into custody while Murray notified a federal judge in Baltimore of what they had done. Because the incident had political overtones, Murray also wrote an explanatory letter to James

---

12. A good general account of this controversy is contained in Alexander De-Conde, *Entangling Alliance: Politics & Diplomacy under George Washington* (Durham, N.C.: Duke University Press, 1958), 204–205; also Thomas, *American Neutrality,* 126–28. Relevant treaty articles may be found in Hunter Miller, *Treaties and Other International Acts of the United States of America* (Washington; D.C.: Government Printing Office, 1931), II, 16–17, 19–20, 39–40, hereinafter referred to as Miller, *Treaties.*

13. Jefferson's *Writings,* VI, 362–64.

McHenry.[14] McHenry was both a friend and a political colleague, but more important, he was also one of Maryland's most prominent Federalist leaders, a man who could give support to Murray if the incident had disturbing political consequences. As it turned out, Murray needed no buffering. He had reasoned correctly that the vessel's American port of origin coupled with its reentry to an American port violated the law of nations. After considerable shifting on this point the administration concurred. Thus Murray anticipated by nearly a month the policy that was ultimately laid down for such cases.[15]

Genêt's impact on factional politics can scarcely be overdrawn. Pro-French Republicans feared that the Frenchman might so severely offend the American populace as to alienate it from the cause of republicanism itself. Moreover, once the administration had set its face against Genêt, the Republican faction faced the ghastly possibility of having to choose between a French minister whose activities might lead to an unwanted war with England and their own President whose neutrality policy smacked of being pro-British.[16] Federalists felt even more strongly. Not only would an English war destroy commerce with their best customer, but they also felt it not unlikely that France intended to uproot the whole structure of the American government, revolutionize it along French lines, and thus hurl the country back into the chaos of the Confederation.[17] Though fears on both sides were undoubtedly exaggerated, the French government's decision to recall Genêt was met with a bipartisan sigh of relief.

Among articulate Federalists, Murray was one of the few who saw clearly through the smoke and flames of that year's partisan denuncia-

14. Written from Cambridge, May 8, 1793; see Bernard Christian Steiner, *The Life and Correspondence of James McHenry, Secretary of War under Washington and Adams* (Cleveland: The Burrows Brothers Company, 1907), 142n.

15. See Jefferson's "Opinion on 'The Little Sarah,'" May 16, 1793, Jefferson's *Writings*, VII, 332–35; also Jefferson to British Minister George Hammond, June 5, 1793, *ibid.*, 367–69; and Jefferson to Genêt, August 7, 1793, *American State Papers, Foreign Relations* (Washington, D.C.: Gales and Seaton, 1832–1834), I, 167; same to Hammond, September 5, 1793, *ibid.*, 174, hereinafter referred to as *ASP FR.*

16. For Madison's worried letters to party leaders see Gaillard Hunt, ed., *The Writings of James Madison* (New York: G.P. Putnam's Sons, 1900–1910), VI, 135–98, *passim,* hereinafter cited as Madison's *Writings.* See also Jefferson's *Writings,* VII, 449, 480, 508.

17. Compare Murray's entry of July 28, 1795, "Commonplace," PUL, with letters written to Hamilton by John Jay, Henry Lee, John Steele, Stephen Higginson, and Rufus King in John Church Hamilton, ed., *The Works of Alexander Hamilton* (New York: John F. Trow, 1850–1851), V, 552–53, 561–73, hereinafter referred to as Hamilton, *Works.*

tions. Looking back on the Genêt crisis he later observed that "the great American ground was overlooked—with eyes & hearts bent on foreign scenes, the domestic ground was not seen." The great American ground to which he alluded was the need for peace—peace not merely because war would have wrecked commerce and dried up the Treasury's tariff receipts, nor because war would have hurt or succored Britain or France, but peace for the sake of securing American nationhood. "Who can comprehend the value of Peace for at least 15 years to this young country," he exclaimed. Given time, the country would "expand into that gigantic size which will in 20 years outgrow the Insolence of Britain & render the U.S. too formidable to be trifled with—The best way to escape injury is to grow strong." [18]

Most Federalist leaders saw only the short-range benefits of staying out of war. Many associated peace with their own private prosperity. Only a few saw how that day's neutrality related to their country's future strength. Washington saw it when he observed that "if this country is preserved in tranquillity twenty years longer, it may bid defiance in a just cause, to any power whatever." [19] Alexander Hamilton also held similar views, but only the few, Murray among them, saw clearly the long-range national advantage of keeping a strict neutrality.

18. Entry of July 28, 1795, "Commonplace," 131–33, PUL.

19. To Gouverneur Morris, Philadelphia, December 22, 1795, in John Clement Fitzpatrick, ed., *The Writings of George Washington* (Washington, D.C.: Government Printing Office, 1931–1940), XXXIV, 401, hereinafter referred to as Fitzpatrick, *Writings*. For Hamilton's views see "Pacificus, No. VII," July 20, 1793, Hamilton, *Works*, V, 484. Merchant Federalists like George Cabot, Stephen Higginson, and Christopher Gore tended to associate peace with their overseas business ventures. See their letters to Rufus King in Charles R. King, ed., *The Life and Correspondence of Rufus King* (New York: G.P. Putnam's Sons, 1894–1900), I, 448, 463, 489, 493–94, hereinafter referred to as King, *Correspondence*.

3

Defender of Jay's Treaty

THE WARS of revolutionary France from 1792 to 1801 constitute, as an epoch, the only major European conflict from which Americans have remained aloof. During nearly a decade of foreign policy crises the Federalist Presidents, Washington and Adams, held firmly to a course of neutrality which they pursued, in part, by negotiating a series of treaties, first with England, then with Spain, and finally with France. For William Vans Murray, the last three years of his congressional career brought him to close quarters with some of these foreign policy crises and prepared him for his own role in solving the last and most difficult, that of keeping the peace with France.

Hard on the heels of the Genêt crisis came a series of British provocations. When Murray returned to Philadelphia in late 1793, the weight of British injury was steadily increasing. Congress had barely convened when Washington sent it a batch of documents that spoke of gathering frustrations on the Northwest frontier and on the high seas. In the Northwest, not only had the British persisted in retaining the military outposts which they had promised to evacuate in 1783, but also, by latest report, British agents had prevented U.S. commissioners from making peace with the Northwestern tribes. Washington's message also exposed how helpless the administration had been in dealing with British maritime policy. By Privy Council order of June 8, 1793, British naval commanders had been ordered to seize all vessels carrying corn, flour, or meal to French ports; the British government would either purchase such cargoes or release the vessels under bond, stipulating their destination as a non-enemy port. Official correspondence made it clear that American protests would not budge London from this sort of interference in Franco-American commerce.[1]

1. *American State Papers, Indian Affairs,* I, 188; *ASP FR,* I, 141–246 *passim.* For a good general account of the crisis see Samuel Flagg Bemis, *Jay's Treaty: A*

Washington's dispirited report evoked from House Republicans a strong impulse to retaliate. On January 3, 1794, James Madison introduced seven resolutions proposing to punish with higher tariff and tonnage duties the ships and cargoes of any nation which had no commercial treaty with the United States. It was Britain, of course, that fell most prominently into this category. Federalists, for their part, feared that such marked retaliation would merely intensify the crisis. On January 13, William L. Smith lengthily denounced the Madison resolutions. Thoroughly briefed by Hamilton, Smith poured forth volley after volley of import, export, and navigational statistics. From these he concluded that all mercantile nations were selfish; that France had been no more generous than England in her trade policies; and that concessions were not to be won by calculated reprisal. Most important, Madison's resolutions were more likely to bring war than they were to bring salutary changes in Britain's maritime policy.[2] Parenthetically, it should be noted that the Federalist position contained an element of political risk. Madison's resolutions have been seen as a Republican flirtation with the mercantile, and thus far predominantly Federalist East. The idea of placing strictures against British trade was not altogether unpopular among merchant Federalists. Despite the risk, however, the Federalist leadership was determined to fight off the anti-British measures.[3]

That Murray was now in substantial accord with a well-defined Federalist position became clear on January 28 when he rose to reiterate the arguments offered by earlier Federalist speakers. He warned, in particular, that if Madison's proposed tariff and tonnage increases depressed the volume of incoming trade, the national government's consequent loss of revenue would endanger the public credit. The warning was distinctively Hamiltonian.[4]

On February 3, Madison's first resolution passed by a slim margin of five votes. Two days later House Republicans won a temporary postponement, a delay which they expected would give them time to

---

Study in Commerce and Diplomacy (New York: The Macmillan Company, 1924), 186.

2. *Annals*, IV, 196, 199–201. For evidence that Hamilton drafted Smith's speech see *The Works of Alexander Hamilton*, Henry Cabot Lodge, ed. (New York: G.P. Putnam's Sons, 1904), IV, 205–24, hereinafter referred to as Hamilton, *Works*.

3. Cf. Cunningham, *Jeffersonian Republicans*, 70; Joseph Charles, *Origins of the American Party System: Three Essays* (Williamsburg, Va.: Institute of Early American History and Culture, 1956), 98–100.

4. *Annals*, IV, 364–65.

sample constituent opinion.[5] During the hiatus, however, the crisis intensified. From the frontier came word that the Canadian Governor General had delivered an inflammatory speech to an Indian conclave on February 10, and from the Caribbean came news that scores of American vessels had been seized in pursuance of a new British order-in-council of November 6. Although by January London had retreated from its wholesale seizures of U.S. shipping, the recantation was drowned out by the report that nearly 250 American vessels had been taken, 150 of them already condemned. Even Madison had to admit that his resolutions fell somewhat short of meeting the exigencies of the new situation.[6]

Urged on by angry voices from the merchant sector, the Federalist party leadership responded adroitly. Madison's resolutions were now dismissed as being too little and too late. Hamilton's party now sounded the call for an outright preparedness program. Specifically, Hamilton urged Washington to ask Congress to increase the size of the Army and to authorize an embargo.[7] By mid-March the Army and embargo proposals had become the Federalist answer to the Madison resolutions. During debate, Murray joined Fisher Ames of Massachusetts in expounding the wisdom of the Federalist alternative. Ames called it "trifling" to talk of regulating a commerce which Britain had "nearly annihilated." More positive measures of defense were clearly in order. Murray was equally scornful. Why, he asked, had Republican members not called for sterner measures in the face of more grievous injuries? Now that war seemed likely, the Madison resolution did not go far enough. "How is an additional ten per cent on importation capable of opposing the torrent of British injustice?" An embargo, on the other hand, would register "a temporary enmity for temporary evil." [8]

In crisis the House was Federalist, and the days that followed bore witness to the skill of Hamilton's leadership. During the last two weeks of March bills dealing with arsenals, harbor defense, and naval armaments were topped off with a House-approved thirty-day embargo and the call for an army of 80,000 militia. Republicans, meanwhile, began to outbid the administration forces. More explicitly retaliatory proposals came from Jonathan Dayton and Abraham Clark, both of New Jersey.

---

5. Madison to Jefferson, Philadelphia, March 2, 1794, *Letters and Other Writings of James Madison* (J.B. Lippincott and Company, 1865), II, 2.

6. Bemis, *Jay's Treaty,* Chs. VIII and IX.

7. Hamilton, *Works,* IV, 506–508.

8. *Annals,* IV, 521–22, 511.

Dayton moved that the federal government block the payment of private debts to British merchants until American shipowners had been indemnified. Clark proposed an outright suspension of Anglo-American commerce until such time as London had not only indemnified shipping losses but also withdrawn her troops from the Northwest posts.[9]

Federalists who had seen a threat to peace in Madison's measures now looked with dismay on the provocative import of the Dayton and Clark resolutions. If the Republican extremists were to be outflanked, the Federalist leadership would have to recover the initiative. Although Washington remained undecided for a month, party Federalists pressed strongly for what promised to be the last best hope for peace: the dispatch of a special diplomatic mission to London. Hamilton's urging, John Jay's tentative acceptance of such a mission, but most of all the specter of extremism in the House, finally moved Washington to send Jay's name to the Senate.[10]

As the Jay mission got under way Murray broke with the party majority long enough to show that he had not been completely mesmerized by the crisis. On April 18 when the House amended the Clark nonintercourse bill so as to delay its taking effect until November 1, Murray voted for it. As a delayed solution he could support it. Thus, for the first time that spring a roll-call vote found Murray in company with Madison, Giles, and other Republican luminaries.[11] His motives can only be conjectured. His willingness to keep nonintercourse alive as a later instrument of policy, however, certainly put him at odds with his own party's leaderhip. Meanwhile, the Clark bill died in the Senate.

Murray's penchant for independent action was most clearly revealed that spring when he put his hand to devising a legislative solution to the problem of impressment. Not only did this British practice touch on his country's national respectability, but it also appeared to Murray to be an abuse that legislation might remedy. What he proposed was that Congress "enable American seamen to obtain and carry evidence of citizenship for the purpose of protecting them from impressment into foreign

9. *Ibid.*, 523–30, 535, 557, 561.

10. For the alarmed reactions of House Federalists, as well as for the speeches of Theodore Sedgwick (Mass.) and Elias Boudinot (N.J.) which foreshadowed the Jay mission, see *Annals*, IV, 566–94 *passim*. The plan to send a mission took definite shape when Federalist Senators King, Ellsworth, Cabot, and Strong, agreed to broach it to the President. See "R. King's Manuscript," March 10, 1794, King, *Correspondence*, I, 517–18.

11. *Annals*, IV, 600–601.

service." This was the first proposal of its kind to suggest that Congress should exercise a protective role. Up to 1794 it was the executive branch which, by a variety of consular "protections" and sustained diplomatic effort, had sought to ward off British press gangs. By 1794 it was also apparent, although Murray refrained from criticism, that the executive arm had failed to give either system or certainty to the remedies that had been tried.[12]

Now, as he reached for leadership on this issue, Murray must have known that the party workhorses on both sides would pull against him. The Republican position, earlier set forth by Jefferson, was that American seamen should not be provided with certificates of citizenship lest the loss of such papers expose them to the certainty of being impressed.[13] In his own party, he could expect opposition both from those to whom it was an article of faith not to interfere with the executive's conduct of foreign affairs, and from those who felt that Jay's mission might be jeopardized by a congressional enactment on a delicate issue.[14]

Murray argued cogently against all these objections. His bill would *permit* American seamen to certify their citizenship, but would not *require* it. Thus, lack of a certificate could not be held as evidence of alien nationality. As for the primacy of the executive branch in handling such matters, he reminded the House that Congress had entered the field of impressment in 1790 when it reimbursed American Consul Nathaniel Cutting for expenses incurred in securing the release of seamen during the Nootka Sound crisis. Congress thus had a precedent for action. Providing certificates was only part of the solution, he admitted, for Britain, on her part, would have to be brought to recognize the validity of American naturalization. But even without this recognition, Murray argued, certificates would provide far more protection to American seamen than they now possessed. His bill proposed to make seamen's "protections" both a personal document and an integral part of a ship's

12. *Ibid.*, 703–704. An act of 1792 had failed to specify the role of consuls in handling impressment cases. See Richard Peters, ed., *The Public Statutes at Large of the United States of America* (Boston: Little, Brown and Company, 1856), I, 254–57. For consular efforts in this regard see James Fulton Zimmerman, *Impressment of American Seamen* (New York: Published Doctoral Dissertation, Columbia University, 1925), 32–35. Diplomatic efforts to solve the problem are touched on in Samuel F. Bemis, "London Mission of Thomas Pinckney," *American Historical Review*, XXVIII (January 1923), 228–29.

13. Jefferson to Thomas Pinckney, June 11, 1792, *ASP FR*, III, 574; Pinckney to Jefferson, March 13, 1793, *ibid.*, 581–82.

14. See Federalist speeches in the House, *Annals*, IV, 155–688 *passim*, in which administration supporters had laid down the dictum that Congress should not legislate foreign policy, an argument used repeatedly in opposition to the Madison, Dayton, and Clark resolutions.

papers. As such, he foresaw that they would carry as much authority as "clearance or other papers certified under the authority of the United States." His colleagues should give the bill a chance to prove its usefulness, he concluded, for if the House refused to act now it would find other reasons for not acting later.[15]

Because Jay's instructions were secret, Murray probably did not know that impressment had been omitted from them. Although Jay and Lord Grenville did discuss the problem, they failed to reach a satisfactory accord.[16]

Murray's bill, meanwhile, was attacked by Republicans and not supported by Federalists. William L. Smith of South Carolina probably voiced the sentiments of the administration when he said the bill was "at present impracticable." One can assume that "at present" meant pending the outcome of the Jay mission. Not again until 1796 did the House debate a legislative remedy for impressment comparable to Murray's of 1794. At that later time Murray fulfilled his own prophecy. He found reasons to vote against it.[17]

In charting an independent course on the impressment issue Murray had been a leader without followers, even among his friends. His failure suggests once again the uncertainty of his relationship with Federalist leaders. That he went ahead anyway is amenable to two explanations. Either he did not know that his party would not support him, in which case his lack of knowledge would place him outside the inner circle of Hamiltonians—or he knew that he had no support and did not care, in which case he presumed by taking a leadership which, in the Federalist view, properly belonged to the administration. Either way, it could still be said of Murray that in 1794 he was *with* the Hamiltonians but not *of* them. In political philosophy and on the roll calls he was found more often with the "friends of government" than with Madison's Republicans, but his place in the Federalist leadership remained uncertain.

Murray and his colleagues had scarcely left Philadelphia in 1794 when the long-smouldering unrest in Pennsylvania burst into insurrection. Once again, as during the Genêt crisis, Washington and his cabinet were left to cope without the benefit of congressional advice. They did so summarily—and with troops. From a political standpoint, the sup-

15. *Ibid.*, 703–704, 710, 727, 772–74.
16. For an explanation of this failure see Bemis, *Jay's Treaty*, 358–59.
17. See Smith's speech, *Annals*, IV, 774; and for Murray's opposition to the impressment bill of 1796, *ibid.*, VI, 104–105, 802–20.

posed complicity of the so-called Democratic-Republican societies made them a welcome target of Federalist oratory during the fall elections. By equating the societies with Republicans as a whole, campaigning Federalists were able to stretch the guilt by association to their political opponents. This equation won seats for the administration, but the charge of either societal or Republican complicity was never proved.[18]

Once the rebels were dispersed, Murray was chiefly concerned with defending the good name of the President. Washington's prestige was, for the moment, badly shaken. Not only had he used armed force against the rebels, but the Chief Executive had flatly diagnosed the origin of the trouble as those "certain self-created societies." [19] When the Republicans said this was not so, Murray hastened to join the chorus of presidential loyalists who insisted that Washington could not be mistaken. The issue was joined in the House when the Federalists demanded that the President's censure of the Democratic-Republican societies be loudly echoed in that body's official "reply" to the President's message. In a week-long debate the Republicans denied that the House had any right to censure groups of private citizens; Federalists warned that unless the House repeated Washington's charges, doubt would be cast on Washington's probity.

Throughout the debate Murray had to ward off Republican efforts to characterize his own views as extreme. At one point Giles accused him of wanting to impose censorship on the Republican press. A confused scene took place in which Murray denied the charge, apologized for being unclear, and insisted that his exact words be read into the record. In fact, his views were generally more moderate than those of the Federalist leadership. He would vote to censure the societies, he said, because he agreed with Washington that they deserved it. As a "source of error" they had cost the American people more than 1.2 million dollars. In the same breath, however, he strongly opposed any suggestion that the societies be legislated against.[20] Long debated and much amended, the House "reply" settled for the phrase "combinations of men" rather than "self-created societies" to account for the origins of the rebellion. Thus the Federalists and Washington were dealt a tactical defeat. In Murray's case, the incident illustrated how unreservedly he gave his loyalty to

18. The tenuous connection between the societies and the rebels has been amply dealt with. See most notably Eugene Perry Link, *Democratic-Republican Societies, 1790–1800* (Octagon Books, Inc., 1965), 145–49.

19. James D. Richardson, *A Compilation of the Messages and Papers of the Presidents, 1789–1897* (Washington, D.C.: Government Printing Office, 1896), I, 163.

20. *Annals,* IV, 906–16.

Washington, even though it meant wading into political quagmires a
more cautious politician would have avoided.

The brief furor over the "self-created societies" was like a distant clap
of thunder in the lowering afternoon of the Third Congress. In the stillness that followed the censure debate all eyes were fixed on the diplomatic horizon. Men who knew their politics foresaw a squall in Philadelphia—perhaps even a declaration of war—should Jay return without
a treaty or with a treaty that was unacceptable.[21] By the end of January
the capital knew that Jay had concluded negotiations; the terms of his
treaty were not known, however, nor would a draft reach the administration before Congress adjourned. The pervasive expectancy bred in Congress a tendency to dawdle over trivia, and in Murray a querulous
anxiety. He was irritated that Edmund Randolph had leaked some of
Jay's early dispatches to the press. He fretted, too, over the cabinet
resignations of Hamilton and Knox.[22] Perhaps the clearest sign of
Murray's uneasiness was that he took issue with a piece of legislation
designed to lengthen the time of naturalization. Though the House bill
would stretch the residency requirement from two to five years, Murray
spoke out in favor of an even longer period. He compared immigrants to
ideological disease-carriers who should be quarantined from political life
until at least ten years of exposure to American ideals had effected the
necessary cure. Otherwise, they might "contaminate the purity and
simplicity of the American character." [23] This allusion to "purity and
simplicity" later returned to haunt Murray in 1799 when William Cobbett, the "Peter Porcupine" of High Federalism, recalled the phrase to
show that Murray was too "sentimental" to be entrusted with the French
peace negotiations.[24] In 1794, however, Murray was more rash than
sentimental when, ignoring the leadership of both parties, he urged a
residency requirement of ten years. His motion failed, and the bill that
passed required only five. Not again until 1798 would a congressional
majority, inflamed by the XYZ Affair, see fit to lengthen the requirement. On that occasion, they extended it to fourteen years.[25]

Murray's petulance over the number of years of residence to be required of aliens applying for American citizenship tended to obscure

21. See, for example, Hamilton's "Camillus, No. II," or Madison's letter to
Monroe, Philadelphia, December 4, 1794, Madison's *Writings*, IV, 222.
22. WVM to James McHenry, Philadelphia, December 16, 1794, McHenry
MSS, LC; same to same, Philadelphia, January 1, 1795, Steiner, *McHenry*, 156–58.
23. *Annals*, IV, 1023.
24. *Porcupine's Gazette*, February 20, 1799.
25. John Chester Miller, *Crisis in Freedom: the Alien and Sedition Acts*
(Boston: Little, Brown and Co., 1951), 41–50.

what really concerned him: a clearer definition of American nationality. He quite agreed that any American who swore allegiance to a foreign power should lose his American citizenship. Conversely, however, he argued that any American could, if he wished, cast off his American citizenship. He saw the anomaly of denying to Americans a right which was presumed to belong to those aliens who forsook their own national allegiances to become Americans. Curiously, Murray's belief that any American might renounce his citizenship was a belief fully shared by nearly the entire leadership of the Republican faction.[26] Federalists, on the other hand tended to deny that such a right existed—partly out of reverence for British common law, partly because contemporary expatriation cases involved Americans defecting to the French cause.[27] That Murray should appear on the "Republican" side, however, was merely incidental to his exasperation with British practice. He was deeply irritated by the British policy of naturalizing persons from other countries while refusing to recognize the right of native-born Britons to become Americans. He perceived how insoluble the impressment controversy would remain so long as London adhered to the doctrine of indefeasible allegiance.[28]

The troubled Third Congress ended on March 3, 1795. Four days later a copy of Jay's treaty arrived at the capital.

The train of events which ignited one of the greatest foreign policy debates in American history began on June 8, 1795, when Washington submitted Jay's treaty to a special closed-door session of the Senate. Less than two weeks later that chamber gave its consent by the narrowest of two-thirds margins. The Senate's acceptance of the treaty, however, marked only the beginning of controversy. A House appropriation of funds would be needed to implement the treaty, and because that chamber would not be heard from for nearly a year, the fate of the treaty remained eminently debatable. Nothing about Jay's transaction would be certain until the House had acted.

Federalists, generally, came to defend Jay's treaty as an honorable

26. Compare Murray's speech of December 30, 1794 (*Annals,* IV, 1028–29), with Jefferson's letter to Monroe, Monticello, May 20, 1782 (Jefferson's *Writings,* III, 301), or the speeches of William B. Giles, John Nicholas, and Albert Gallatin in the House on June 21, 1797, *Annals of the 5th Congress, 1st Sess.,* 350, 354.

27. I-Mien Tsiang, *The Question of Expatriation in America Prior to 1907* (Baltimore: Johns Hopkins Press, 1942), 34–37.

28. *Annals,* IV, 1029, 703–704.

and very real alternative to war. Republicans tended to denounce it as
a calculated submission to British maritime policy. Murray himself had
grave doubts about it, and they were doubts that were finally resolved
less because of party loyalty than by a careful weighing of what he
believed to be the national interest. While few Federalists claimed perfection for the treaty, even fewer examined their doubts as meticulously
as Murray in the summer and fall of 1795.[29]

What might be considered the official Federalist position on Jay's
treaty was a series of thirty-eight essays written by Hamilton and Rufus
King over the pseudonym "Camillus." Although the authors pictured the
treaty as being virtually flawless, a good many misgivings were privately
expressed within the administration.[30] Nearly all Murray's assessments
of the treaty approximated those rendered by the authors of "Camillus."
The dates of Murray's entries in his "Commonplace," however, show
that he arrived at his conclusions independently, some weeks before the
"Camillus" series began to appear in the *New York Argus*.

As Murray saw it, Jay's treaty was flawed but defensible. He sympathized with shipowners who would object to the slowness of settling
maritime claims by arbitration, but he reasoned that claims cases would
probably fare better before an arbitral commission than they would in
British courts of law. Jay's failure to incorporate the neutral principle of
"free ships, free goods" was, in Murray's views, a sinless omission. While
technically this meant that Britain might seize French-owned cargoes
from American bottoms while France was still treaty-bound not to
seize British-owned cargoes, the fact was that France herself was violating this principle. Harder to swallow was Jay's inability to get compensation for American slaveowners whose Negroes had been "liberated" by
British officers during the Revolutionary War. These "Negro claims"
were hard to forego, Murray thought, but they were "not worth a *war*."
Jay's worst mistake, he believed, had been to stipulate naval stores as
contraband. Of all the soft spots in the treaty, the contraband article
was "the most vulnerable." Sails, cordage, and ship timber were important items of American export. To sacrifice them to the name of contra-

29. Murray's commentaries on the treaty are scattered randomly from pages
118 to 239 in his "Commonplace" (PUL); some entries are dated, as early as
July 19 and as late as August 27, but others are not dated.

30. See, for example, Washington to Randolph, Mount Vernon, July 22, 1795,
Fitzpatrick, *Writings*, XXXIV, 244; Hamilton to Wolcott, New York, August 10,
1795, in George Gibbs, *Memoirs of the Administrations of Washington and John
Adams, Edited from the Papers of Oliver Wolcott, Secretary of the Treasury* (New
York: William Van Norden, 1846), I, 223–24, hereinafter referred to as Gibbs,
Wolcott.

band—when neither the "usage of nations" nor "our treaties with others" required it—was Jay's sorriest error. Moreover, to accommodate Britain with a more inclusive designation of contraband than had been agreed to with France was at least untimely, if not also unneutral.[31]

Though chilled by doubts Murray nonetheless warmly embraced the treaty's promise of peace. Not for a moment did he doubt that war had been avoided. And for that saving grace Jay's diplomacy could be forgiven its failure to win any spectacular concession. Peace would assure that continuance of Anglo-American trade which, by producing revenue from tariff and tonnage duties, kept the national government solvent. Perhaps no other peril so dominated Federalist thinking as that a war with England would starve the nation's revenues and thus threaten the very existence of the federal government.[32]

The Senate's consent to Jay's treaty now focused Murray's attention on George Washington. The President must decide whether or not to ratify. "He must risk the most alarming discontent if he *ratifies*," wrote Murray, "& War if he does not . . . unless he goes on negotiating to gain time." Though determined to accept whatever decision the President might make, Murray continued to toy with the idea of prolonging the negotiation. So, too, did Washington, although Murray did not know it. The unpopularity of the treaty, coupled with news that Britain was again seizing American cargoes, had given Washington reason enough to postpone final action.[33]

What disturbed Murray most was the prospect that the President, caught in a cross fire of partisan volleying, might cease to be the great symbol of national unity. Writing an article for the press, he urged confidence in the man who had led Americans through so many difficulties. Only Washington, he wrote, had the experience and the wisdom to make the right decision on the treaty. Could anyone doubt that he would fail to make it? [34]

When, in August, Washington decided to ratify, Murray at first hoped that further controversy had been averted. He sensed a "silent acquiescence," doubtless ascribable to "the fruit of reflection over sudden passion," or more likely due to the "prodigious & virtuous ascendency of the President over the good men of this country." [35] This optimistic as-

31. "Commonplace" entries of July 19, 1795, 118; July 28, 1795, 128; and undated August entries, 187–89, 201, 226–27, 233–34.
32. Entries of August 1, 3, and 4, 1795, *ibid.*, 137–44.
33. Entry of August 5, 1795, *ibid.*, 152–54.
34. Manuscript article signed "Union" (place of publication is unknown). See entry of early August, 1795, "Commonplace," 174–83.
35. Entry of September 8, 1795, *ibid.*, 247.

sessment turned to despair when the other horn of the dilemma poked itself into the foreground in the fall of 1795. The Republicans were still to be heard from, and their plans to block the treaty in the House were clearly visible well before Congress was due to reconvene. It would be a "warm" session, Murray knew, and the issue would be one of vital constitutional significance: Did the President and Senate have the authority to treat on matters which fell within the province of Congress as a whole? He foresaw how the Republicans would answer this question. They would contend that although the power to regulate commerce was vested in both Houses, the commercial regulation inherent in Jay's treaty had been made binding by President and Senate alone. On that constitutional ground they would object.[36]

Washington's announced intention not to submit Jay's treaty to the House until after Britain had ratified it had the effect of postponing the great debate for several months. Not until March 1, 1796, did the House officially receive a copy of the treaty. While the treaty issue lay fallow, Federalists were able to attack their opponents across the unlikely terrain of the Randolph Affair. The Secretary of State's supposed complicity in a French plot was suggested by captured dispatches written by the French minister, Joseph Fauchet, just before his departure. The captured documents hinted that Randolph had counseled Fauchet how best to buy public support in this country for French policy aims. When confronted with Washington's brusque demand for an explanation, Randolph resigned. Republicans unwisely injected a partisan note into the affair by their precipitate, almost reflex assertions of Randolph's innocence.[37] Because Randolph could not be defended without also questioning Washington's ready acceptance of his resignation, the Federalists made capital in the press by balancing innuendoes of Randolph's supposed wrongdoing against the dead weight of presidential infallibility. Throughout, Murray could not quite bring himself to believe that Randolph had become a French agent. Doubtless the Secretary had been involved in "some sort of corruption," but more important to Murray was the likelihood that the publication of Fauchet's dispatches would so far discredit France as to melt any lingering opposition to Jay's treaty. In this Murray was too sanguine. The image he hoped France would project—that of would-be buyer of American influence—did not come through clearly. With an

36. Entries of November 1 and December, 1795, *ibid.*, 317, 366–71.
37. Stephen G. Kurtz, *The Presidency of John Adams: The Collapse of Federalism, 1795–1800* (University of Pennsylvania Press, 1957), 33; Charles, *Origins*, 108; Irving Brant, "Edmund Randolph, Not Guilty!" *William and Mary Quarterly*, 3rd Series, VII (April 1950), 197–98.

assist from Fauchet, Randolph published a *Vindication* which left open to partisan interpretation both his own and France's roles. If the cause of Jay's treaty was served at all, it was perhaps by the multiplicity of targets that were now available to Republican snipers. To the extent that treaty foes were disconcerted as to whether to attack the treaty, or the Constitution, or the slanders against Randolph, Federalist supporters of the treaty could find some consolation.[38]

Debate on the treaty continued to be postponed as long as Washington refused to be hurried into submitting it formally. During the lull Murray found another kind of excitement in helping to expose the efforts of two land speculators to bargain away from Congress some twenty million acres of the Michigan peninsula. The two men, Robert Randall and Charles Whitney, proposed to give or to sell (this was the crucial point) more than half of the acreage to those congressmen whose votes could be won over. The Randall-Whitney scheme came to light when Smith of South Carolina, believing that Randall was trying to bribe him, confided in Murray, who in turn sought the counsel of Maryland Senator John Henry. The three men decided to alert the President. Meanwhile, Murray carefully arranged an interview with Randall from which he concluded that certain members of Congress were about to become, perhaps unwittingly, parties to a land swindle. Out of further conferences, including one with Washington himself, came the decision that Murray and Smith should announce their suspicions to the House before any member could compromise himself by introducing Randall's proposal. This they did on December 28; whereupon the House ordered Randall and Whitney arrested. Randall was found guilty of contempt, but amid so many charges that the House was improperly preempting the functions of a court that he was shortly released. During the House "trial" Murray's insistence that Randall had offered to give him land (not sell it) met with conflicting stories from other members, some of whom made the longest speeches of their careers on this occasion. In the end it appeared that Randall had broached not one scheme by many, tailoring his approach to individual congressmen.[39]

Once quit of the Randall affair, the House slipped back into a torpor that was to last through January and most of February. Then, on February 29, Washington officially proclaimed Jay's treaty. With a pre-

38. A point made by Stephen Kurtz, *Presidency of John Adams*, 35–36. For Murray's speculations see entry of December 20, 1795, "Commonplace," 376, PUL; also Murray's letters to James McHenry, one of December 24, 1795, the other undated, both in Steiner, *McHenry*, 159–60n.

39. Details may be found in the *Annals*, V, 166–229 *passim;* and in Murray's "Commonplace" entries of December 23–25, PUL.

mature sigh of relief Murray wrote in his "Commonplace" that the treaty was "now the *Law of the Land*." In point of fact, it was the skirmishing that had ended. The real battle was about to begin.

Edward Livingston fired the opening round on March 2 when he moved that Washington be asked to send to the House all of the correspondence relating to Jay's mission. When Livingston's resolution came off the table, Federalists took the tack of questioning its purpose. If the treaty were unconstitutional, why was it necessary to examine Jay's correspondence? Why not simply lay the treaty itself against the Constitution and see if a disparity existed? Perhaps, they suggested, Livingston intended to lay the basis for an impeachment proceeding. If so, did he propose to impeach John Jay, or perhaps the President himself? Uncowed by this mention of the "great name," Livingston replied calmly that an impeachment might be forthcoming, but that his main purpose was simply to shed light on the conduct of Mr. Jay.[40]

Though Federalists pretended to be mystified, they well knew that the Republicans had only one purpose: to defeat the treaty. Murray, for example, learned from Giles of Virginia that the Livingston motion would be followed by others which, if adopted, would kill the treaty for lack of enabling legislation.[41]

Had Murray been a passive follower of Alexander Hamilton he would have kept silent until after Hamilton's accredited spokesman, William L. Smith, had set forth the Federalist position. This Smith did on March 8, lengthily denouncing the idea of House obstruction to treaty-making. Because Smith often served as Hamilton's mouthpiece, and doubtless did so on this occasion, historians have accorded the South Carolinian a certain primacy in stating the constitutional position of the Federalists.[42] It was William Vans Murray, however, who on March 7 anticipated Smith and, firmly grasping the constitutional nettle, sketched in most of the major arguments that Smith presented at greater length the next day. It was "dangerous doctrine," said Murray, for the House to think it had a right "to adjudge, to adopt, or to reject treaties." Were impeachment or inquiry into fraud among Livingston's purposes, his resolution might be properly entertained; but such were not its announced intentions. As it stood, Jay's treaty was now supreme law, and because the House had no power to question a constitutionally permitted

---

40. *Annals*, V, 400–401, 427–28.
41. Entry of March 7, 1796, "Commonplace," n.p., PUL.
42. Brant, *Madison, 1787–1800*, 434; see also Volume VII of Douglas Southall Freeman's *George Washington*, written by Alexander Carroll and Mary Wells Ashworth (New York: Charles Scribner's Sons, 1957), 351, hereinafter cited as Carroll and Ashworth, *Washington*.

action of President and Senate, the tendency of the Livingston resolution to raise that question made the resolution itself unconstitutional. The House might ask for Jay's correspondence if such documents bore on the treaty's constitutionality, but the resolution had not alleged this possibility. At this point Murray was forced to break off when the Speaker ruled that his allusions to the powers of the Senate were out of order.[43]

Out of the welter of arguments that followed emerged this fundamental question: Did the House have a right to inquire into a treaty which touched on legislative matters ordinarily requiring the consent of both chambers? Albert Gallatin thought so. So did Madison, Giles, Nicholas, and lesser Republicans, many of whom felt that the President and Senate had encroached on the prerogatives of the lower house as set forth in Article I, Section 8, of the Constitution. Federalists chose instead to construe strictly Article II, Section 2, which described the treaty-making power of President and two-thirds of the Senate. Throughout debate each side stood, figuratively, on separate clauses of the Constitution and refused to touch hands across the gap.

The day before Livingston's motion came to a vote Murray gave such a powerful summing-up that Gallatin himself felt compelled to answer. The historians Carroll and Ashworth have used the word "skilful" to describe Murray's March 23 speech. It was more than that: it was climactic. Except for final rebuttals by Chauncey Goodrich and Robert Goodloe Harper, the duel between Murray and Gallatin was an oratorical reckoning which plucked the essentials from more than two weeks of debate.[44] Murray once more questioned the motives of those who wanted to see Jay's correspondence. Those documents could serve no purpose, he said, because the House could not question either the validity or binding effect of a treaty. Were the House to assert an "active agency" in treaty-making, the Constitution would be violated. Moreover, the Constitution recognized an important reality in conferring the treaty-making power on President and Senate alone. Nearly every treaty that could be imagined would touch somewhere on powers reserved to Congress as a whole. But if the President and Senate were compelled to defer to the House for its approval of every clause of every treaty, the foreign policy of the United States would be undone. Perhaps members misunderstood the nature of diplomacy. Treaties were usually reciprocal, assuring benefits to one's nationals in return for benefits granted. Congress might bestow such favors through legislation, but it could not secure reciprocal

43. *Annals*, V, 429–30.
44. See Carroll and Ashworth, *Washington*, 352. For the speeches alluded to, see *Annals*, V, 684–703, 726–46, 717–25, 747–59.

favors unless it entered the field of diplomacy. Treaties by their very nature must be negotiated, cannot be legislated. In the present case, Murray continued, Jay's treaty was a contract as constitutionally perfect and therefore as fully binding on the House as if that body had given its express consent. The House might choose its own mode or method of implementing the treaty, but there its authority ended. Only if a particular clause were believed to be unconstitutional or fraudulent, he repeated, could the House rightfully ask for the correspondence which had attended the negotiation. No irregularity of either sort, he believed, had been imputed by Livingston's resolution.[45]

The power of Murray's argument was evidenced by the extent to which Gallatin, next day, directed much of his own summation for the Republican side to an explicit rebuttal of Murray's points. Treaties, he admitted, were designated as "supreme law," but so too were "laws of the United States." Between treaties and laws the latter might be considered to take precedence because of House involvement in their enactment. For Murray to contend that the House was bound to execute the will of President and Senate was to violate the "sacred principle that the people could not be bound without the consent of their immediate representatives." And for Murray to say that the House was confined solely to the *mode* of implementing treaties was an absurdity that would become startlingly apparent should some future treaty require the raising of an army and thus leave the House powerless except to determine how the army was to be paid for. Moreover, Murray's point that the House might legitimately inquire into fraud or unconstitutionality seemed to Gallatin to place Murray among the sponsors of the resolution who, after all, hoped from Jay's papers to determine the constitutional validity of the treaty. Finally, Gallatin assailed Murray's use of the word "making" as applied to "treaty-making." The House, he said, did not presume to "make" treaties in a constitutional sense, but it had every right to decide whether or not its consent was needed to make a treaty valid. Although the House could claim no active voice in diplomatic negotiation, it was entitled to consent to treaties which appeared to infringe on its legislative prerogative.[46]

Only more convincing than Gallatin's rebuttal was the size of the majority in favor of the Livingston resolution. That same day, by a resounding 62 to 37 votes, the House gave persuasive proof that in calling for Jay's correspondence it believed itself competent to examine the treaty-making process. From George Washington, however, came a blunt

45. *Ibid.*, 686, 689–94, 696–98.
46. *Ibid.*, 738–45.

refusal to transmit any of the papers which the House had asked for. To soften the blow, Washington also sent along for House action the very popular Spanish treaty recently negotiated by Thomas Pinckney. This offering was eagerly seized by House Federalists who, in a "strategy of desperation," [47] devised an omnibus bill calling for simultaneous approval of the British and Spanish treaties. The strategy was not only desperate but also unsuccessful. With the defeat of the omnibus proposal, debate began on the all-important resolution to carry Jay's treaty into effect.

Although Murray did not speak at all to this resolution, he was the first person to designate the central issue of the debate that followed. On a motion to reduce the size of the Army, which he opposed, Murray remarked that troops would be needed to man the Northwest posts or, if the treaty failed, to fight the war with England that would probably ensue. So inflammatory was this prognostication that Gallatin himself rose to denounce it. How sensitive a nerve Murray had touched was evident thereafter in the frequency with which speakers returned to the question: would or would not a negative action by the House result in war with England? [48] Unerringly, Murray had put his finger on the two factors that ultimately eroded Republican opposition in a flood of pro-treaty petitions: fear of war with Britain, and the West's desire for the Northwest's posts. As the tide of petitions rose in late April, opposition to the treaty began to wash away. Gallatin, after presenting both pro-treaty and then antitreaty memorials, announced reluctantly on April 26 that he would vote for treaty appropriations when the question was called. Hope for the treaty leaped higher when Edward Livingston, the original leader of the radicals, presented a petition which could be interpreted as favoring the treaty.[49] For the Federalist "faithful" and perhaps for a few waverers, the last doubt was dispelled when the Massachusetts Federalist, Fisher Ames, lived up to his high reputation as an orator with a stirring appeal for treaty approval. Ames's "most beautiful speech," as Murray termed it, may not have changed any votes, but if John Adams was to be believed, it left "not a dry eye" in the House.[50]

47. Phrase used by Carroll and Ashworth, *Washington,* VII, 361.
48. *Annals,* V, 908–10, 986–1153 *passim.*
49. For historians' agreement on the effectiveness of the petition campaign, see Kurtz, *Presidency of John Adams,* 55–72; DeConde, *Entangling Alliance,* 137–40; or Brant, *Madison,* 438–39.
50. Cf. Murray's entry of April 28, 1796, "Commonplace," PUL; John Adams to his wife, Philadelphia, April 30, 1796, Charles Francis Adams, ed., *Letters of John Adams Addressed to His Wife* (C.C. Little and J. Brown, 1841), II, 227, hereinafter cited as *Letters to His Wife.*

Had Ames's speech changed but one vote, however, it was worth the hearing. The treaty passed its crucial test on April 29, but only by the Speaker's tie-breaking vote (49–49) on the motion to make the necessary appropriation.

The victory was nearly undone the next day when the Bay State Republican, Henry Dearborn, sought to smear the motion with a preamble that would have described the treaty as being "highly objectionable" and possibly "injurious to the United States." [51] Murray was instantly on his feet. Foes of the treaty, he warned, would vote against execution in any event; so, too, might friends of the treaty if this slur were attached. What little authority the national government possessed, he said, would be further diminished by Dearborn's amendment. At this juncture the House must not only

> carry the Treaty into effect, but . . . carry it into effect with good faith. The object was not merely the posts—it was conciliation of the differences long existing between the two nations; and it was their duty to execute it so as to produce the greatest advantage; whereas, if they were to agree to the amendment proposed, so covered with odium, it would weaken the power of the Executive.[52]

Whether or not Murray rescued Jay's treaty from last-minute defeat, his assault on the Dearborn amendment put the Republican strategists to rout. The House first altered the phrase "highly objectionable" to read merely "objectionable," and struck out altogether the reference to injuriousness. Before the day was over, even the remnant stigma of the word "objectionable" was removed. Thus purged, the motion to execute the treaty passed its final test, 51–48. The Federalist victory was complete.[53]

Murray wrote that night in his diary: "Thus has the great Drama wound up—the nation is in much agitation & the prospect critical on its rejection," to which he added modestly: "we carry'd it clean & clear of all amendmt. of odium wh. they moved to attach to it." [54] Whatever its effect on events, Murray's last-day speech made one thing clear: he had spoken out in the best of the Federalist tradition, voicing his party's will to make the nation strong and to keep it at peace.

51. *Annals*, V, 1282.
52. *Ibid.*, 1285–86.
53. *Ibid.*, 1287, 1289.
54. Entry of April 30, 1796, "Commonplace," PUL.

4

Campaigning for John Adams

BACK AMONG HIS constituents in June Murray learned, somewhat to his surprise, how deeply the Eastern Shore had been stirred by the treaty debate. Though now mollified by the administration's victory in the House, the Federalist gentry, he wrote McHenry, had been "much alarmed & extremely indignant at the Southern party." Testifying to that alarm was a bundle of protreaty petitions which Murray now belatedly forwarded to the Secretary of War.[1]

After the bustle of Philadelphia Murray found the isolation of Cambridge depressing, the more so because he planned not to stand for reelection. His reason was his need to recoup personal finances. By early August, his mind made up, he told McHenry that he had publicly notified "their majesties the people" that he would serve them no longer. Financial necessity was tinged with regret. Public life was no longer convenient for him, he told his old friend, but neither did he welcome retirement. He would miss what he called "the full tide of Philad. information," but added philosophically, "what ought to be—must be." [2] Of some consolation, and certainly indicative that his finances were not altogether straitened, Murray bought land that spring and began plans to build a house. His new estate was a tract of land overlooking the Choptank River, about a mile downstream from Cambridge, of which he wrote enthusiastically:

> it stands with an elevation & boldness & variety of view worthy of a better country—& will, I am certain, be healthy. It contains 150 acres—40 of wh. are woods—in these woods I shall soon give the raccoons & squirrels "notice to quit," that I may burn brick to advantage on the spot for the foundation of a small neat house.[3]

1. Cambridge, June 24, 1796, McHenry MSS, Ac. 3847, LC.
2. See letters of August 8, 12, and 21, 1796, *ibid.*
3. To McHenry, June 24, 1796, *ibid.*

Though determined to retire at the end of the lame-duck session Murray gave no sign of retreating from the political battle that would attend the first contested presidential election. With Jefferson the candidate of congressional Republicans, he fretted lest the Federalists fail to unite behind a candidate of their own. Much as he revered Washington, he observed, it would be "vain to lament" the latter's departure while the choice of a successor remained undecided. Now that Congress was out of session, he urged cabinet members to take charge of coordinating the party's strategy, "for a party dispersed act without concert, unless a rallying point is understood among them." John Adams was his own choice, and he reminded McHenry that at the time Congress adjourned it had been "understood" that the friends of government would support an Adams-Pinckney ticket. Adams electors would poll heavily on the Eastern Shore, he predicted.[4]

Unaware of the Hamiltonian "plot" to elect Thomas Pinckney instead of John Adams, Murray was nonetheless acutely mindful of the danger of offering two Federalists against Jefferson. Somewhat bewildered, he relayed to McHenry the news from Delaware that John Jay, as well as Adams, was being talked of. Either Jay or Adams would suit his constituency, he wrote, "but I understood that Mr. A. was the man," adding, "if they divide the friends of Govt., the State of Virginia will again have a President." [5] Silence from the party chieftains in Philadelphia led him to inquire as late as November 2 whom they were supporting for Vice President. Sometime during the next week he heard from McHenry that it was Pinckney. In that event, he replied, the party leadership must "take care & write to every seat of Govt. where the Electors meet, to run Pinckney as Vice, that we may have two strings." [6] Nowhere in his correspondence, however, did Murray indicate that he looked on Pinckney's candidacy as more than insurance against Jefferson's winning the second place.

As the campaign progressed Murray divided his attention between the local and national arenas. His own district, he was pleased to note, had given a 582–1 margin to an Adams elector who was personally unpopular. That his constituents had in this instance put party considerations ahead of personality led him to write that he had never before seen "an election so much of *principles*." Describing the scene to McHenry, he wrote:

4. To McHenry, Cambridge, September 9, 1796, Steiner, *McHenry,* 197; see also William L. Smith to Rufus King, Charleston, July 23, 1796, King, *Correspondence,* II, 66; and the *Philadelphia Aurora,* September 13, 1796.

5. Cambridge, September 24, 1796, Steiner, *McHenry,* 198.

6. *Ibid.,* 201–202.

The farmers came in without leaders to support government, they said, by voting for a Fedl. man as Presdt. I assure you I never saw such an election before, in which real good sense appeared unmixed.[7]

Because electors were constitutionally unable to designate which of their two ballots was being cast for President and Vice President, the significant aspect of the Maryland balloting was that three of the seven Adams electors withheld their second ballot from Thomas Pinckney. Of these three, two went to Senator John Henry and one, anomalously, to Jefferson. Thus Maryland followed the pro-Adams pattern of New England where some eighteen electors, determined that Pinckney should not be elected by a deficit of Adams votes in the South, also scattered their second ballots. Whether the Maryland scattering was Murray's work, as one historian has suggested, is a moot question.[8] Murray obviously did not know that the covert effort to bring in Pinckney was of Hamiltonian origin; nor did he balk at McHenry's suggestion that Pinckney should be backed for the vice-presidency. Just as certainly, however, his political instinct told him that a straight Adams-Pinckney ticket in the East, augmented by Pinckney votes from South Carolina and possibly Pennsylvania, would make Pinckney President.[9]

If ever a presidential candidate lacked for a champion, it was John Adams in 1796. Characterized by his foes as a political conservative in whom they pretended to see an avowed monarchist, Adams was too complex an expounder of political philosophy to suit the ideological simplifiers; not all his enemies were Republicans. To the Federalist hierarchs, whose natural leader was Alexander Hamilton, Adams appeared dimly as a high-ranking appendage of the Washington "court," as a man whose ability to lead the party—or, if necessary, to be led by it—was conjectural. A strong-minded, obstinate man, Adams had never shown that he could project his will among a national political following. And should he try, what of Hamilton's leadership? Already the Adams brand of Federalism, with its agrarian doubts about the felicity of Hamilton's financial program, was sufficient to cause uneasiness in the ranks of merchants and speculators.[10] Small wonder that Federalists should toy with a Pinckney candidacy. Not only was Thomas Pinckney a more

7. Cambridge, November 9, 1796, *ibid.,* 201.

8. Manning J. Dauer, *The Adams Federalists* (Baltimore: Johns Hopkins Press, 1953), 109.

9. WVM to McHenry, September 24, 1796, Steiner, *McHenry,* 198; also Murray's articles appearing in the press, *infra.*

10. See "A Federalist," *Gazette of the United States,* November 30, 1796; also Dauer, *Adams Federalists,* Chapter IV.

recognizable party man than John Adams, but, best of all, Pinckney looked like a sure winner. The Federalist chieftains, like President-makers ever since, were drawn to the man most likely to be elected. Praised for his treaty with Spain and untainted by association with Jay's treaty, Thomas Pinckney possessed the additional asset of being a Southerner. To a party whose Northern base was secure, no matter who the candidate, the prospect of using Pinckney to make inroads in the Republican South held an irresistible attraction.[11]

Meanwhile, to the uninitiated, Murray among them, the existence of a Pinckney "plot" against Adams appeared most starkly in the pages of the *Gazette of the United States.* Throughout November a writer who styled himself "A Federalist" used the party's chief press organ to keep up a drumfire attack on Adams, all the while giving reasons why Pinckney should be supported. Even so, Murray might not have plunged so vigorously into a newspaper campaign in Adams' behalf had not William L. Smith, Adams' supposed defender, so badly bungled the job. Smith's "Phocion" articles, which began to appear in the *Gazette* on October 14, dwelt more on Jefferson's inadequacies than on Adams' merits. Evidence suggests that Smith was trying to scotch a pro-Jefferson movement among South Carolina Federalists, but was not a party to the Pinckney "plot." [12] His coolness toward Adams, however, evoked from "A Federalist" the pointed remark that Smith had not denied that Adams was a monarchist (*Gazette,* November 9). The implication—that is, that the charge could not be denied—brought Murray to the fray. Murray well knew the source of the slur: it came largely from Adams' *Defence of the Constitutions of the United States,* the work written during Murray's earliest acquaintance with Adams. In the *Defence* Adams had noted the recent emergence of wealthy and talented persons whose increasing influence in American politics had clearly marked them as a "natural" aristocracy.[13] In failing to denounce this group, Adams had given offence to Republicans.

Murray's effort to rescue his old friend and mentor from the reproaches of his critics consisted of several newspaper articles. The most widely distributed piece was entitled "Short Vindication of Mr. Adams's 'Defence of American Constitutions.'" First published in the *Gazette*

11. See, for example, the King-Hamilton correspondence of May 1797, Hamilton, *Works,* VI, 113–14.

12. George C. Rogers, Jr., *Evolution of a Federalist: William Loughton Smith of Charleston (1758–1812)* (Columbia, S.C.: University of South Carolina Press, 1962), 289–91.

13. The most recent analysis of Adams' political views and of the *Defence* in particular is John R. Howe, Jr., *The Changing Political Thought of John Adams* (Princeton: Princeton University Press, 1966), 137–42.

on November 5, Murray's "Vindication" was later appended to Smith's "Phocion" letters in a campaign tract called *The Pretensions of Thomas Jefferson to the Presidency Examined: and the Charges Against John Adams Refuted.*[14] This pamphlet was unquestionably the major piece of Federalist campaign literature in the 1796 election, excepting, of course, Washington's "Farewell." Moreover, in view of Smith's virtual neglect of Adams, Murray's contribution was probably the most influential written commitment to the candidacy of John Adams outside of his native New England.

Adams' purpose in writing the *Defence,* Murray explained, had been to refute the mistaken assertion of the French publicist, Robert Turgot, that American state governments were servilely imitative of the British. Turgot, of course, had overlooked the significant absence in America of either nobility or monarchy. Because he had chosen the comparative approach, Adams had also remarked on certain praiseworthy features of the British system as contrasted with the less free governments on the Continent. But, wrote Murray emphatically, whenever Adams had compared the American and British systems, "we always, in every instance, find that he is exultingly in favor of the free constitutions of America. . . . No where does he even insinuate, that we ought to adopt hereditary first magistrates, or kings or nobility." Adams himself had written that Americans *"have not made their first magistrates hereditary: here they differ from the English constitution, and with great propriety,"* to which Murray added: "Can language be more explicit?"

Signing himself "Union," "Union Among Federalists," and "Eastern Shore," Murray kept up a flow of pro-Adams letters to the Maryland press. One of these, the lengthiest, may never have seen print unless it appeared in the Georgetown *Potomack,* whose issues for this period are not extant. It pointed to Adams' prominent leadership of the independence movement, his primacy among the peace commissioners at Paris, his success in securing loans from the Dutch. As for the *Defence,* again defended, readers were challenged to discover in what manner Adams' credo disagreed with the principles of the Constitution. In all, Adams was pictured as a firm, enlightened man who "seems to have got above party passions," and whose election would assure continuance of Washington's policies of peace, neutrality, and treaty observance. Jefferson, by contrast, would be "a President of Experiments," under whom the country would risk being "polandized." [15]

14. Pamphlet published in the United States, October 1796; Part II, November 1796.

15. This long article appears in draft in Murray's "Commonplace," PUL, with the notation that he had sent it to the *Maryland Herald and Eastern Shore Intelli-*

Again in the *Gazette* on December 5, Murray varied his themes under the pseudonym "Eastern Shore." Putting the "great name" to good use, he urged that Washington's successor be one "who will carry into practice that system which our beloved Washington has adopted and recommended to his fellow citizens." In Adams, Washington's wisdom would be extended and immortalized. Murray must have gasped at the typographical error which followed: "This is the immorality [*sic*] that is due to such a man as Washington."

Wisely, Murray did not balloon Adams' vice-presidency as an argument for succession. He explained to McHenry that he thought it best "to associate him with *Revolution Services* as most unquestioned & most splendid & long *past*." [16] The italics bespoke the well-recognized fact that Adams' term as Vice President had been undistinguished. Murray nonetheless put the best light on Adams' recent, though negative, record as U.S. minister to London, and made a virtue of Adams' failure to negotiate a treaty with Britain in the 1780s by blaming the weakness of the Confederation on the one hand, and the King's personal antipathy toward Adams on the other. As for Adams' still more recent advocacy of high-sounding titles for federal officials, Murray reminded Marylanders that their governors were styled "excellency" and their state senators "honorable." [17]

Whether or not Murray's relentless campaigning for Adams tipped the election to the Vice President is impossible to determine. It is noteworthy, however, that seven of the twelve electoral votes which the South gave to Adams came from Maryland. And it was only by three votes that Adams beat Jefferson.

If during the campaign Murray retained any lingering doubts as to the potentially treasonous affiliations of the opposition party, they were erased when the French minister, Pierre Adet, tried to frighten the voters into electing Jefferson. Using the vehicle of the *Aurora,* the leading Republican journal of Philadelphia, Adet on November 2 published

---

gencer (Easton, Md.) over the pseudonym "Union Among Federalists," also to the *Potomack* (Georgetown, Md.) and the *Maryland Journal and Baltimore Advertiser,* both signed "Union." In none of these newspapers has the author been able to find the piece. An article signed "A Federal American" appearing in the *Maryland Herald* of November 1 and 8, and another signed "A Whig and a lover of Old Whigs" appearing in the *Maryland Gazette* of October 18 and 19, are written in Murray's style.

16. November 1796, Steiner, *McHenry,* 202.
17. Draft article, October 1796, "Commonplace," PUL.

his earlier note to the State Department protesting Jay's treaty in threatening terms. The administration felt impelled to answer publicly the next day. With only two days remaining before Pennsylvania chose electors, the cabinet foresaw that if the Quakers of that state, heretofore counted safe for Adams, became alarmed by Adet's warlike blast, they would swing to Jefferson as the likeliest pacifier of Franco-American relations. Political pundits, looking back on the swift succession of blast and counter-blast, later concluded that the administration's reply to Adet, because it preceded the Pennsylvania election by only one day, had been unable to stay the shift of Quaker votes to Jefferson. On November 4, Pennsylvania returned fourteen of its fifteen electors for the Virginian. To all appearances, Adet's masterful timing had outflanked the Federalists in a pivotal state.[18]

Two weeks later, with other elections still pending, Adet sought to influence the outcome by announcing his own recall. This threat to break off official relations could be removed, he suggested, were Americans to elect Jefferson and return to the French orbit.[19] By this time, however, the Federalist strategists in the cabinet were beginning to feel Hamilton's influence. The New Yorker, whose advice had arrived too late to prevent the first exchange, strongly disapproved of engaging Adet in the press.[20] Hamilton's counsel now prevailed: Adet's threat of rupture went unanswered until Congress, back in session in December, received the administration's public defense of its French policy in the form of a letter of instructions to Charles C. Pinckney, minister-designate to Paris.[21] Murray, though he had found the administration's published effort to save Pennsylvania for Adams "firm & temperately retortive," wholeheartedly concurred with Hamilton's urging that the administration keep silent during the later stages of the election. Adet, he supposed, would like nothing better than to engage the Federalists in a "newspaper dispute." Broadly viewed, Adet's electioneering antics spoke to Murray of France's long-settled plan to use the United States as a pawn in her contest with England. That an Adams victory would defeat this plan had led the Frenchman to show his teeth. If any good came of Adet's

18. William L. Smith to Ralph Izard, November 8, 1796, Ulrich Bonnell Phillips, ed., "South Carolina Federalist Correspondence, 1789–1797," *American Historical Review*, XIV (July 1909), 781; Oliver Wolcott to his father, November 27, 1796, Gibbs, *Wolcott*, I, 401; John Adams to his wife, December 4, 1796, *Letters to His Wife*, II, 231.

19. *ASP FR*, I, 579–83.

20. See Hamilton's letters to Washington and Wolcott, Hamilton, *Works*, VI, 162–63, 180–82.

21. This letter was a full-dress review of U.S. policy toward France. In pamphlet form it ran more than 100 pages. See text in *ASP FR*, I, 559–76.

ill wind, Murray hoped it would be the awakening of Americans to the essential selfishness of French policy.[22]

Murray and Charlotte returned to Philadelphia in mid-December to find the capital locked in the grip of a French crisis, easily explained. By winning the presidency, John Adams had convinced Paris that no further obstacle could be raised against the fulfillment of Jay's treaty. France, having lost any hope of preventing what she believed to be the pro-British drift of Federalist foreign policy, was striking back. Amid reports that French corsairs were committing wholesale depredations on American shipping, Philadelphia settled down uneasily to see whether Washington and his lame-duck Congress would respond in kind and take the counter-measures that would lead to war. Whether or not the crisis could be resolved peaceably seemed to hinge on the temper of Washington's annual message, on Charles Pinckney's reception at Paris, and on the possible variations of congressional reaction to France's maritime spoliations.

Washington, as might be expected, proved no incendiary; his last formal message to Congress breathed conciliation, even optimism. Pinckney, to be sure, was not received by the French Directory, but news of the rebuff reached Philadelphia only after Congress had adjourned. As for Congress itself, members engaged in what a later age would call a "silly season."

On January 19, 1797, the House received Timothy Pickering's strongly worded reply to Adet, together with a copy of Pinckney's instructions and all of the papers relating to more than two years of Franco-American controversy. So voluminous was this documentary offering that the House unwisely sent it all to the printers without having it read. By the time it was published, any opportunity for debate had passed. Earlier, a full-scale airing of foreign policy had appeared imminent when Republicans tried to force the Federalist members to admit that they would welcome a French war, especially if it produced a British alliance. Charges of warmongering died, however, when John Nicholas of Virginia termed the French crisis "not yet ripe for discussion," and counseled his fellow Republicans not to impede the efforts of the executive branch to find a peaceful solution.[23] What little debate transpired thereafter on foreign policy reverted to familiar

22. WVM to McHenry, Cambridge, letters of November 9 and 22, 1796, Steiner, *McHenry,* 201, 190.
23. *Annals,* VI, 1661–62; also 1615–55 *passim.*

dialogue: Federalists spoke of peace but urged preparedness; Republicans warned of war but voted against bills designed to improve the military.

Faced with increasing French raids on American shipping, both Houses seemed apathetic. The Senate defeated an embargo bill lest it embarrass the incoming President.[24] The lower house, meanwhile, refrained from anti-French measures because a sense of crisis had so far disintegrated the Federalist bloc as to give virtual control of that house to the still Francophile Republicans.[25] Hard-core Federalists, Murray among them, had to be content with a rearguard action that session, defending the party's policies until the new Congress, ostensibly more Federalist in composition, could take over. Primarily, it was the nation's military establishment that ran the greatest risk of partisan-inspired dismemberment. From the Republican side came an apparently unstoppable drive to cut the number of regiments in the regular Army from four to three. Albert Gallatin led the forces of retrenchment, preaching economy and dilating on the awful and unrepublican spectacle of a "standing army." Fortunately, Gallatin overstated his alarms, and laid himself open to ridicule for suggesting that four regiments totaling 1,660 men could pose a threat to the Republic. With Gallatin silenced, House Federalists won a minor victory for preparedness when the House voted, 50–44, to keep army strength at four regiments.[26]

Having failed to prune back the Army, the economizers, still led by Gallatin, now appeared ready to scuttle the Navy. On January 30, Gallatin won House approval for striking the word "Naval" from the title of a military appropriations bill. Congress, Gallatin declaimed, had yet to decide whether the country should have a naval establishment. Furiously, Murray reminded the Republican budget-cutters that whether or not they recognized the existence of a naval establishment, three frigates belonging to the United States stood in varying stages of near-completion at shipyards in Boston, Baltimore, and Philadelphia. Should the House refuse to finish these vessels, they would become "a monument of disgrace to the country." Murray's impassioned plea to save the frigates and thus lay the "foundation of a future navy" ultimately ran aground on the shoals of compromise. The House, on February 11, yielding to a motion shaped by Gallatin and Nicholas, voted to complete

24. See Senate Proceedings of March 1, 1797, *ibid.*, 1569; also Theodore Sedgwick to Rufus King, Stockbridge, Mass., March 12, 1797, King, *Correspondence*, II, 157–58.

25. See, for example, Fisher Ames to Hamilton, Philadelphia, January 26, 1797, Hamilton, *Works*, VI, 200–203.

26. *Annals*, VI, 1981–82, 2066–72, 2094.

the construction of the three frigates but not to man them! This decision naturally led Republicans to cast a suspicious eye at the appropriation figure of $172,000. Would not this amount buy crewmen as well as rigging and canvas? Finally, enough Republicans were persuaded either that the figure was low enough to prevent the vessels from being manned or that John Adams would send them to sea anyway, to win passage. Again, as with the Army bill, the Federalists had barely held the line against the economizers.[27]

As his days in the House drew to a close, Murray grappled with two long-cherished issues: the matter of raising salaries for public officials, and the continuance of the Neutrality Act of 1794.

Since his entry into public life, Murray had always championed the cause of adequate salaries. The opportunity to do so again came in late January of 1797, when a House committee recommended $500 increases in the salaries of the Attorney General and the Secretary of War. Murray's argument was straightforward: cabinet-level salaries should be high enough to enable competent men to serve without personal sacrifice. It was not guileless enough for Thomas Henderson of New Jersey, however, who felt that the bill's supporters were a little too eager in "volunteering" as petitioners. As one of the more prominent petitioners, Murray replied heatedly that it would be a "miserable justice" to require Charles Lee and James McHenry to petition, in person, to redress a grievance "so glaring as the present." [28] Murray did not record what must have been his personal chagrin when the House raised Lee's salary, but not that of his old friend McHenry. Even where ties of friendship played no part, however—as in the proposal to raise the pay of high federal office-holders by 25 percent—Murray strove to win points for the axiomatic relationship between price and worth, warning that low salaries would draw to office those who, while boasting of their republican simplicity, would "as a reward for this kind of penance . . . probably take care of themselves." [29] If this view was somewhat cynical, it was also representatively Federalist. The pay-raise bill itself was swept aside, 57–32, by the economizers, now in full swing.

One last echo from the past was sounded by the Senate's end-of-session proposal to keep the Neutrality Act of 1794 on the statute books indefinitely. Once more Murray and Gallatin came to grips, this time

27. *Ibid.*, 2050–53, 2113–25 *passim*, 2149–50, 2339, 2351.
28. *Ibid.*, 1987–95. The additional $500 would have brought McHenry's salary up to $3,500, Attorney General Lee's up to $2,400. The latter was expected to supplement this from private law practice.
29. *Ibid.*, 2011–12.

on the question of whether the neutral duties required by the law were also required by international law. To Murray, a congruence between domestic and international law was not as significant as that they should coincide in intent. International practice might not impose such rigid restraints on neutral persons as did the law of 1794, but both had the same purpose: to prevent third parties from giving offense to a belligerent. Gallatin argued, conversely, that no domestic law which put greater restraints on Americans than were put on them by the law of nations should be made permanent. Ultimately, the House, heeding Gallatin, voted a two-year extension only. Not until April 24, 1800, was Murray vindicated; on that later day a bill was signed into law extending the act of 1794 "without limitation of time." [30]

By that time, however, Murray could look back over nearly three years of foreign service during which the congressman's concern for the permanency of U.S. neutrality laws had long since been overshadowed by the diplomat's active role in dealing with the practical problems of neutrality and noninvolvement.

30. *Ibid.*, 1530, 2227–32; U.S. *Statutes at Large,* II, 54.

5

Watching Paris from The Hague

MURRAY WAS NOT altogether surprised by the news of his appointment
to The Hague. Earlier, McHenry had told him that Washington was
considering him for the post. Until that day in late February of 1797,
when, as he stood on the floor of the House, word reached him that
his appointment was certain, Murray had steeled himself against the
possibility that he would be passed over and allowed to retire to Cambridge. In that event, he wrote, "I will try to be a good farmer." [1] Having
said earlier that he would no longer serve "their majesties the people,"
Murray would have stepped far out of character had he declined the
honor of accepting appointment from George Washington, the man he
most revered. Moreover, the prospect of a $4,500 annual salary must
have removed any doubts as to the financial desirability of continuing
in public life. [2]

More than a month before his appointment Murray had yielded to
Adams' urging that he let Timothy Pickering show him the old diplomatic files. The purpose of the visit seems obvious: to give the Francophobic Secretary of State an opportunity to test the reflexes of a
prospective diplomat. Here in his office Pickering could observe Murray's reactions to those documents dating from the War for Independence which testified to the long-standing ill will of France toward this
country. Here Murray was shown the documentary evidence that France
had once opposed the American claim to fishery rights along the Canadian coasts. Here, too, he saw the proof that France had sought, during
the peacemaking, to prevent the United States from obtaining a western
boundary on the Mississippi River. [3] If this visit with Pickering was in

1. Entry of February 16, 1797, "Commonplace," PUL.
2. Even at this salary Murray had difficulty meeting expenses. See his letter
to McHenry, The Hague, April 12, 1798, Steiner, *McHenry,* 299–301.
3. What Murray saw was the Barbé-Marbois letter and a copy of the Rayneval
mémoire. See Richard B. Morris, *The Peacemakers: the Great Powers and
American Independence* (New York: Harper and Row, 1965), 322–26.

fact a testing, Murray's responses needed no prompting, for if he conveyed to Pickering the same sense of outrage at France's treachery which found its way into his diary that night, the colonel must have been amply satisfied that John Adams' young protégé was politically sound. Testing or not, Pickering subsequently recommended that Murray be given The Hague post, only to discover that Washington had already determined to do so.[4]

Eager to be off, Murray busied himself throughout the month of March, packing trunks full of books, clothing, and household linens—carefully listing the contents of each parcel—while also concerning himself with the more formal details of leave-taking: a social visit to Washington, an informal dinner with the Adamses, and a brief but ominous encounter with the Dutch minister-resident in Philadelphia. This last gave Murray an ideological foretaste of the diet he could expect at The Hague. R. C. Van Polanen was a doctrinaire Dutch republican whose utterances against the Stadtholder had forced him to flee to Philadelphia in 1795. About a year later Van Polanen had been appointed as his country's emissary to the United States when, following a French invasion, the Netherlands had been republicanized, French-style, and renamed the Batavian Republic by its new rulers.[5] When Murray conferred with the Dutchman in early March of 1797, he was greeted with a mixture of flattery and cautionary advice. While Murray was gratuitously informed that the Batavian regime believed him to be "neither British nor French," the Dutchman also warned him that his predecessor, John Quincy Adams, had become unpopular, not because of any misconduct but because the American "Jacobins" living in Paris had pinned a pro-British label on him. Murray shrugged at this, remarking that he himself would doubtless suffer the same obloquy, if for no other reason than that he, too, despised the American expatriates and their pro-French sympathies. With that, Murray invited the Dutchman to take tea with him the next day.[6]

Besides Charlotte and their Negro servant, Will, Murray's entourage

4. Entries of January 21 and February 25, 1797, "Commonplace," PUL.
5. The administration agreed to receive Van Polanen in the fall of 1796 largely because, as Washington put it, there was no reason not to. See Washington to Pickering, Mount Vernon, July 25, 1796, Fitzpatrick, *Writings,* XXXV, 155–56; also Pierre Adet to the French Foreign Minister, Philadelphia, October 4, 1796, Frederick Jackson Turner, ed., "Correspondence of French Ministers," *American Historical Association Report of 1903,* 952–53.
6. Entry of March 3, 1797, "Commonplace," PUL.

would necessarily include a private secretary, a post usually given to the sons of political luminaries. In this instance Murray was especially pleased to honor Washington. At a meeting with the President on March 1 it was arranged that Bartholomew Dandridge, kinsman and recently secretary to the President himself, would fill the position. Washington, who had not always found Martha's nephew reliable, nonetheless gave his blessing.[7] Dandridge proved to be a good choice. He and Murray came to enjoy an easy, congenial rapport, occasionally glimpsed in the older man's correspondence. Later, at The Hague, they found a common interest in fencing, took lessons in it together, and, as Murray related to John Quincy Adams, became "quite belligerent," adding gaily, "we . . . both hope to shine in at least militia feast days, if this country becomes too hot for us." [8] By early fall of 1798, however, Dandridge's health had been so impaired by the damp chill of the Dutch climate that Murray, very reluctantly, had him transferred to Rufus King's legation in London.

Not a man to leave the instruction of a departing diplomat entirely to his Secretary of State, John Adams offered his own personal counsel to Murray during a dinner to which the Adamses invited the Murrays shortly before they sailed. Now that Pinckney's mission was known to have been rebuffed at Paris, Adams foresaw the recriminations into which Murray might be drawn. Should French foreign policy become a topic of official conversation, Murray was warned to speak softly. He was not, for example, to stir the ashes of outrage at Adet's electioneering the previous fall. And if asked whether the United States would entertain further negotiations with Paris, he was to answer affirmatively. Then, recalling his own mission to The Hague, Adams advised Murray to be "short & sincere" when he addressed the Dutch government. If the latter wanted a new commercial treaty, Murray was to accommodate them, but at all events, keep the old treaty inviolate. At some point during the dinner Adams suggested that Jay's treaty might also have to be explained. Murray needed no instruction on that score.[9]

Three days before his party sailed from Philadelphia, Murray received his written instructions from Pickering. His "most constant and laborious" task would be to oversee payment of the United States debt, to which end he was to correspond regularly with the Treasury Department. Otherwise, his "principal duty" was to maintain harmony between Phila-

7. On at least one occasion Washington had been irritated when Dandridge left the capital without telling him where or why he was going. GW to Bartholomew Dandridge, Philadelphia, June 5, 1796, Fitzpatrick, *Writings,* XXXV, 77–79.
8. July 17, 1798, *AHA Report of 1912,* 433–34.
9. Entries of April 8 and 9, 1797, "Commonplace," PUL; see also WVM to JQA, October 5, 1798, *AHA Report of 1912,* 480.

delphia and The Hague. Should the Dutch undergo a change of regime, he was to follow John Quincy Adams' precedent of 1795 of dealing with any new government that gave evidence of being based on majority rule. In more general terms, Murray was urged to take full advantage of The Hague's usefulness as a listening post. More or less centrally placed among the capitals of Europe, The Hague had long been the crossroads of fact and rumor. Like his predecessor, Murray was to be "watchful and diligent," and to send to the State Department any intelligence he might gather.[10] Meanwhile, two problems in particular would occupy his attention: the apparent desire of the Batavians for a new commercial treaty, and the settlement of a long-standing claims case involving the Dutch seizure of an American merchantman, the *Wilmington Packet*.

Nothing came of the treaty proposal. Nor, as Murray discovered later, did the Dutch appear truly to want a new treaty. The Batavian Republic, as a satellite of France, apparently chose the treaty question as a sounding board from which to echo France's hostility toward Jay's treaty. That the Dutch republicans seriously considered giving up the liberal maritime principles of their 1782 treaty in favor of the more restrictive terms of Jay's treaty, as a sort of ideological masochism, is open to much doubt. John Quincy Adams was probably nearer the mark when, noting the perfunctory quality of the Dutch treaty feelers, he explained them in terms of France's "irresistible external impulse" on Dutch politics. The Dutch overtures for a new treaty told more of The Hague's eagerness to demonstrate Franco-Batavian solidarity than anything else.[11] The case of the *Wilmington Packet* was not so easily disposed of. For more than six years Adams and then Murray were to assail a succession of Dutch regimes for their refusal to admit liability for a clear-cut violation of the principle of free ships, free goods. The *Packet*, a vessel of American registry, had been captured by a Dutch privateer while en route from Bordeaux to St. Thomas at a time (1793) when the Dutch were at war with France. Confiscation had followed on grounds that the *Packet*'s cargo was French-owned—this despite the "free ships" clause of the 1782 Dutch-American treaty by which the

10. See Vol. IV, Instructions to U.S. Ministers, Record Group 59, Department of State, National Archives.

11. JQA to the Secretary of State, No. 85, The Hague, November 1, 1796, Netherlands Despatches, I, Record Group 59, Department of State, National Archives, hereinafter cited as Netherlands Despatches, I; same to same, No. 86, November 4, 1796, *ibid.* See also Pickering's memorandum of May 15, 1797, Pickering MSS, 37, 158, Massachusetts Historical Society, hereinafter abbreviated as MHS.

vessel's neutral flag should have exempted its cargo from capture. Not until 1800 did Murray finally succeed in persuading the Dutch government of its liability, and thus win for the owners a compromise settlement of 20,000 florins.[12]

Of some solace to the pragmatic statesmen who must deal with revolutionaries is the comfortably predictable need of the latter to be consistent. Had Timothy Pickering been more alive to this weakness, he might have foreseen what he learned from reading the pages of the *Leyden Gazette* shortly after Murray had sailed. In the *Gazette* Pickering found the disturbing speculation that Murray might not be officially received. Should the Dutch follow the example of their French masters— and revolutionary fraternity suggested they might—Murray might be handed the same rebuff that Pinckney had suffered at Paris earlier. With this sobering thought, Pickering wrote Murray that it was quite possible his mission would end before it had begun. But even if he were received, Pickering continued pessimistically, another problem had arisen —also involving French influence at The Hague—that was bound to cause difficulty. On May 19, Congress had received from the President a number of diplomatic dispatches, among them extracts from a letter written by the younger Adams the previous fall. These extracts, now made public, showed all too clearly that John Quincy Adams believed the Batavian Republic to be the servile puppet of France.[13] As Pickering correctly surmised, Dutch officials would shortly register anger at Adams' portrait of them. Thus, together with the *Wilmington Packet* case, John Quincy Adams' slurring depiction of Dutch dependency on Paris was to become, for Murray, the object of prolonged, and in this case bitter, recriminations. It was June of 1799 before Murray could close this unpleasant chapter in Batavian-American relations.[14]

From the deck of their vessel, *Good Friends,* Murray and his party first sighted land on May 31. The next day as they ran before the wind

12. For a survey of Murray's lengthy negotiations on the *Wilmington Packet* case, see the major documents collected in Miller, *Treaties,* V, 1075–1103.

13. Pickering to WVM, Philadelphia, May 24, 1797, Instructions to U.S. Ministers, IV, RG 59, NA; see also, *ASP FR,* II, 1; and Worthington C. Ford, ed., *The Writings of John Quincy Adams* (New York: The Macmillan Company, 1913–1917), II, 35–40, hereinafter cited as Ford, *Writings of JQA.*

14. See Chapter 9. In making this diplomatic correspondence public, Pickering was following a deliberate policy of exacerbating relations with France and her allies. See Gerald H. Clarfield, *Timothy Pickering and American Diplomacy, 1795–1800* (Columbia, Mo.: University of Missouri Press, 1969), ix.

Murray described the islands: "Shetland on our Left—like a cloud—Land off the Orkneys high," and proceeded to sketch the airy island profiles in his Commonplace book. A week later, and two months out of Philadelphia, Murray and his official family debarked at Helder, where he learned from a port officer that Adams had not yet left the country. In his first letter to McHenry, Murray unconsciously revealed with what alacrity he had fallen into a standing Dutch joke. It was current, he wrote, that the King of Prussia was dead.[15] Almost two years later, when the rumor recurred, his friend Adams explained that the Dutch loved to report the death of the Prussian monarch. "It was so fashionable to announce that event in my time," Adams chuckled, "that I know one of our countrymen (Clarke) who knew little more of the language than to say 'De Koning van Preussen is dood,' which he retained from hearing it so often repeated." [16] Frederick William II did die the following November.

Murray hastened to join Adams at Amsterdam, where the two conferred so intensively that Adams, who had started to write a letter to his father, did not complete it until nearly two weeks later. What the two diplomats discussed as they "briefed" each other can only be speculated on. A safe guess would be that they ranged the field of foreign policy from developments at Philadelphia to those of London, Paris, Madrid, and, of course, The Hague. But whatever direction their talk may have taken, inevitably the conversation must have swung back to Paris and to the growing threat of war with France. By despoiling American commerce and by refusing the right of embassy, the French Directory had chosen a dangerous course. Surely Murray must have told the younger Adams that his father planned to play out the role of conciliator, that there would be no retreat from Jay's treaty, and that Federalist leaders, taking their cue from Hamilton, supported the President's proposal to send another mission to France so that if war came, the party could not be accused of lacking the will to peace.[17]

Despite earlier rumors in the *Leyden Gazette,* Murray encountered no difficulty in assuming his official duties. He admitted to McHenry, however, that he had been officially received "with as little active politeness here from any one, as ever minister or traveller did." [18]

Once Adams had left for Berlin, Murray busied himself gathering the intelligence which he knew the State Department expected. How-

15. Helder, June 9, 1797, Steiner, *McHenry,* 227.
16. JQA to WVM, Berlin, March 9, 1799, Adams MSS, MR 130.
17. Hamilton to Pickering, New York, March 29, 1797, Hamilton, *Works,* VI, 216–18.
18. The Hague, June 22, 1797, Steiner, *McHenry,* 227–30.

ever time-consuming his official dealings with the Dutch government, he
realized that any information gleaned from a Paris source would be
far more welcome in Philadelphia than a dozen dispatches relating to the
progress of the *Wilmington Packet* case. Considering Pinckney's failure
at Paris, the administration would be eager to know whether its new
mission, this time linking Pinckney with John Marshall and Elbridge
Gerry, had any reasonable prospect of success. Pinckney was then at
The Hague, waiting to begin again; Marshall and Gerry would join him
in September. In the interim, Murray sifted the uncertain soil of rumor
and speculation, hoping to find some solid evidence that by the time
Pinckney, Marshall, and Gerry reached Paris the Directory would be
ready to make its peace with Jay's treaty and call off its corsairs. Hopeful
at first, Murray saw several contingencies that might bring France to
seek an accommodation: one, should she find the price of outright war
too high; or, two, should the peace-minded moderates in the French
legislative Councils gain the upper hand over the war hawks in the executive Directory; or, finally, should peace break out in Europe, leaving
France with no further reason to pursue hostilities against the United
States. One by one, Murray dismissed these hopes as summer lengthened
into fall. But at first, certainly, he thought, France must realize how high
a financial price she would pay if her Dutch ally were cut off by war
from the profits of American commerce. France was supplying herself
indirectly from this lucrative trade by the loans which she forced from
the Dutch. Assuming that Batavia would be dragged into a French war
against the United States, France would lose an important source of
revenue. How little such financial considerations weighed against the
vindictiveness of French policy-makers, Murray soon realized.[19]

As for the second contingency—that moderates in the French Councils
might overrule the Directory—this, too, proved ephemeral. It shortly
became apparent that these moderates were more intent on challenging
the dictatorial powers of the Directory than they were on working for a
rapprochement with the United States; their outcries against the Directory's belligerent foreign policy merely manifested an internal power
struggle. Moreover, the faint hope that Franco-American good will might
be reborn in the French legislative councils disappeared abruptly when
on 18 Fructidor (September 4) the Directory moved decisively against
its critics, unseated them from the councils, repealed their laws, and

19. WVM to Pickering, No. 1, The Hague, June 20, 1797, Netherlands Despatches, I; same to same, No. 3, June 27, 1797, *ibid.* For the toll taken by French
wars, French taxes, and French manpower levies, see Bernard H.M. Vlekke, *Evolution of the Dutch Nation* (New York: Roy Publishers, 1945), 276–85.

proscribed their leaders. To Murray, the Directory's triumph over its opponents spelled the end of hope in that direction.[20]

There still remained, however, the possibility that Pinckney, Marshall, and Gerry might arrive at Paris at the moment of a general European peace settlement. By the summer of 1797, France had vanquished all her enemies save Britain. Prussia and Spain had fled the field in 1795. Austria, reeling under the blows of Bonaparte's Italian campaign, was moving from the truce of Leoben to the peace of Campo Formio. Only Britain remained, and even she seemed bent on ending hostilities. Just as Murray was taking up his duties at The Hague, a British emissary, Lord Malmesbury, was on his way to Lille to hear what France's terms might be. Should Malmesbury make peace, the way might be opened for the American mission to do likewise. Murray's hope on this score dimmed quickly as his assessment of French motives grew sharper. Quite likely, he reasoned, France was merely sparring for enough time to conclude peace with Austria so that she might then turn her full wrath on England. To McHenry he ventured that France might next try a cross-Channel invasion. To Pickering he noted ominously that troops and ships were being mobilized at the Texel. Whatever the next phase might be, however, Murray was convinced that the Directory could not afford to make peace because its hold on power depended on keeping France embroiled in war. When the Lille negotiation broke down, Murray laid it to a combination of French insincerity and British clumsiness.[21]

Though his reading of the French scene gave Murray little hope for the success of the new American mission, his profoundest pessimism was directed toward that infuriating French attitude which held all other nations to be either enemies or satellites. Moderates might call for peace in the Council of Five Hundred, negotiators might talk of peace at Lille or Udina, but the hard fact was that France continued to make war on American shipping. France, her policy fixed, would have the United States repudiate Jay's treaty, abandon her neutrality, and swing into the French orbit. Should Americans be worn down by the alternation of French threats and blandishments, should they give up

20. WVM to Pickering, No. 10, The Hague, September 9, 1797, Netherlands Despatches, I; WVM to McHenry, The Hague, September 21, 1797, Steiner, *McHenry*, 275–85. For details of the coup see Georges Lefebvre, *The Thermidorians and the Directory; Two Phases of the French Revolution* (New York: Random House, 1964), Ch. VII, hereinafter cited as Lefebvre, *The Thermidorians*.

21. Murray's assessments of French policy accord with those of recent scholarship. Compare, for example, his dispatches Nos. 2, 3, and 8 (of June 23, June 27, and August 17, 1797, respectively) in Vol. I of Netherlands Despatches with Lefebvre, *The Thermidorians*, 326–27, 361–64. The letter to McHenry is that of June 22, 1797, Steiner, *McHenry*, 227–30.

the British treaty and embrace the French fraternity, what further disgraces could they expect to their nationhood? To Murray, the answer was obvious: France would complete the design begun by Genêt, Fauchet, and Adet. The power which had just sold the Venetian Republic for Belgium and was rapaciously plundering its Dutch ally out of pocket would end by making the United States another victimized appendage of the French revolutionary *dominium*.[22]

Small wonder Murray harbored ambivalent feelings toward the impending mission to Paris. What could it accomplish against such settled hostility, he asked McHenry, except, perhaps, to gain time for Americans to look to their defenses? Meanwhile, every whisper of peace that floated deceptively from Paris would sap the will of Congress to take the necessary measures. Armed force was the only language France understood. Only "a united & most decided tone, attended by armed preparations . . . can lead her to listen to reason." [23]

Murray's worst fears came alive on September 2 when John Marshall arrived bearing letters from Pickering which told how feebly Congress had responded to the President's urgings of preparedness. Congressional Republicans, he learned, had strongly opposed measures that might have a character of hostility while the outcome of a peace mission was still awaited. Too, the prospect of a general European peace had caused not a few defections among Federalists.[24] Even before these letters from Pickering, Murray was not unaware of congressional complacence. He confessed to McHenry that he was hard put to explain to the diplomatic corps at The Hague why Congress had acted so weakly during its special spring session. To those who asked, he had answered that American policy was to treat amicably and sincerely; since France was not arming against the United States, the latter would not arm against France. To McHenry, however, he deplored the reactive, wait-and-see policy which the administration seemed compelled to follow.[25]

One hope remained: that France herself would force matters. Should Paris once more rebuff the overtures from Philadelphia, Americans might find that unity of response in which, as Murray put it, "the national mind will become truly National." One more insult from Paris might finally give the administration the impetus it needed to prepare the country for

22. WVM to McHenry, The Hague, July 14, 1797, *ibid.*, 230–43.
23. *Ibid.*
24. Pickering to WVM, Philadelphia, June 12 and 15, 1797, Instructions to U.S. Ministers, IV; WVM to Pickering, No. 10, The Hague, September 9, 1797, Netherlands Despatches, I; see also entry of September 1, 1797, "Commonplace," PUL.
25. The Hague, August 11, 1797, Steiner, *McHenry*, 248–49.

war, might even spare his countrymen that war if they were shown to be armed and united. Meanwhile, the mission to Paris would doubtless be greeted with "a flood of sentiment" coupled with demands for treaty concessions which no American diplomat could make without compromising American sovereignty. In the end, the mission would fail, and the Paris ideologues would be to blame. To Murray's mind, only a French government less doctrinaire, or better yet, monarchical—though this last was too uncertain to be looked for—could effect a lasting reconciliation.[26]

Thus did Murray, with considerable accuracy, predict the ill wind of XYZ and the good that would come of it. Pinckney, Marshall, and Gerry did fail, largely because they were unable to swallow the outrageous French demands for a *douceur,* a loan, and certain changes in one of Adams' speeches. Congress also choked on these demands and answered France with warlike measures that fell just short of war itself. And when the Directory had seen enough of American hostility to put out peace feelers, it was the less-than-republican Bonaparte who concluded that peace.

The ill-fated mission began on September 18, 1797, when Murray saw Pinckney and Marshall off to Paris; they left without waiting for Elbridge Gerry, an oversight of some symbolic significance, perhaps, in view of Gerry's later desertion of his colleagues during the latter stages of the negotiation. But haste was imperative, as Pinckney explained, because the Paris press was beginning to attribute "very false and improper motives" to the delay. Also, the two envoys had heard that Gerry would probably land at Le Havre. Such was not the case, however: Gerry arrived at The Hague two days later, conferred briefly with Murray, on whom he left an impression of extreme naiveté, and followed his colleagues to Paris on September 24.[27]

That the envoys would encounter the Directory at an inopportune moment for negotiation Murray scarcely doubted. The three-man radical rump, composed of Barras, Reubell, and La Revellière-Lépeaux, having smashed their moderate opponents, would almost certainly renew the attack on England and probably on Austria. With ideological certainty, the war hawks of Fructidor would try once more to work France's revo-

26. To McHenry, The Hague, July 14, 1797, *ibid.,* 230–43.
27. C.C. Pinckney to McHenry, Rotterdam, September 19, 1797, Steiner, *McHenry,* 274–75; and WVM to McHenry, The Hague, September 21, 1797, *ibid.,* 275–85.

lutionary will on American domestic politics. Again, no effort would be spared to alienate the American people, the bulk of whom were believed to be friendly to France, from their elected leaders, known with conviction to be pro-British. "That idea," wrote Murray, "so baneful and so humiliating and so false works at the bottom of every project and every proposition . . . and is discoverable in every conversation upon American affairs." So believing, the Directory would not send the American envoys away, but rather use them as a sounding board for threats and promises and, by delay, hold the initiative. It might even attain its chief end: the repudiation of Jay's treaty. Murray observed that many Americans were ignorant of what the treaty actually contained, but they were keenly sensitive to French expostulations. His countrymen might well be convinced, if the negotiations were stormy, that they had best give up the treaty.[28]

Earlier, Murray had suggested that France might conciliate the United States if peace became general in Europe. Now, to Pickering, he ventured that a renewal of active Anglo-French warfare might yield the same result. A warring France, he reasoned, might welcome the opportunity to neutralize American hostility. Quite oppositely, then, an awareness of France's self-interest in keeping Americans neutral might override that otherwise provocative revolutionary logic which dictated that France should begin again her meddling in American politics. If Paris were so moved, the envoys might be received after all.[29] Whatever transpired, however, Murray privately wished that if the mission must fail, it fail decisively—and from causes that might be laid squarely on France. Then, with Britain active in the field, Congress might dare strong measures. "The existing war is equal to an alliance in our favour," he wrote to the younger Adams. The direction of his thinking was evident. Should his own country be brought to war, it would be a short step to pronouncing Britain the ally. That, too, would come.[30]

As autumn wore on, the news from Paris was disconcerting. First came a cheerful letter from Elbridge Gerry, informing Murray that Charles Maurice de Talleyrand, the Directory's Foreign Minister, had greeted the emissaries "politely & in a familiar & easy style." Gerry expected negotiations to open shortly. Next came a letter from all three

28. To Pickering, No. 10, The Hague, September 9, 1797, Netherlands Despatches, I; see also WVM to JQA, The Hague, October 1, 1797, *AHA Report of 1912*, 361–66.

29. To Pickering, No. 13, The Hague, October 10, 1797, Netherlands Despatches, I.

30. To JQA, October 1, 1797, *AHA Report of 1912*, 362.

envoys: they had been twice refused an audience in a single afternoon.[31] Then, on October 21, John Marshall may have missed an opportunity to change the course of history. He wrote Murray that the mission had not been officially received. He did not expect it to be received. But he gave Murray no explanation. In failing to tell Murray the sordid proposals made by Messieurs X, Y, and Z, Marshall delayed for a full month the State Department's knowledge of that episode. Had Marshall confided to Murray the substance of Talleyrand's machinations, word would have reached the administration in early February.[32] Instead, the envoys' decision to route dispatches through Lisbon, plus the slowness of Atlantic crossings that winter, meant that news of the XYZ Affair did not arrive in Philadelphia until the evening of March 4, 1798. Timing may well have been a significant factor in the crisis that followed. When the dispatches did arrive, they came all at once; the whole story of the envoys' humiliation could be read at one sitting. Thus, when House Republicans called for the correspondence, and subsequently published it, the impact on Congress and on public opinion was extreme. Preparations for war were begun at once. Had it been otherwise, had Murray been apprised of what was happening in Paris—at the time it happened —his piecemeal relaying of dispatches to Philadelphia might have had a less exciting effect.

Why the envoys did not use Murray as a channel of communication is as tantalizing a question as any answer must be speculative. Not until mid-January of 1798 did Murray learn (possibly from Pinckney) that "the French want a forced *loan* from the United States." Not until May 28 did he hear the whole story from Rufus King. The simplest explanation is that the envoys chose to send dispatches via Lisbon, rather than The Hague, because, although the Lisbon route was slower, it was safer from British interception. This does not explain, however, their failure to show Murray the same confidence they showed Rufus King. The American minister in London knew the details of XYZ as early as December 23, and was advising the envoys not to yield to French demands for loans and bribes.[33] It is difficult to resist accepting the likelihood that Murray was deliberately kept uninformed and that his colleagues in

31. Gerry to WVM, Paris, October 9, 1797, Misc. Letters, WVM MSS, LC; also U.S. Commissioners to WVM, Paris, October 10, attached to Murray's No. 15 to Pickering, October 17, 1797, Netherlands Despatches, I.

32. Marshall's letter was enclosed in Murray's No. 16 to Pickering, October 28, 1797, *ibid.*

33. King to the U.S. Commissioners, London, December 23, 1797, King, *Correspondence*, II, 262–63.

Paris, too gentlemanly, perhaps, to send him coded dispatches without
divulging their contents, were determined simply not to tell him anything. Obviously, Murray had little rapport with Elbridge Gerry who,
to his disgust, was too willing to believe the best of the Directory; but
neither did he have close personal or political ties with his fellow Federalists, Pinckney and Marshall.[34] Nor, remarkably, did Murray signify
that he expected confidences from the Paris mission. Though by axiom
politics make strange bedfellows, it was even truer that Federalist politics
made few bedfellows. Within the inner circle, the chosen few did not
include William Vans Murray. The silence from Paris, therefore, may
be taken as another measure of Murray's exclusion from the Federalist
establishment.

34. For a fuller treatment of the envoys' oversight see Peter P. Hill, "A
Speculative Footnote to XYZ," *Maryland Historical Magazine* (March 1966),
68–72.

6

Satellite Politics and a Touch of War Fever

ALTHOUGH THE Paris scene continued to hold Murray's fascinated attention, it was to The Hague that he owed his education in diplomacy. When he arrived at the Dutch capital in June, 1797, Murray found himself thrust into the midst of a revolution *à la française,* whose stormy progress John Quincy Adams had been reporting for more than two years. French influence had triumphed in January of 1795, when an invading force of French troops and "Batavian" legionaries had put an easy end to the ancient Republic of the United Netherlands. That same month the Hereditary Stadtholder, William V, had fled to England, leaving his government to the revolutionary ministrations of a patrician-hating party of *petite bourgeoisie.*[1] Out of these events had come the Batavian Republic, a regime whose underpinnings were so deeply buried in the volcanic sands of French politics and French ideology that every Parisian earthquake of the period shook The Hague with almost equal force. At first the Batavian "Patriots" had bought golden opinions by ousting the oligarchs from the places of power. What soon became apparent, however, was that in casting off their traditional leaders, the Dutch had put themselves in the hands of the French Directory. By May of 1796 the Batavian puppets had been forced into an alliance with France whose cost totaled a "contribution" to France of one hundred million florins, the cession of Maastrict, Venloo, and the province of Zeeland-Flanders, an agreement to outfit, feed, and quarter a French occupying force of 25,000, and a submission to the introduction of

1. See Robert R. Palmer, *The Age of Democratic Revolution: A Political History of Europe and America, 1760–1800* (Princeton: Princeton University Press, 1959), 324–40, for details of the disordered state of Dutch politics prior to the French invasion.

assignats. Four months later, this alliance with France had thrust the
Dutch into a ruinous war with England. Not only was Dutch commerce
interdicted by a close British blockade but, by the time Murray arrived,
the Batavian Republic had lost to England all of its overseas possessions except Surinam and Java.[2]

As Murray found his bearings in Dutch politics, two questions impressed him with their importance. First, did the supporters of the
deposed House of Orange stand any chance of overthrowing the puppet
regime? Or, barring that, could the puppets be persuaded to remain
neutral if their French ally went to war with the United States? Both
questions seemed to yield negative answers. Orangist prospects were
bleak: the British who might be expected to assist in a Stadtholderian
restoration were virtually alone in their contest with France, and their
navy was beset by mutiny. Moreover, the Orangists could scarcely take
matters into their own hands as long as French garrisons occupied every
Dutch province. Nor did Murray expect the Dutch to be able to exercise an option for war or neutrality should their French ally decide on
war with the United States. Where France led, Batavia must follow, no
matter what the cost.[3]

Though unhopeful of great changes, Murray nonetheless probed the
small fissures which might weaken the Franco-Batavian monolith. Careful not to exaggerate its importance, he noted, for example, the
humiliation visited on the Dutch in their not being asked to participate
in the Lille negotiations during which Ceylon and the Cape Colony were
topics of Anglo-French parleying.[4] More significant was the rudeness
with which the Dutch "fundamental" assemblies refused, in August, to
ratify a new revolutionary constitution. Here the battle centered on the
question of how much the old provincial sovereignties should give way
to a strong central authority. Through their disagreement, the revolutionaries had suffered a three-way split. The Radicals, styling themselves
"the Friends of the People," wanted a powerful unitary regime in which
the legislature would play a major role. The Moderates, called "Patriots,"
preferred that the provinces should retain some of their powers, and
favored a balance between executive and legislative branches at the top.
The Federalists, whom Murray called "the real Dutchmen, the friends
of Batavian independence," were the least enthusiastic about creating a

2. George Edmundson, *History of Holland* (London: Cambridge University
Press, 1922), 344–46.
3. WVM to Pickering, No. 1, The Hague, June 20, 1797, Netherlands Despatches, I.
4. Same to same, No. 6, The Hague, July 21, 1797, *ibid.*

strong central organ. This last group, he wrote, though few in number, would "as soon cut down their dykes as destroy the old provincial sovereignties." [5]

As it came from the hands of the National Assembly, the constitution reflected most nearly the views of the Moderates. A bicameral legislature was coupled with a strong executive, and by no means were the provinces reduced to mere appendages of the central government. Much to the chagrin of the Radicals, the French Directory signified its approval. This put the Radicals in the position of being more revolutionary than the French. Having fought the constitution on the familiar revolutionary ground that it was "too federal and too aristocratic," they listened in vain for an answering echo from Paris. By the time the constitution had reached the fundamental assemblies, the Radicals were being publicly embarrassed by the open support which the organic law was receiving from the French minister at The Hague, Jean François Noël.[6] Figuratively, the Dutch "Jacobins" were now out of phase with Paris and were caught between "Thermidor" and "Fructidor." In August of 1797, they were strong enough to defeat the Moderates' constitution, but their own dispensation would have to await the resurgence in Paris of the Directorial radicals. Throughout the constitutional battle Murray lacked nothing for accurate intelligence. He correctly predicted that the fundamental assemblies would not ratify, that M. Noël, himself embarrassed by this turn of events, would be recalled, and that it would take a conjuncture of "jacobinism" at both Paris and The Hague to unseat the Moderates.[7] The day would come in January 1798. Meanwhile, both Murray and John Quincy Adams were sorry to see Noël replaced. To Murray he was "as good as French politicians can be—mild & bookish —& too good for the guilty violence which the Jacobins here wish for & which they call ENERGY." [8] His replacement was the recent head of the French Foreign Office, Charles Delacroix, whose arrival at The Hague in October set the stage for the Radicals' *coup d'état* in January.

Noël may have been "too good for guilty violence," but in Murray's hardened view, no minister of revolutionary France could yet resist a political gaming table whereat France might call a turn. Noël's unre-

5. Cf. WVM to Pickering, No. 4, The Hague, June 30, 1797, *ibid.*; Edmundson, *History of Holland*, 349.

6. WVM to Pickering, Nos. 6 and 8 of July 21 and August 17, 1797, respectively, Netherlands Despatches, I.

7. *Ibid.*; also WVM to McHenry, The Hague, August 7, 1797, Steiner, *McHenry*, 246–48.

8. Entry of October 23, 1797, "Commonplace" dated 1797, 66, WVM MSS, LC, hereinafter referred to as "Commonplace" of 1797.

warded effort to win the Dutch to their new constitution was a species of
meddling which confirmed to the American his long-held belief that
"certain death . . . awaits the liberties and happiness of any people
among whom the French obtained a finger breadth of political ground." [9]

Murray ceased to be merely a watcher of diplomatic events when,
somewhat belatedly, in the fall of 1797 the Dutch regime requested an
explanation of the so-called "Adams Letter." His predecessor's asper-
sions on Batavia's susceptibility to Parisian influence would, in any
case, have evoked a protest from The Hague. It was apparent to Murray,
however, that the Fructidorian strengthening of the French executive
power now made it easier for the Dutch to pick a quarrel with the
United States. At issue was a letter which John Quincy Adams had
written to the State Department a year earlier. It dealt with a Batavian
complaint that the United States appeared to be powerless to prevent the
British from seizing Dutch cargoes from American merchantmen. Not
only had the Dutch complaint been insultingly worded, but to Adams,
who was then trying to bring The Hague to recognize a free-bottoms
claim in the *Wilmington Packet* case, it was infuriatingly incongruous.
In writing to Pickering, Adams had angrily put a Paris label on the
whole affair. The Dutch, he wrote,

> can have no avowed will different from that which may give satis-
> faction to the government of France. They feel a dependence so
> absolute and irremovable upon their goodwill, that they sacrifice
> every other inclination, and silence every other interest, when the
> pleasure of the French government is signified to them in such a
> manner as to make an election necessary.[10]

Unfortunately for Murray, Adams' father had incorporated excerpts
from this letter in the diplomatic correspondence which he sent to
Congress on May 19, 1797. Pickering explained why: the administration
hoped to educate the public to recognize the pervasive nature of the
French peril.[11] Only gradually did the Dutch learn who had written so
unkindly of their regime. In July the *Leyden Gazette* had published the
Adams' indictment but without identifying the author. As late as August

9. WVM to Pickering, No. 6, The Hague, July 21, 1797, Netherlands Despatches, I.
    10. JQA to Pickering, The Hague, November 4, 1796, *ibid.*
    11. To WVM, May 24, 1797, Instructions to U.S. Ministers, I, Record Group
59, National Archives, hereinafter cited as Instructions to Ministers, RG 59, NA.

23 Murray was able to tell Adams in Berlin that "not a word has been said to me by men in government about the extracts of your letters." [12] Then, on September 19, Murray met a routine request from Jacob Hahn, a member of the Dutch foreign relations committee, for a copy of Pickering's published instructions to Charles Cotesworth Pinckney in which the Adams extracts were mentioned. The next day Hahn asked the American minister to call on him. [13]

It was "an unpleasant scene," Murray recalled. Hahn was civil enough, but the letter to Pinckney which lay on the table before him called for an explanation. As to the Adams letter to which it alluded, the Dutchman said he had not seen it but he understood it to describe the Batavian Republic as a French province. He was not even sure that Adams was the author, but he could believe it because Adams "was consider'd here as British & Orange." Murray, as earlier instructed, explained to Hahn that his government had published diplomatic extracts

> not flattering to this country—but . . . related to a state of facts which all lamented & from wh. all men were free to draw conclusions that Batavia had been invaded & overrun by foreign troops . . . that a revolution had taken place—that one hundred mil'n Flor. had been exacted by public treaty—that 25,000 of these troops occupy'd this country. [14]

His government's purpose in publishing these facts, Murray explained, was to warn the American people of what might be their own fate, were French diplomats allowed to meddle in American public policy as they had in that of the Netherlands. Nor did Murray allow Hahn's characterization of John Quincy Adams to pass unchallenged. Adams, he said, was neither pro-British nor pro-Orange, but, like himself, believed that Britain was too powerful on the sea and France too powerful on the land. Moreover, Adams had never uttered a derogatory word about the Dutch without also expressing his regret at the sad estate to which their country had fallen. Hahn replied sulkily that were Adams still at The Hague his recall would have been asked for. Murray, he hoped, "entertained different sentiments" about the Batavian Republic. To this Murray answered evasively: "A minister must always write with freedom what he wrote with confidence & for the good of his own nation." Then, softening a little, Murray assured Hahn of his esteem for the historic Netherlands and its institutions.

12. *AHA Report of 1912*, 360.
13. Entry of September 20, 1797, "Commonplace" of 1797, 37.
14. Undated entry, *ibid.*, 127–28.

Finally, the Dutchman came to the point. Adams' insults, he re-marked fretfully, had given the French another handle in Dutch politics. Should France wish to push Batavia into "unfriendly measures" toward the United States, she would merely have to say: " 'See what they think of you. They openly insult you & call you a province of France.' " [15] Hahn's pique at Adams obviously weighed lightly against his anguish that the administration had given France this means of inciting ill will. Behind the facade of outraged dignity Murray clearly saw that the Dutch regime was determined to remain on good terms with the United States.[16]

Believing that his explanations to Hahn had settled the matter, Murray was intensely chagrined to learn a month later that Van Polanen had been instructed to lodge a formal protest at Philadelphia. Why, Murray asked, did the Dutch think this was necessary? Had he not already con-veyed Philadelphia's regrets at the discomfiture caused by the publica-tion of the Adams Letter? The answer was simple: the Dutch Foreign Office believed that Murray had devised his own explanation without official authorization. To this Murray hastened to reply that although he had brought with him no explicitly worded message of apology, he had nonetheless been formally instructed to express his government's regret. From the Dutch came the reaction: why didn't you say so in the first place? Murray was aghast. He explained to Pickering, "I had so said I was authorised"—but apparently Hahn had misunderstood him. In re-trospect, Murray guessed that his conversation with Hahn had been too informal; Hahn had mistakenly assumed that he was not speaking officially. At the time, Murray explained, it had seemed appropriate to avoid formalities because

> they would have expected from me a note to the committee . . .
> containing wider apology than was due, and a discussion upon the
> truth of certain positions complained of, to which . . . it would be
> unpleasant to be brought.[17]

Formalities now became unavoidable. While Van Polanen was told to extract from Philadelphia an explicit disavowal of Adams' strictures on Dutch impotence, Murray also was called upon to write a formal

15. *Ibid.*, 128–31. Other accounts of this meeting appear in Murray's letter to JQA, October 1, 1797, *AHA Report of 1912*, 361–66, and in Murray's No. 13 to Pickering, October 10, 1797, Netherlands Despatches, I.

16. WVM to JQA, October 1, 1797, *AHA Report of 1912*, 364.

17. To Pickering, Nos. 15 and 16 of October 17 and 28, 1797, respectively, Netherlands Despatches, I.

note of explanation.[18] Anxious lest this note not coincide with Pickering's reply to Polanen, Murray took the safest course and drafted a generalized response along the lines of his original instruction. Inwardly, he squirmed at the obvious awkwardness of being dunned for an explanation at the same time that an explanation was being sought at Philadelphia.[19] Outwardly, however, he told the Dutch foreign office that he was "now extremely rejoiced" to be able to make a formal acknowledgment "which ought to satisfy the Batavian government." Because his own government had "a sincere respect" for the Batavian Republic, it regretted the necessity of making public the Adams Letter. He recalled, however, that Adams had written disparagingly "not without cause and provocation."

At the root of the present controversy was the Dutch note to Adams of September 27, 1796, wherein the United States had been urged to "take to heart the numberless insults daily committed on their flag by the English." No minister, Murray observed, likes to be told that his country is "not sufficiently alive to daily insults." How else but by French influence could Adams have explained this departure of the Dutch government from its usual politeness and goodwill? By counterattacking, Murray succeeded in creating a diversion, at least to the extent that Hahn was put to searching the files of the foreign office in a vain effort to find a copy of the original offending note.[20] From Adams in Berlin, meanwhile, came the advice that Hahn should be told to look carefully, and if he found the note to mark it well because it and it alone had provoked his own dispatch to the State Department.[21]

Batavia's rulers may have winced painfully at having been characterized as puppets, but their later protests had a perfunctory quality. How could it have been otherwise when Murray's dialogue with Hahn was suddenly interrupted by a most disastrous proof of The Hague's subservience to Paris? On October 7, at French insistence, the Dutch war fleet, which had been gathered at the island of Texel, put to sea against the advice of its commanding admiral, Jan de Winter. Under a master plan drafted by French General Lazare Hoche, this squadron

18. Batavian Committee of Exterior Relations to WVM, The Hague, October 31, 1797, WVM MSS, I, 15–18, Pierpont Morgan Library, NYC, hereinafter abbreviated as ML.
19. WVM to Pickering, No. 21, The Hague, November 5, 1797, Netherlands Despatches, I.
20. WVM to the Batavian Committee of Exterior Relations, November 4, 1797, WVM MSS, ML.
21. To WVM, November 24, 1797, Adams MSS, MR 130.

was to land troops on the Clyde in a diversionary maneuver designed to force the British to pull troops out of Ireland. Meanwhile, the major French effort against Ireland was to be launched from Brest.

The plan miscarried badly. On the eve of de Winter's departure General Hoche died; the Brest fleet never sailed, but the Dutch did— into the waiting guns of a British squadron under Admiral Duncan. On October 11 off the Dutch town of Kamperduin (Camperdown), de Winter's sixteen ships of the line met an equal number under Duncan and were badly beaten. Throughout the day of the battle Murray, along with other residents of the Dutch capital, listened tensely to the sound of cannonading out to sea. What they heard but could not see was Duncan's bold attack, striking at the rear and middle of the Dutch line from both the leeward and windward sides, a risky maneuver which ended with the British capture of nine ships, two frigates, and the Dutch admiral. A premature victory celebration was cut short at The Hague when the devastating news arrived. For days afterwards, Murray reported, bodies and spars washed up on the beaches nearby.[22]

Duncan's victory at Camperdown ended any immediate threat to Britain of invasion from the Dutch coast. For the Dutch, it meant a further decline in prestige. And for Murray, whose heart went out to the Dutch in their distress, there was satisfaction in knowing that France had lost a useful auxiliary to her naval strength.[23] The American minister was also gratified at the "symptoms of dissatisfaction" which Camperdown had caused at the Dutch end of Franco-Batavian relations. Dutch assemblymen, usually amenable to French direction, bitterly denounced France for having "urged this battle wh. has ended in the total crippling of the navy." The assembly's anger showed most plainly in its overwhelming refusal to send a deputation to attend the funeral of General Hoche, the architect of French invasion plans. If Murray's intelligence was correct, the deputies had excused themselves on grounds that they "had not time to attend every French Fete." Were it not for the French military presence in Belgium, he concluded, the Dutch might well have made peace with England in the wake of their naval disaster.[24] So preoccupied was Murray with the possible diplomatic consequences of

22. For general accounts see Edmundson, *History of Holland*, 347; and *Cambridge Modern History*, VIII, 481–82. Murray's accounts of the disaster are contained in his Despatch No. 14 to Pickering, Netherlands Despatches, I, and his letter of October 13 to McHenry, Steiner, *McHenry*, 285–87.

23. WVM to JQA, The Hague, November 4, 1797, *AHA Report of 1912*, 366–70; also entry of October 28, 1797, "Commonplace" of 1797, 68, LC; and Murray to Pickering, No. 14, Netherlands Despatches, I.

24. Entry of October 22, 1797, "Commonplace" of 1797, LC.

Camperdown that he overlooked its effect on the Dutch domestic scene. What he failed to foresee was that the Radical faction would now come to the fore. Disappointed by the constitution, which they had refused to take from the hands of the Moderates in August, the Radicals now purposefully laid the blame for Camperdown on the Moderates' provisional government. Thus, the naval disaster, plus the encouragement they derived from witnessing the ouster of Moderate forces in Paris, inspired the Dutch Left to engineer their own *coup d'état* at The Hague the following January.[25] As the waters of Dutch politics rolled to a boil, quite naturally the affair of the "Adams Letter" fell into the limbo of forgotten trivia. In retrospect, Murray, although discomfited at the memory of his awkwardness in dealing with Jacob Hahn, was consoled by the thought that his first serious diplomatic encounter had, after all, produced more "inkshed" than bloodshed.[26]

The belief intoxicatingly shared by most American diplomats of this era was that, given the right moment, the tangled skein of European power politics could be unraveled to yield some vital advantage to American national interest. As the historian Samuel F. Bemis has so fully demonstrated, Europe's distress often worked to America's advantage. In his efforts to discover what the next windfall might be, William Vans Murray ventured somewhat extravagantly into the realm of political speculation during the darkening autumn of 1797. The path of logic which he took seemed straight and clear; that it would end in a wilderness of unreality was not at first apparent. His reasoning began with the thesis that his country's major interest lay in avoiding war. Ranged against this was the antithetical near-certainty that France would force war upon the United States. The synthesis that resulted was that if war did not destroy American nationhood, it might somehow strengthen it. It was in this speculative piecing together of possible advantages that Murray ultimately lost touch with reality and had to be rescued by his friend, John Quincy Adams.

For his initial thesis—that war should be avoided—Murray held out slim hope. Should Duncan's fleet, now released from its watch on the Dutch coast, be sent to the Caribbean, France would become more than ever dependent on American shipping to supply her West Indian islands. That the Directory would awaken to this possibility, and therefore choose to deal amicably with the American commission, Murray thought

25. Edmundson, *History of Holland*, 350.
26. Entry of October 22, 1797, "Commonplace" of 1797, 65–66, LC.

problematical. Another frail hope was that the Directory could be persuaded that it had too much to lose by involving either France or the Dutch in a war that would deprive Paris of the tribute she was wont to levy on Dutch-American commerce.[27] To nurture this hope, Murray assiduously gathered trade statistics which he urged the Dutch to relay to Paris; these statistics showed how heavily France depended on revenues derived from Dutch-American trade. The financial argument against dragging Batavia into a Franco-American war would, he hoped, act equally to deter France herself from war. And lest France construe his arguments to mean that he expected the American negotiation in Paris to fail, Murray urged the Dutch to assure their French allies that the United States earnestly sought a peaceful denouement.[28] Not surprisingly, the Batavian Committee of Foreign Affairs gave Murray a favorable hearing. Their life-giving commerce already hard hit by British blockades, the Dutch were eager to avoid any worsening of trade that would surely result from war with the United States. Murray was assured that the Batavian Republic sincerely wished to remain at peace. He was warned, however, that Dutch entry into a Franco-American war might well hinge on whether the United States came to war as a formal ally of Great Britain. In that eventuality, Batavia would be forced to make common cause with France.[29]

Against these fragile hopes for peace Murray saw a far greater likelihood that the Directory, now dominated by Merlin de Douai and Talleyrand, would capitalize on Austria's exit from the war to attempt another invasion of England. Americans could scarcely expect France to remain at peace with a government whom they looked on as British lackeys. Moreover, the quickening tempo of French depredations on American shipping, coupled with the Directory's refusal to receive Pinckney, Marshall, and Gerry, made the prospect for peace look even more bleak. This last—the French refusal of embassy—was patently the most critical factor. Federalists generally, Murray among them, were beginning to see no alternative to war should France completely close down the channels of diplomacy.[30]

27. WVM to McHenry, The Hague, October 13, 1797, Steiner, *McHenry*, 285–87; WVM to Pickering, No. 11, The Hague, September 10, 1797, Netherlands Despatches, I.

28. WVM to McHenry, The Hague, September 21, 1797, Steiner, *McHenry*, 275–85; WVM to JQA, The Hague, October 21, 1797, *AHA Report of 1912*, 365.

29. WVM to Pickering, No. 16, The Hague, October 28, 1797, Netherlands Despatches, I; see also Murray's conversation with Hahn, entry of October 27, 1797, "Commonplace" of 1797, 40–41, LC.

30. See, for example, John Adams to the Heads of Departments, Philadelphia, January 24, 1798, Adams' *Works,* VIII, 561–62; and Oliver Wolcott to John

Had war come in late 1797, Federalist chieftains were ready to make the most of it. Murray was not alone in testing the ill wind of war which might also bring national advantage. Not only were Federalist leaders calling for a staunch defense, but they were already actively contemplating a counter-stroke against France in the West Indies. Here, ostensibly, a conjuncture of American manpower and British seapower would win for England the French island of Santo Domingo, and for the United States possession of Louisiana and the Floridas, to be seized from France's Spanish ally.[31] Not content to stop there, men like Hamilton and Rufus King were already encouraging the South American revolutionary, Francisco Miranda, to enlist British support for a grand Anglo-American liberation of all of Latin America.[32] A declared war with France and a formal alliance with England seemed to be the essential ingredients. The prize, if Spain's grip to the south were shaken, would be a great new area opened to American commerce.

Although Hamilton tended to equivocate on the question of a declared war, some of his most influential followers had no hesitations. Federalists like King, Pickering, Ames, and Cabot not only expected war and urged warlike measures, but they also openly expressed the wish that it would come.[33] These men were to become the Warhawks of '98, spokesmen of an abortive policy of manifest destiny. Their more moderate colleagues, however, would hold back. John Adams—and Murray, too, once his excitement had subsided—would shy away, both from the notion of a British alliance and its concommitants, war and expansion. To Adams, as to Murray, war would remain an expression

---

Adams, Gray's Gardens, October 24, 1797, Gibbs, *Wolcott*, I, 571–72, as well as WVM to Pickering, No. 23, The Hague, November 10, 1797, Netherlands Despatches, I; JQA to WVM, Berlin, November 18, 1797, Adams MSS, MR 130; and King to Gerry, London, December 24, 1797, King, *Correspondence*, II, 264–65.

31. See, for example, Col. John Trumbull to Oliver Wolcott, London, January 15, 1798, Gibbs, *Wolcott*, I, 474; King to Pickering, London, February 7, 1798, King, *Correspondence*, II, 281.

32. Among the most recent secondary works treating with the Hamilton-King-Miranda intrigue is Alexander DeConde, *The Quasi-War: the Politics and Diplomacy of the Undeclared War with France, 1797–1800* (New York: Charles Scribner's Sons, 1966), 116–19, hereinafter cited as DeConde, *Quasi-War*.

33. King to Hamilton, London, July 31, 1798, King, *Correspondence*, II, 374–76; Pickering to King, No. 7, Philadelphia, April 2, 1798, Instructions to Ministers, IV, RG 59, NA; Ames to Pickering, July 10, 1798, Seth Ames, ed., *Works of Fisher Ames* (Boston: Little Brown and Company, 1854), I, 234; George Cabot to King, October 6, 1798, King, *Correspondence*, II, 438–40. Dauer finds that even Hamilton was not reluctant for war, although the latter's elliptical prose makes it difficult to settle this point. Cf. Dauer, *Adams Federalists*, 188n; DeConde, *Quasi-War*, 171.

of national honor requiring widespread public support. To the mercantile Federalists, war was to be the occasion for broadening the range of American commerce and for maintaining the ascendency of the Federalist party. In these divergent purposes lay a major difference between the Moderate and High Federalists.

Murray caught the war fever early. It lasted from November 1797 into the summer of 1798. First came the tentative communing with John Quincy Adams. Suppose we came to war with France? Should we not look to Britain for help? Yes, Murray thought, the United States should at least seek "cooperation" in that quarter, but "without alliance." A simple cooperation with Britain against a common enemy would, he believed, "work out our safety cheaply and with greater conformity to the public feelings in the United States." [34] Murray's allusion to "public feelings" showed his perceptiveness. To an American public already afflicted with one alliance, the very word "alliance" was fast becoming synonymous with "entanglement." Even Alexander Hamilton recognized the public's sensitivity when, two months later, he urged that Rufus King explore various avenues of cooperation with the British, warning, however, that "it is believed to be best, in any event, to avoid *alliance*." [35]

Anglo-American "cooperation," however, connoted something less pejorative, and perhaps equally useful. This thought occurred to Murray during that conversation with Jacob Hahn in which the Dutchman had warned that Batavia could remain aloof from a Franco-American conflict only if the United States were not formally allied with Britain. War with France, he reasoned, need not entail a formal alliance with England. "In fact wh.out [without] a formal alliance we sh'd have all the benefits of one." But would London agree merely to "cooperate" on an informal basis unless the United States pledged itself not to make a separate peace? Murray doubted that it would.[36] Later, when a British alliance was seriously talked of in the administration, this fear that Britain would "tie our hands" was one of John Adams' reasons for holding back. Too, Murray perceived that in any cooperative venture Britain, because of her seapower, would doubtless emerge disproportionately aggrandized by the taking of French, Dutch, and Spanish possessions in the Caribbean.[37]

34. To JQA, The Hague, November 4, 1797, *AHA Report of 1912*, 367.
35. To McHenry, January, 1798, Steiner, *McHenry*, 291.
36. Entry of October 27, 1797, "Commonplace" of 1797, 40–41, LC; see also WVM to Washington, The Hague, November 4, 1797, WVM MSS, III, 55–60, ML.
37. WVM to John Marshall, The Hague, November 2, 1797, *ibid.*, 53; same to C.C. Pinckney, November 6, 1797, *ibid.*, 63. For John Adams' view of an alliance

At this point in his speculations, Murray thought he had hit on the perfect solution. Perhaps the heirs to French, Dutch, and Spanish colonies could be found among the lesser powers of Northern Europe. If the thrust southward were bilateral—British and American only— Britain would surely be the chief gainer. But suppose Prussia, Sweden, and Denmark were baited into an anti-French coalition by the prospect of acquiring Caribbean holdings? The result, he predicted, would be "to change the face of Europe in 20 years." [38] With this, Murray began to elaborate what he later fondly called his *"projet."* In letters to Pickering and to the younger Adams Murray pursued his coalition project intermittently for nearly a year. Its substance changed as circumstances changed, and from time to time Adams threw cold water on it from Berlin. Nevertheless, Murray's *projet* illustrated a persistent characteristic of Federalist diplomacy: its awareness that in the changing power patterns of a Europe at war lay possible advantage to the United States. It may also have stimulated that later architect of the Monroe Doctrine, John Quincy Adams, to think of Latin America in broader terms than he might otherwise have done. To Pickering, even before he sounded out Adams, Murray boldly put his proposal in these terms:

> The more I consider the present state of commerce, & thence the existing and the potential marine ability of France, Spain & other nations, the more I am persuaded, Sir, that, however irksome a co-operation with the British marine might be, with it, a total change might be worked in the commerce of Europe. The only good to the United States would be present aid. The avoidance of the evil to the U.S., which might arise from too great an aggrandisement of Great-Britain, would be the transfer of the colonies to other powers. The present is the only opportunity for such a plan since the discovery of America.[39]

Though wholly at variance with the later American policy of nontransfer, Murray's proposal to reshuffle the colonial empires of the New World illustrates the fluidity of contemporary diplomatic conjecturing. It was of a piece, for example, with Rufus King's contemporaneous intrigue in London with the Latin American revolutionary, Francisco Miranda. A month later, and again to Pickering, Murray named Prussia,

see Charles Francis Adams, ed., *The Works of John Adams, Second President of the United States* (Boston: Little, Brown and Company, 1850–1856), IX, 268, hereinafter cited as Adams, *Works.*
38. Entry of December 1, 1797, "Commonplace" of 1797, 200, LC.
39. No. 25, The Hague, December 16, 1797, Netherlands Despatches, I.

Sweden, and Denmark as possible partners in an Anglo-American concert.

> Our temptations for them are in the West Indies, and in a co-operation with the British marine. These possessions may be transferred. Since the discovery of America there was never such an opportunity of dividing, if not transferring these.[40]

In mid-January Murray's *projet* took wings when the French government decreed a maritime measure so hostile to neutral shipping that the Northern neutrals seemed certain to rise up against their French oppressor. Should France succeed in driving both the United States and Northern Europe into war against her, his plan for the redistribution of Caribbean islands, he believed, might come to fruition. Enthralled, now, by the sweep of what he proposed, Murray became briefly the most ardent of war hawks. "Yes," he exclaimed to Adams,

> we can *at this moment* (but not again for five centuries perhaps) transfer or revolutionize all the colonies of Europe hostile to the United States. The value of this to the United States would be ten times the cost in a free West Indian and South American trade, besides the crippling of a foe. So far from having fears [of war], I assure you I feel a pride which rises as the occasion advances.[41]

March found Murray convinced that it was time to put the question of war to the American people. Pickering had been repeatedly warned not to expect an accommodation with France. And although Murray was not entirely sure of the Secretary's receptivity, he wrote the younger Adams that he planned to take a stronger line in warning the State Department of the imminence of war. The great majority of Americans, he believed, would actively support a war against France, although a resistant minority might have to be crushed. In one of the most virulently partisan passages he ever wrote, Murray came murderously close to the highest of High Federalist passions.

> The call of the present hour is for the worthy and the free to bring over the unworthy and the base to their standard, or to force them into submission or to know their lot. The division must soon take place. . . . The delay of this distinction, practical and clear, but nurses treason against our glorious liberties and country.[42]

Despite its implacable rhetoric, this passage nonetheless revealed a

40. No. 27, January 16, 1798, *ibid.*
41. February 3, 1798, *AHA Report of 1912*, 377.
42. To JQA, March 12, 1798, *ibid.*, 386.

major difference between the High and the Moderate Federalist. To the hard-core partisan, a war with France was devoutly to be wished because it would confer the positive benefit of discrediting the Republican party. To men like Murray, however, the extinction of political opponents were merely incidental to the more important end of vindicating the national honor. To the Marylander who was always more patriot than partisan, crushing Republicans was not so important as trying to win them over with good arguments and appeals to national unity.[43]

Back in the context of his *projet,* Murray considered other questions. Could France hurt America in war? He doubted it; French principles were more dangerous than French armies. Would the neutrals be persuaded to join a coalition? They might be, if France showed signs of weakening; already there was unrest in the satellites. Moreover, French prestige would surely reach its nadir when, as Murray was convinced, the Directory would try again but fail to invade England. And finally, should both the United States and the powers of Northern Europe be swept into an active anti-French coalition, would London then see the expediency of bestowing former French and Spanish colonies on her co-belligerents? Murray had no ready answer. He knew only that "these times demand a blow—a vast convulsion—a fundamental attack." [44] And yet, curiously, though Murray envisioned the annexation of Louisiana and the Floridas to the United States, he consciously rejected the notion that his own country become a colonial power. Like some Americans a century later, he found imperialism incompatible with "the genius of both government and nation." Statehood was the proper mode—even statehood for South America was not unthinkable—but not the imposition of colonial status on a subject people.[45]

John Quincy Adams, on whom Murray tried his *projet,* responded with sober disparagements. Prussia, he noted, had neither the fleet nor the funds to undertake a venture in the New World. Moreover, if the French invasion of England succeeded, the neutral powers would be rendered helpless; if the invasion failed, France would be left so weak on the high seas as to no longer offend the neutrals with her maritime strictures; the motive for coalition would quickly disappear. The two men did agree, however, that Europe's wars would continue to loosen the ties between the Old World and the New. Even now, Adams pointed

43. Dauer notes this distinction in his *Adams Federalists* (pp. 200–201), and this passage, taken from Murray's correspondence at the peak of his enthusiasm for war, seems to illustrate it.

44. To JQA, The Hague, March 12, 1798, *AHA Report of 1912,* 385; see also WVM to Pickering, No. 35, March 12, 1798, Netherlands Despatches, I.

45. Letters to JQA of March 12 and July 6, 1798, *AHA Report of 1912,* 385, 428.

out, a France that was ascendant in Europe was losing its grip on its overseas possessions. Foreshadowing the statesman who would one day set forth "the law of political gravitation," Adams predicted that the United States would ultimately fall heir to some sort of hegemony over the New World.[46]

Murray took Adams' dampening commentary in stride, writing:

> You have at a stroke dashed my projet through and through. Certainly I did not predicate upon a supposed understanding and energy in other powers; still with a paternal bias I do think there are parts of this plan that war would render a respectable subject for reflection, and I suppose every projector feels the same.[47]

Although by July Murray had virtually given up hope for his *projet,* he and Adams continued to ruminate over the future of Latin America. Almost casually, Murray suggested that perhaps the continental part of South America could "be made a State or States" of the Union. Adams disagreed: alliances would be profitable, perhaps, but not annexation. "In close alliance," he wrote, "leaving them as to their Government totally to themselves, we can protect their Independence, furnish them with necessaries and stipulate for the exclusive carriage of their produce." Murray, meanwhile, dropped the whole question of statehood. He even showed misgivings at the prospect of Latin American independence. Santo Domingo, for example, with its large Negro population would, he suspected, "fall into chaos and negroism." Should the United States assist in liberating the French islands, it would be salutary for France "after the war to regain them, and then, *know that we can wound her,* or any mother country! And we can do that, and more! and I hope will!" Thus, if neither annexation nor liberation were desirable, the islands might retain some value as hostages for the future good behavior of France. Again Adams disagreed: France should be expelled entirely from the New World. Let France have Europe, was Adams' view, but "no part of America."

On July 20 Murray yielded to his friend's superior arguments. As for his own *projet,* he wrote, he had "half given it up" because it hinged on too many unlikely contingencies. Adams' proposal for "close alliance" between the United States and the former colonies had the

46. JQA to WVM, Berlin, letters of March 3, 13, and 20, 1798, Adams MSS, MR 130.

47. For this series of exchanges see Murray's letters of July 6 and 17, 1798, in *AHA Report of 1912,* 428, 433–34, and Adams' responses of July 14 and 24, 1798, in the Adams MSS, MR 133.

virtue of simplicity; it did not depend on the cooperation of other powers, and it might serve to prevent what he called "negro despotism . . . with a set of white Devils as counsellors and council." Of their respective views, he wrote, "yours is a longitude established in your room, and mine a circumnavigation dependent on wind and weather to get at it." [48] Not to be outdone in graciousness, Adams conceded that in foreseeing the likelihood of native misgovernment Murray had, after all, made a strong case against independence.[49]

Murray lived to see an abortive fulfillment of his coalition project in the "Armed Neutrality" of 1800. Those same nations—Prussia, Sweden, and Denmark—which Murray had earmarked for an anti-French coalition were, at this later time, ranged against Britain under French and Russian leadership. The petty jealousies which soon arose to prevent any effective cooperation, even in the weightier presence of Napoleon and the Czar, led Murray to conclude that "perhaps the history of every coalition upon speculative points will prove the same truth." [50] Had he lived to see the downfall of Napoleon, Murray might have thought better of coalition warfare, although considering the time it took to shape a coalition effective to that end, he might simply have been confirmed in his doubts.

If, in hindsight, a pipe-dream quality lingers over Murray's coalition scheme, it should be recalled that the French Revolution manifested itself not only in the minds of men but also in their arts of war. Murray was deeply impressed by the boldness and success of French armies in overcoming the legions of the old regimes. The French soldier's maxim, he noted, was "nothing is impossible." Small wonder that Murray, himself an apostle of vigorous nationalism, should dream no little dreams for his own country and yearn for a call to its destiny because "these things demand a blow." [51]

For Murray, this willingness to abandon the Washington policy of neutrality and noninvolvement proved to be a passing aberration. Unlike the High Federalists, who persisted in hoping for war until Adams came down decisively on the side of peace, Murray had relinquished any grand design for promoting coalition warfare by midsummer of 1798. Once cured of his enthusiasm for war, Murray was to step readily into the role of peacemaker which events were to thrust upon him.

48. The Hague, July 20, 1798, *AHA Report of 1912*, 438–39.
49. Berlin, July 28, 1798, Adams MSS, MR 133.
50. WVM to the Secretary of State, No. 132, The Hague, May 7, 1801, Netherlands Despatches, I.
51. To Pickering, No. 22, The Hague, November 6, 1797, *ibid.;* and to JQA, The Hague, March 12, 1798, *AHA Report of 1912*, 385.

7

Revolution, Dutch-Style and a Rebuke

ON MONDAY MORNING, January 22, 1798, Murray, much to his disgust, witnessed his first *coup d'état*. That day the Dutch Radicals, with Paris backing, unseated the Moderate regime and established at The Hague a provisional government more in keeping with the political bent of Fructidorian France. In the parlance of the day, Batavia had been "fructidorized," which was to say, purified by being pushed to the left, and thus reborn, ostensibly, in the image of those who had asserted power in Paris the previous September. No matter how loudly the Dutch Radicals proclaimed the spontaneity of what happened at the Hague that morning, Murray was thoroughly convinced that France had called the tune. From first to last he saw the January coup for what it was: a French manipulation, planned by a French secret agent named Guillaume Bonnecarrère, heralded by a manifesto denouncing the Moderates as aristocrats, and brought off by the French minister himself. With "armed burghers and Dutch troops" standing by, the Radicals had simply arrested enough Moderate members of the National Assembly to permit the remaining Radical rump to announce the establishment of a new provisional government.[1]

Murray was quite clear in his own mind as to what had happened and why. The Radicals had been unable to gain control of the National

1. Murray's accounts of the coup and the events which foreshadowed it may be found in three places: his letters to JQA in the *AHA Report of 1912,* 371–378 *passim;* his dispatches to Pickering, Nos. 17 and 25, of October 29 and December 16, 1797, respectively; and later Nos. 27, 28, and 29, of January 22, 23, and 31, 1798, respectively, in Netherlands Despatches, I; and his entries in his "Commonplace" of 1797, 73, 127, 137, 275, 281–304 *passim.* Edmundson's *History of Holland* (p. 350) substantiates the accuracy of what Murray read into this revolutionary situation.

Assembly during the autumn elections. Not only were they frustrated by their minority position, but they also found it unendurable that the Assembly's constitutional committee should be so reluctant to sweep away the provincial sovereignties in favor of their own proposal for a highly centralized "unitarian" regime. Now, on signal from Paris, their hopes were to be realized. Nor were the motives of the French Directory obscure: any faction which came to power at The Hague by dint of French connivance would be forced to submit to French direction, especially if that faction had only minority support. Thus, as Murray saw it, the new regime could not but be the instrument of France. If the new Dutch government proved to be more highly centralized, the more easily it would be controlled from Paris. Such control was important, for the French would need Dutch cooperation in the forthcoming invasion of England.[2]

Led by a Radical luminary named Pieter Vreede, whom Murray described as being bold, energetic, and decisive, the Radicals accomplished their coup bloodlessly. The Moderates were systematically proscribed and arrested, among them "poor Hahn," Murray noted. Supporting Vreede in the near background were Charles Delacroix, the recently arrived French minister; General Herman Willem Daendels, the Dutch officer who in 1795 had led the "Batavian" legion in Pichegru's invading army; and General Barthelémy Joubert, commander of the French occupation forces. It was Charles Delacroix who fascinated Murray by the obviously pivotal role he played. Murray had heard that Delacroix, while dining with a group of Moderate leaders during the first week in January, had prescribed for the assembled diners that "you must have a constitution on such and such principles. If you will not agree, I will give you one!" [3] Delacroix' part in the coup was confirmed when, at an official banquet on March 21, Murray overhead the French minister brag in a loud voice that he had spoken "very plainly to these men at Citoyen Hahn's Dinner *& I resolved from that day to make the Revolution!*" [4] Murray could readily believe the boast. At one o'clock on the day of the coup he had heard Delacroix' speech of "confratulation" given to the National Assembly amid cheers of *"vive la République."* He strongly suspected that the Frenchman had been awaiting the call, his speech prepared in advance.

The coup itself was not without wry detail. An assemblyman named

2. See especially, WVM to Pickering, Nos. 25, 27, 28, Netherlands Despatches, I; and his "Commonplace" entries of January 22 and 23, 1798.
3. Undated entry, "Commonplace" of 1797, 227.
4. Entry of March 21, 1798, *ibid.,* 265.

Voss, Murray noted, had been laid up with gout when the arrests were made. When the list of proscribed members was published, Voss discovered that his name was not included and wrote immediately to the new chairman of the Assembly demanding that it be added to those of his colleagues whom "he was proud to be among." Instead of being confined under house arrest, Voss was thrown in prison. Murray recorded the incident in his "Commonplace" entry of January 24, 1798.

Raw, sensitive, and doubtless unsure of themselves, the Radicals showed little sense of humor. In February Murray told of a mounted soldier, stationed in front of the Directorial palace, who, as he put it, "got into trouble by his wit—a rare thing to disturb the Peace here."

> His horse, a great, black, heavy, long tail peaceable animal, became tired of standing on the pavement & grew restive. He flounced a little & the soldier damned & giving him a blow with the flat of his sabre said "What I suppose you are a revolutionary too damn you!" he was overheard by some of the Quintuple Kings & was put in prison.[5]

There was also a touch of the sardonic in Murray's description of the "Quintuple Kings" themselves. At an audience on January 31 he stood with other members of the diplomatic corps when, suddenly, four of the five Directors appeared in full regalia,

> en costume with Henry 4th Hats plumé—& superb sashes and scarfs of red blue & white with rich gold fringe at bottom. . . . they were in a row & for new made sovereigns looked well. [Wybo] Finje very erect indeed—toes out—head up—but he is a very pleasant & well informed man. . . . Vreede, who is the Revolution, as Robespierre said "je suis le Peuple" looked well & like a man of energy as he is. [Johan Pieter] Fokker is one of the most diminutive little fellows I ever saw. With his back to you he looks like a runted thin boy of thirteen. [Stephanus] Van Langen is a handsome fresh & genteel looking man.[6]

Though reputed to be honest men, not one of the five Directors, Murray felt, carried any political weight in the nation as a whole. They were merely puppets chosen by Delacroix. As such, they were not likely to put themselves out (perhaps in actuality) by straining for neutrality if France bade them go to war. Dutch neutrality was not to be counted

---

5. February 10, 1798, *ibid.*, 316.
6. Murray's "Photostat Diary", LC pp. 195–96v) gives further description of the Directors, their vocations, reputations, and personal appearance.

on as long as the influence of France prevailed. Clear enough to Murray, however, was that no Dutch faction—not even the newly crowned Radicals—actively wanted war with the United States; but it was equally clear that if France should insist, Batavia would comply. Superficially at least, the members of the new regime struck him as being as well disposed toward the United States as they dared to be. Wybo Finje, the President of the Directory, confided to Murray that he had been one of the early supporters of the cause of American independence, and expressed the hope that the two republics could form closer ties in the future. Even the French minister, Charles Delacroix, "is suspiciously civil to me," Murray observed, adding warily, "I fear this kindness from Greeks." [7] With reason, he bore the Frenchman a hearty dislike. On February 13, only three weeks after the coup, he wrote in his "Commonplace" that Delacroix was the only man in all Batavia "who durst open his lips or write a word against the late measures." How influential the French minister was Murray learned with astonishment, when it was announced that the principle of Franco-Batavian solidarity was to be written into the new Dutch constitution. That the formality of alliance should be incorporated in an organic law struck Murray as being peculiarly humbling. What, now, could Batavia expect but to be dragged "groaning airs of Liberty through all the mud & misery into which the triumphs of France may force her?" [8]

With French influence ascendent at The Hague, the only real hope Murray saw for the future of Batavian-American amity lay in the remote possibility that the Dutch Moderates would recover from their political defeat and, in turn, oust the Radicals. The most he could report, however, was that the January regime was unpopular: the old provincial estates balked at voting themselves into oblivion; the provinces that were relatively debt-free objected to sharing the burden of a consolidated debt; and the people themselves were demonstrating publicly against the purging of Moderates from the fundamental assemblies.[9] Between discontent and overt opposition, however, lay a world of difference. On the day of the coup Murray was assailed by mixed feelings of sympathy and disgust as he watched the placid Dutch burghers allow their "mock sovereignty" to be dragged to the "scaffold" without remonstrance, with-

7. WVM to Pickering, Nos. 28 and 36, The Hague, dated January 23 and March 18, 1798, respectively, Netherlands Despatches, I. See also entries of February 7 and March 21, 1798, "Commonplace" of 1797, 310, 263–64.

8. WVM to Sylvanus Bourne (U.S. consul at Amsterdam), The Hague, April 4, 1798, Misc. Letters, WVM MSS, LC.

9. To Pickering, Nos. 31 and 37, The Hague, February 11 and March 27, 1798, respectively, Netherlands Despatches, I.

out question, and with only 1,500 troops in the capital. Neither the ousted Assemblymen nor the members of the provincial estates offered even token resistance.[10]

Individual Dutchmen, Murray knew, felt the hurt and disgrace of what had happened. "There is a great deal of Dutch smothered turf burning in the hearts of many," he wrote, "but they are as cautious as if a French grenadier had his bayonet at their bosoms." [11] And again: "Men in and out of public station . . . have told me of the utter undoing of their country. . . . It cannot be otherwise among a people whose character is moderation and justice." [12]

It was this very trait of moderation, Murray thought, that would make the Moderate political faction slow to rise in insurrection. But once aroused, they might "do wonders." In this last Murray was not disappointed. By June the Moderates, having put up long enough with Delacroix' puppets, overthrew them by counter-coup. Where Murray misgauged, however, was in supposing that a restoration of the middle faction would free Batavia measurably from French influence. In fact, when the Moderates came back to power, it was with the explicit permission of Paris. The writ of France would continue to run to The Hague for many years to come.

Though the January regime was short-lived and soon over, Murray's official recognition of it taught him a lesson he never forgot. Innately a courteous man to whom verbal pleasantries were the balm of existence, Murray made the horrendous diplomatic error of greeting the new government too cordially. His friend Adams tried to warn him that his niceties had been too nice, but the warning came too late.[13] Timothy Pickering, when he heard of it, breathed such flames of wrath that the sensitive Marylander was scorched to his inmost being.

It all began on January 31 when Murray attended a diplomatic reception and listened impatiently while the Dutch revolutionary leader, Pieter Vreede, directed a lengthy encomium to Charles Delacroix and the "great republic of France." Although Vreede made not even passing reference to the goodwill of the United States, Murray suppressed his resentment and later, on receiving a copy of the speech, wrote back that he received it "with the greatest pleasure and deference." Then, com-

10. To Pickering, No. 31, Netherlands Despatches, I; also entries of January 22, 23, and 25, 1798, "Commonplace" of 1797, 283, 289, 304.

11. Entry of January 23, *ibid.*, 292.

12. To Pickering, No. 29, The Hague, January 31, 1798, Netherlands Despatches, I.

13. JQA to WVM, Berlin, February 13, 1798, Adams MSS, MR 130.

pounding his insincerity, he informed the new regime (when its existence was announced to him) that President Adams would welcome its accession "with greatest satisfaction." And as if this were not enough, Murray also expressed to Vreede his belief that one result of the revolution would be to strengthen "the power of the Batavian nation against their enemy [i.e., Britain]." [14]

Pickering was thoroughly outraged. Why, he wanted to know, had Murray not withheld recognition until Vreede had explained why all reference to the United States had been omitted from his speech to the diplomatic corps? Why had Murray expressed pleasure on receiving a copy of that speech when by its omission it constituted an insult to the United States? Why had he conveyed President Adams' "greatest satisfaction" in recognizing the new regime when, in fact, the administration detested the whole revolutionary faction? And finally, by what stretch of courtesy was it necessary to wish Batavia strengthened in her war with England? Layer by layer, Pickering tore away the fabric of Murray's verbiage. He was sure that Murray had seen "the necessity of 'going with the government de facto,' 'of following the stream' while in your heart you felt 'the sentiment of sorrow at the whole of this revolution.' " Indeed, Murray had been authorized to recognize new regimes, but, Pickering queried, "may not such respect and acquiescence be manifested without paying a pointed homage to unworthy usurpers . . . ?" The Secretary then lectured Murray at some length on the proper uses of meaningless phraseology, concluding that the American government was wont

> to speak to foreign governments in the language of sincerity; to express no strong sentiments that are not felt; and where customs require certain formal expressions of civility, to use such as, like common professions of respect at the close of a letter, are universally understood to mean nothing.

In closing his own letter Pickering was more than civil. He regretted the unpleasantness of being candid because

> I risked an injury to the feelings of a man who is too respectable and too amiable to be wounded by a friend; yet you will forgive me in the reflection, that "faithful are the wounds of a friend" and such I am proud to call myself in addressing you.[15]

Mortified not so much by the rebuke itself as by the scathing form it had taken, Murray wrote back that a much milder criticism would have

14. Entry of January 31, 1798, "Commonplace" of 1797, 305–307; WVM to Pickering, No. 30, The Hague, February 4, 1798, Netherlands Despatches, I.
15. Pickering to WVM (private), Philadelphia, April 20, 1798, *AHA Report of 1912*, 397–99.

sufficed to make him more cautious in the future. His overly complimentary language he defended halfheartedly as a thing of expediency. The reproof was accepted, however, and Murray assured Pickering that he would give him "no further trouble upon this subject." No harm had been done, he thought. The January regime had been cast aside, and he did not expect the new government to make an issue of his too flowery greeting to its predecessor. He also made clear that he bore Pickering no grudge, that he was proud to work with the colonel, and was consoled that the Secretary's personal feelings toward him remained friendly.[16]

To Adams in Berlin, Murray complained mournfully that he thought Pickering had been unduly harsh, that "a very little disapprobation would have been very impressive on me." Worse, "the Colonel's friendly expressions added keenness to the reproof." [17] John Quincy Adams, far from being sympathetic, added a few friendly wounds of his own. He was sorry that Murray had been embarrassed, but he tended to agree with Pickering's finding of insincerity. Formal messages, Adams admitted, were difficult to compose; one said either too much or too little. His own maxim was that "we are not bound to utter what we think, but we are to think what we utter." In all, it was better to risk coolness by saying too little, especially when an "empty compliment" might offend the faction that was out of power.[18]

Much later, in the fall of 1799, it was a maliciously partisan Pickering who deliberately reopened the old wound by relating to Murray what the President's reaction had been. On learning earlier of Murray's gaucherie, John Adams had been overheard to say, "that young man will ruin me." [19] Pickering's motive for conveying this cheerless sequel, more than a year after it had been uttered, can easily be guessed. By late 1799 the High Federalist war hawks were making a last-ditch effort to defeat Adams' plan to send a peace mission to Paris. Pickering undoubtedly hoped he might alienate Murray from the President at a time when the success of the mission depended on the fidelity of its members, Murray among them. In short, Pickering was not one to forego even the smallest opportunity to produce dissension in the ranks of the Adams men.

Meanwhile, aside from having been taught a lesson in diplomatic niceties, Murray came to expect that henceforth his least activities would not go unnoticed, and that his medium-sized mistakes would receive

16. The Hague, June 23, 1798, Pickering MSS, 22, 231, MHS.
17. The Hague, June 25, 1798, *AHA Report of 1912*, 422–24.
18. Berlin, July 3, 1798, Adams MSS, MR 133.
19. Pickering to WVM (private), Trenton, October 25, 1799, *AHA Report of 1912*, 612.

detailed correction. The caution which he exhibited in his later dealings with Louis Pichon, the French agent of rapprochement, was undoubtedly sharpened by an awareness that Pickering would be watching and would tolerate no missteps.

At his post that spring Murray continued to observe, report, and interpret the rush of events. Like his colleagues at home and abroad, he sought an answer to the central question: Would France, aggrieved by Jay's treaty, and the United States, outraged by French maritime depredations, finally come to open warfare? The answer, he knew, lay largely in another question: did France intend war? Only Talleyrand and the French Directory knew the answer to that one. Americans in the field could only read the signs, report the rumors, and speculate on the most obvious variables in French policy. What they did not know was that sometime in early 1798 Talleyrand had proposed, and the Directory had accepted, a clearly defined but flexible policy toward the United States. Punishment was to be the keynote, but not to the point of provoking war; peace would follow at France's convenience. "After we have chastised this government as vigorously as we can," Talleyrand recommended, France might then "terminate in a durable manner the differences which divide the two republics." Meanwhile, reprisals against American shipping were amply justified by that "revolting partiality" which the United States had shown toward England in signing Jay's treaty. When time came for a peace settlement, the battered Americans might be required to pay for peace by purchasing, at par, depreciated Batavian rescriptions. "This would not be the first time," mused Talleyrand, "that political wrongs had been compensated by the payment of money."

Either way, France stood to gain. The plundering of American commerce was itself a source of profit; to stop the plundering, for a price, would be equally rewarding. Outright war, however, would not be profitable, Talleyrand warned, lest it thrust the United States into alliance with Britain. To prevent this last, he proposed to continue to "negotiate" with the American envoys. Pinckney and Marshall, he believed, were too hopelessly Federalist to bother with. They should be *"écarté"* so that he, Talleyrand, could deal separately with Elbridge Gerry whom he described as "truly conciliatory." [20]

Until July, Talleyrand's calculations proved well founded. Gerry was

20. For Talleyrand's report of Pluviôse, An 6 (January 20–February 18, 1798) to the Directory see Archives des Affaires Etrangères, Correspondance Politique, Etats Unis, 49, folios 174–87v, photocopied volumes of which are in the Library of Congress, hereinafter referred to as AAE EU.

told that war would be instantaneous if he left Paris and, so believing, made himself captive to the pretense of continuing "negotiations." Marshall and Pinckney, sick of being put off and even sicker at what they supposed to be Gerry's apostasy, broke off their own efforts and left Gerry behind. Meanwhile, according to plan, French privateers continued to "chastise" American shipping while the American Congress, predictably, remained lethargic. If anything, Talleyrand was further heartened by the news from Philadelphia that the rising fortunes of the Jeffersonian party might enable him, when the time came for a settlement, to write the terms of peace even more fully to suit the will of France.[21] In short, his policy of half-war, half-peace seemed to be unfolding as he had expected. It would cease to be desirable, however, the moment the half-war threatened to become a full-scale operation. And that moment would come when news arrived in Paris that the XYZ disclosures had fired Congress to the brink of declaring war outright.

In the interim, those whose ears were attuned to the rumors that swarmed ceaselessly through the chanceries of Europe were more immediately excited by the prospect of a French invasion of England. Now, if ever, in the early months of 1798 an invasion of England seemed most propitious. One by one, Britain's continental allies had been beaten into peace. She alone remained at war with France. And on the homefront, troubles were accumulating faster than the Pitt ministry could effectively deal with: heavy taxes, low morale, sporadic revolt in Ireland, and a dangerous naval mutiny. In short, Britain's low estate suggested a vulnerability that seemed to invite a French-administered coup de grâce.

Murray and Adams, contemplating the event, were torn between their doubt that France would be so foolhardy and their hope that she would be. That Bonaparte was rumored as leader of the invasion made Adams wonder if this was the Directory's way of ridding itself of a dangerous rival, and whether the French government could afford to pay the political price of almost certain military disaster. Murray was also convinced that France would fail, and wrote that he had been glad to drink an official toast to "a descent on England," because its certain failure would bring an end to France's warring.[22] Both men were agreed that if France were resoundingly defeated in her efforts to cross the Channel, a

21. French Consul General Létombe to Talleyrand, Philadelphia, January 17, 1798, AAE EU, 49, 144–46. See also E. Wilson Lyon, "The Directory of the United States," *American Historical Review*, XLIII (April 1939), 524.

22. See Murray's letters to JQA of February 20 and March 12, 1798, *AHA Report of 1912*, 379–80, 384–85; and his entry of March 21, 1798, "Commonplace" of 1797, 263–64; also JQA to WVM, Berlin, March 29, 1798, Adams MSS, MR 133.

Franco-American settlement could be easily arranged. To Adams, the only justification for the American commissioners' remaining in Paris was to make such a settlement in the wake of an invasion disaster.[23]

Murray, on the other hand, worried lest France abandon her invasion plans, so pregnant with calamity, and make peace with England instead. For France to be able to deal with the United States at her leisure would not work to American advantage. The possibility that the American ministers were being detained in Paris pending an Anglo-French peace settlement had occurred to Murray during a conversation he had had in December with Guillaume Bonnecarrère, the French agent who was then preparing the January 22 coup. Suppose, Murray had inquired, that when France and England had made peace, "we do not like the terms of France?" Murray was sorely discomfited to report that Bonnecarrère had "absolutely laughed outright." [24] As the spring of 1798 wore on, and it became apparent that the American commissioners *were* being detained in Paris and that an Anglo-French peace *was* possible, Murray's suspicions turned to alarm. On March 17 he wrote Pinckney in Paris strongly urging the envoys to break off. And to John Quincy Adams he wrote that if war was the only honorable course, his countrymen "ought to have some pride and not seem . . . to fight with that doubtful spirit which despair assumes when driven into a corner." [25]

This melancholy mood was lightened only momentarily when Murray heard from Paris on April 1 that the artful Talleyrand had failed to separate the envoys, only to learn two weeks later that Gerry had decided to stay and negotiate alone. Thereafter, Murray put his hope in Britain's remaining in the field, knowing that his own country could wage neither war nor peace effectively if the two great rivals should come to terms.[26] Fortunately, England and France did not make peace that spring. Nor, anticlimactically, was the French "army of England" put to the test of invasion. Bonaparte visited the Channel coast early in the year, saw the hopelessness of the project and, with Directorial blessing, turned his energies toward Egypt. The Toulon fleet, which carried him there, later met Horatio Nelson's forces in early August. Nelson's victory in the Battle of the Nile not only left Bonaparte stranded for more than a year

23. JQA to WVM, March 29, 1798, Adams MSS, MR 133.

24. WVM to JQA, The Hague, letters of February 20 and March 12, 1798, *AHA Report of 1912*, 378, 385; same to Pickering, No. 34, The Hague, March 9, 1798, Netherlands Despatches, I.

25. To JQA, The Hague, March 19, 1798, *AHA Report of 1912*, 388–89, in which the letter to Pinckney is mentioned.

26. WVM to Sylvanus Bourne, The Hague, letters of April 2 and 15, 1798, Misc. Letters, WVM MSS, LC.

at the eastern end of the Mediterranean, but it also encouraged Russia and Austria to join England in forming the Second Coalition.

Murray's own energies that spring were given over to more than mere speculation about the Toulon fleet. Zealously, and with some success, he set out to dissuade France from enforcing a new maritime decree that was highly damaging to American and other neutral shipping. Dated 29 Nivôse (January 18), this decree ordered the condemnation of any vessel laden wholly or in part with British-produced goods. Neutral, not British, vessels were the principal victims of this law, Murray contended, because British merchantmen usually sailed under convoy. In a memorial addressed to the Dutch Foreign Office, though intended for French eyes, Murray supposed that the law was intended to strike at British manufactures and to divert neutral ships from British to French ports. In point of fact, however, the law would stimulate a more widespread use of protected British bottoms while forcing up insurance rates on unprotected neutral vessels. The law would "injure neutrals, benefit G. Britain and produce no good to France." Britain herself, he concluded, could scarcely have devised a law more beneficial to her own interests.[27]

Murray's warning was borne out almost immediately. The day after he submitted his memorial a French privateer brought an American merchantman, *America,* into the Texel, where a French consul threatened to confiscate that part of the *America*'s cargo which consisted of British West Indian coffee. Murray seized the occasion to put some hard questions to Willem Buys, the Batavian Foreign Secretary. Did Batavia intend to join France in war against the United States? Or did it merely intend to permit French consuls to extend jurisdiction over American vessels brought as prizes into Dutch ports? Would the Dutch, in fact, enforce the French law of 29 Nivôse, or were they merely planning to allow French consuls to enforce that law within Dutch jurisdiction? From Buys he learned that these questions might be answered as soon as the Batavian government heard from its minister to Paris, one Casper Meyer, who was even then preparing a protest against the French law. On March 13, with the fate of the *America* still pending, Murray was told that his memorial had been forwarded to Meyer. When in early April Murray met Meyer on the latter's return from Paris, he was delighted to discover that his arguments against the Nivôse law had been incorporated in the Dutchman's protest to the French Directory.[28]

27. Murray enclosed a copy of this memorial, dated February 26, in his dispatch to Pickering, No. 32, February 23, 1798, Netherlands Despatches, I.

28. See Murray's dispatches to Pickering, Nos. 33, 34, 35, and 38, of February 28, March 9 and 12, and April 6, 1798, respectively, *ibid.;* also entry of March 3,

Not content to work solely through official channels, Murray took a direct approach when he urged the merchants of Rotterdam and Amsterdam to join in a petition of protest. Through an unnamed intermediary, he conveyed to the mercantile community of those cities the telling argument that any interruption in the flow of American commerce to Dutch ports would delay the payment of interest on the United States debt owing to Dutch bankers. Thanks to Murray's initiative, some sixty leading businessmen signed a petition directed to the Batavian Directory protesting the Nivôse law. To assure the regime's receptivity to this petition, Murray kept his own instigative role carefully concealed.[29]

Murray's effort to save American shipping in Dutch waters brought mixed results. The Amsterdam merchants who took their complaint directly to Delacroix were rebuffed by the French minister's defense of privateering and told to consult with "one of my secretaries." When the merchants approached the Dutch Directory they were told: "Go and speak to Mr. Delacroix." [30] Eventually, Murray secured the release of the *America,* but the question of French jurisdiction in Dutch waters lingered on. Not until early fall did the Batavian Directory succeed in putting an end to French privateering off the Dutch coast. Nor even then would this have transpired had not the Dutch Moderates returned to power or, more importantly, had not France by then begun to move toward conciliation of the United States.[31]

By early summer of 1798, nearly a year into his mission, Murray had learned some hard lessons but he had also begun to make a visible impression. His initial awkwardness in handling the messy business of the "Adams Letter" had been followed by still more gaucherie in his greetings to the regime born of the January coup. But where a vital American interest had been at issue—as in the case of the Nivôse decree —he had moved with the surefootedness of a maturing diplomat. His closely-reasoned critique of French maritime policy had, of itself, had a measurable impact in both official and commercial circles. That he was acquiring a reputation for intelligence, vigor, and integrity can hardly be doubted.

The time now was fast approaching when, as the search for peace

---

1798, "Commonplace" of 1797, 237–40; and memorandum in AAE EU, 50, 65–65v. For Willem Buys' note to Murray of March 13, 1798, see WVM MSS, I, 32, ML.

29. WVM to Pickering, The Hague, Nos. 36, 37, and 41, of March 18, 27, and April 22, 1798, respectively, Netherlands Despatches, I.

30. Undated entry, "Commonplace" of 1797, 374.

31. WVM to Pickering, No. 61, The Hague, September 3, 1798, Netherlands Despatches, I.

would begin in earnest, France and the United States would need a reliable intermediary. But even before that need became evident, Murray was demonstrating that he was a man who was willing to take initiatives, or respond to them, and most particularly when those initiatives would serve what he perceived to be his country's best interests.

8

Lessons from Paris and London

BY MID-1798 Murray had acquired a profound distrust of Revolutionary France. Like many Americans, he had greeted with applause the first stirring of upheaval nearly a decade before. He had expected France quietly to join and become a prestigious addition to the small sisterhood of republics. Instead, he had been horrified to see the revolutionaries move from one excess to another, uprooting institutions, indulging bloodshed in the name of liberty and conquest in the name of fraternity. As one who preferred orderly change within a framework of a stable political order, Murray had been by turns puzzled, disgusted, and outraged. As a Federalist among Federalists he had leaned toward the stereotype that possibly all revolutionaries were natural "disorganizers," and its corollary, that American Republicans might well become their accomplices in radically changing an American political system which he believed had already achieved a certain perfection. Like many Federalists, he used the term "Jacobin" without differentiation to describe loosely any group or individual proposing radical change.

The stereotype had been strengthened when Murray saw at closer range the disruptive activities of French ministers. Genêt's violations of American neutrality, Fauchet's mysterious dealings with Randolph, and Adet's intrusion into the 1796 election had broadened his distrust, convincing him that France would make his country a satellite if she could. His year at The Hague—in the front lines, so to speak—seemed only to confirm his belief that wherever French revolutionaries or their ideals appeared in strength, nations lost not only their internal political stability but also their national independence. He sensed that by war, or more likely by intrigue, Revolutionary France would not rest until all monarchies became republics, and all republics were cast in the French mold.

Nor did Murray ever quite understand how offensively ungrateful

France conceived Jay's treaty to have been. To him, the treaty with England had been a necessary assertion of American neutrality. That France should have seen it as the final act of betrayal eluded him, for he scarcely realized how badly disappointed Frenchmen themselves had become when the French and American revolutionary experiments had failed to mesh either politically or ideologically. He saw only the end-result of that disappointment in the recurrent and odious distinction which Frenchmen made when they extolled the American people but damned the American government. What he failed to see was that in making that distinction, Frenchmen were merely writing *finis* to a once-cherished sentiment of good will, long in decline.[1]

Although Murray distrusted all Paris politicians of revolutionary stripe, he did not give up hope that someday France would find it a matter of national self-interest to reach an accommodation with the United States. This latent hope came to life with news from Paris in mid-April. On Saturday evening, April 14, he wrote in his "Commonplace":

> A Ray of light seems to me to break the gloom. Talleyrand persuaded Gerry to stay—telling him [that] nothing but his staying could prevent an immediate rupture! This convinces me they would make an open rupture now if they durst, but it does not suit them to make it, nor to have it made by the U. S. They keep Gerry because as long as they can keep him there . . . they delay us from being decisive. . . . If they wish a rupture, if they did not *dread one*—they would not persuade Gerry to stay.

Obviously, Murray's optimism was clouded. Gerry's remaining in Paris meant that France would retain a diplomatic initiative. But insofar as it signified France's unwillingness to go to war immediately, the sign was hopeful.[2]

As the American mission dragged out its last days in Paris, Murray continued to hear its dialogue with Talleyrand only indistinctly. The

1. For the somewhat mystical French attitudes toward the American experiment and their gradual disappearance see Durand Echeverria, *Mirage in the West: a History of the French Image of American Society to 1815* (New York: Octagon Books, Inc., 1966), especially Ch. V.
2. WVM to Pickering, The Hague, Nos. 39 and 40 of April 12 and 14, 1798, Netherlands Despatches, I; also same to JQA, April 17, 1798, *AHA Report of 1912*, 395–97.

secretiveness of the envoys left much to conjecture. Murray, however, felt keenly the dubious role that Elbridge Gerry had chosen to play. That Gerry was a sincere and well-meaning person has never seriously been questioned, either by his contemporaries or by later historians. That he showed poor judgment, however, in separating himself from his colleagues in order to pursue peace under Talleyrand's threat of war is still a debatable point. Gerry later wrote in self-justification: ". . . had I left Paris with the other envoys, war without doubt would have been the consequence: & this was suspended by my remaining there." [3] Murray was one of those who most seriously questioned this judgment. Talleyrand's insistence that Gerry stay behind led Murray to just the opposite conclusion: that France was trying to avoid war.

It had been with some hesitation that John Adams had picked Gerry to fill the third place in the three-man commission. He had once expressed the wish that Gerry were "more correct in his views." Like Adams himself, Gerry had had a political career stretching back to the days of the Revolution, but it was a career marked by a high degree of independence. The knowledge that his old friend from Marblehead could be willfully obstinate had given Adams pause and had made the High Federalist vocally uneasy. But to Adams, Gerry's impartiality, his integrity, were more to be valued than party-line regularity.[4]

Murray at first gave a tolerant account of Gerry during their meeting at The Hague in the fall of 1797. At that time Murray had hoped that the envoys would be quickly rebuffed at Paris, and would break off negotiations immediately in order to take advantage of the relative unity of American sentiment for war. He was vaguely disturbed when Gerry suggested that more advantage could be gained from delay. Otherwise, he remarked, Gerry seemed "well made up upon the American points in contest with French ambition." [5] Not until Gerry had refused to leave Paris with his colleagues did Murray recount the full unpleasantness of their first meeting. He had "stuck" close to Gerry, he told John Quincy Adams, and had gone to Amsterdam with him. He had been impressed

3. "Remarks of Mr Gerry on Mr Pickerings report communicated to Congress on the 21st of January 1799 respectfully submitted by the former President of the United States," as published in Russell W. Knight's *Elbridge Gerry's Letterbook, Paris 1797–1798* (Salem, Mass.: The Essex Institute, 1966), 71.

4. JA to Gerry, Philadelphia, letters of June 20, 1797, and July 8, 1798, Adams' *Works*, VIII, 546, 547–48. For an account of the Adams-Gerry friendship see Eugene Kramer, "John Adams, Elbridge Gerry and the Origins of the XYZ Affair," *Essex Institute Historical Collection*, XCIV (January 1958), 57–68.

5. To JQA, The Hague, October 1, 1797, *AHA Report of 1912*, 361–62.

by what he believed to be Gerry's naiveté: "a thousand truths were new
to him." Apparently Gerry was not aware that "the French were not
all purity, philanthropy and real liberty; that the affiliated countries were
abject and enslaved." The French, he had told Gerry, were probably
incapable of true republicanism; their government, even now, was a military despotism, and their hostility to the United States unmistakable.

On venturing to wish the French had never had their revolution,
Murray was provoked but not surprised when Gerry "turned short and
said 'Then you deny our right to Independence and the principles of
Our Revolution! !' " Murray continued: "I was not surprised because he
had harrast me on other occasions by voluntary conclusions of this sort."
Thereafter, Murray avoided political discussion with Gerry because "the
latter seemed to have taken some concealed badness of design for
granted in me." Except for these encounters, Murray admitted to liking
the man for his kindliness and, perhaps for that reason, pursued him to
Paris with several letters dwelling on the current evils of French republicanism.[6]

Through the long months of the Paris negotiation, Murray remained
starved for news from the envoys. As late as November 28, 1797, he
wrote William L. Smith, his former House colleague now posted at
Lisbon, complaining "I know not *anything* from them scarcely." Finally,
in a point-blank effort to pry information out of Charles Cotesworth
Pinckney, Murray wrote on December 19 expressing curiosity as to the
motives of the Directory. Had the envoys discovered those motives?
Pinckney's reply (not extant) apparently lifted a corner of the veil,
enough for Murray to recognize the political explosiveness of the XYZ
demands. "No," he wrote back, "no tribute—no thieving will be the
word from south to north. . . . The quarrel put in that shape will
seventy-six us." [7] How little Pinckney actually disclosed was revealed by
Murray's astonished reaction to the full publication of the XYZ dispatches. "Never," he exclaimed, "never were there such scoundrels." [8]

Gradually the story unfolded. Although a number of coded dispatches
passed through Murray's hands, he knew only vaguely of their contents
from the accompanying letters Pinckney wrote. On January 31, 1798, the
envoys made their final effort: a long note to Talleyrand setting forth the
American position on the salient issues and asking that they be received

6. The Hague, April 27, 1798, *ibid.*, 402. See WVM's letters to Gerry of
November 2 and 10, 1797, WVM MSS, III, 54–55, 65–67, ML.

7. That is, a demand for tribute would evoke the sort of warlike response
which characterized the national temper in 1776. *Ibid.*, 67–72, 79, 87.

8. To JQA, The Hague, May 29, 1798, *AHA Report of 1912*, 410.

officially or given their passports.[9] Not until March 19 did the envoys receive Talleyrand's reply. Pinckney described it to Murray as "weak in argument, but irritating and insulting in style." Most provocative was Talleyrand's blunt proposal that thereafter he deal with Gerry alone. All three envoys signed a note rejecting this suggestion, only to have Gerry reverse himself and agree to continue talks with the Frenchman on an unofficial basis.[10]

Murray at first refused to believe that Gerry had allowed himself to be separated from his colleagues. As late as mid-May he urged Sylvanus Bourne, the U.S. consul at Amsterdam, to quash the rumor that Gerry had stayed behind.[11] As the truth became less deniable, Murray tried to put the best face on it. At least he had no intention of denouncing Gerry to Colonel Pickering, to whom he wrote that "some very striking demonstration must have been seen by Mr. Gerry before he would take on himself such responsibility at such a period." [12] To his friend in Berlin he expressed more nearly his real feelings: that Gerry would be ruined unless he could bring off a favorable treaty—and that appeared very unlikely. More probable, he thought, Gerry had merely yielded to Talleyrand's persuasion. The French would now "seventy-six-him-up in such a manner that he will be softened into the warm hope that now is the time and opportunity for saving the two republics—through him." Meanwhile, the French could choose "to strike when it suits them" while continuing to work a further division in American public opinion. John Quincy Adams generally agreed.[13]

On April 15, Murray tried his own hand at persuasion. He wrote Gerry that, "as an old Colleague and acquaintance," he would presume to give some advice. He could understand Gerry's decision to stay in Paris, but only if Talleyrand had already offered some major concession. Should the French agree to stop their maritime depredations, for example, Gerry would be warranted in staying. But Talleyrand's civilities, he warned, were more likely "a cover to further political management on their Part—as a Means of Delay favorable to them—as DISARMING

9. See *ASP FR*, II, 169–82, for the envoys' summation, and Bernard Fay, *The Revolutionary Spirit in France and America* (New York: Harcourt, Brace and Co., 1927), 405, for Talleyrand's argumentative reply.

10. For a paraphrase of Pinckney's letter to WVM, Paris, March 23, 1798, see WVM to JQA, The Hague, April 3, 1798, *AHA Report of 1912*, 391; see also Marshall's Journal, April 3, 1798, Pickering MSS, MHS; and *ASP FR*, II, 188.

11. The Hague, May 14, 1798, Misc. Letters, WVM MSS, LC.

12. No. 39, The Hague, April 12, 1798, Netherlands Despatches, I.

13. See Murray's letters to JQA of April 13 and 27, and May 1, 1798, *AHA Report of 1912*, 393–94, 402–403; and JQA's answering letters of April 19, 27, and 30, 1798, Adams MSS, MR 133.

AMERICA and leaving her bare to the French." As to Talleyrand's threats, war was preferable to the loss of American honor and independence. But Talleyrand did not intend war, Murray argued, and this was proved by the Foreign Minister's insistence that he stay. France merely wanted to retain the initiative, to choose the time at which she would declare war. And should Gerry doubt her hostility, Murray reminded him of the consistently provocative language of the Directory, not to mention the ruinous effects of the maritime decree of 29 Nivôse.[14]

Gerry was unmoved; he replied from Paris that he believed France would declare war unless he continued to talk to Talleyrand. It was Murray's opinion, vouchsafed to Adams, that Gerry had become thoroughly confused. But it was also possible that Gerry had confused Talleyrand, first by agreeing to stay, and now by refusing to deal with the Frenchman on substantive questions. As Murray put it, "that same turn of mind that made him stay now operates against their further views on him." [15]

Pickering's letter recalling the envoys passed through The Hague on May 28. Murray hurriedly forwarded it to Paris lest Gerry and Pinckney (the latter was still in the south of France) be arrested during the furor that was bound to occur when the Directory learned that the XYZ dispatches had been published. "Gerry," he observed to Pickering, "has had warning enough. I hope he will take it." [16] In July, Murray reported that Talleyrand had told Gerry that he was ready to deal on all particulars but that "Mr. Gerry will do *nothing*. Says he has no powers, and *will* go away." Not until August 23 could Murray verify that Gerry had actually left France (by way of Le Havre).[17]

To Murray, who was shortly to be himself a recipient of French peace overtures, the lesson of Gerry's misadventure was plain. If France wanted a reconciliation with the United States she must make some preliminary concession. Mere assurances of French good will, of the sort which Gerry was now conveying to President Adams, were not the substance of a conciliation that would satisfy Murray. Nothing less than a solid concession from Paris would persuade him that the Directory

14. WVM MSS, III, 250–52, ML.
15. See Gerry to WVM, April 30, 1798, WVM MSS, LC; and WVM to JQA, The Hague, May 14, 1798, *AHA Report of 1912,* 406.
16. No. 47, The Hague, June 5, 1798, Netherlands Despatches, I.
17. To JQA, The Hague, July 20, 1798, *AHA Report of 1912,* 437; and to Pickering (private), The Hague, August 23, 1798, *ibid.,* 459.

had had a change of heart. For all Gerry's lingering, he observed, the French "have not yielded a single point—they pledge themselves to nothing—everything is left in doubt." [18]

Despite this appraisal, a steady undercurrent of optimism ran through Murray's correspondence in late April and early May. It began in a carefully worded letter to Pickering analyzing the significance of Gerry's detention. To Murray it signified a weakening, perhaps only temporary, in the French position. Had France wished to provoke an open rupture, he wrote, she would have sent all three envoys packing. To Sylvanus Bourne he was less guarded. "In truth," he wrote the consul general, "they dread a rupture & keep Gerry till it suits them to have it." To John Quincy Adams he was equally emphatic: ". . . *France dreads a rupture with the United States, at PRESENT.*" And again to Pickering on May 5: "my own idea is yet as it was when I last wrote that this Threat [to Gerry] was a proof that *they* feared a rupture." [19]

But why did France hold back? Was it because her plundering of American commerce was already inflicting maximum damage—the most that France was capable of? This was Talleyrand's view. Murray guessed it, and John Quincy Adams was sure of it.[20] Murray also considered other possible explanations. Fear of American naval power, perhaps? While hardly a match for France on the high seas, his country's new warships, Murray believed, must appear "more formidable in their eyes than they were eight months since." Or was France's reluctance to declare war outright the consequence of her rapidly deteriorating position in Europe? This possibility led Murray to tick off such recent embarrassments as the failure of the Rastadt Congress to meet French demands in the Rhineland, the restlessness of the northern neutrals under French maritime strictures, the instability in Italy since Bonaparte's departure, the imminence of peace between Britain and Spain, and a rumor that Austria and Prussia had made an alliance in early April. Were there an American mission in Paris at this juncture, he speculated, it might reasonably have demanded that France cease her

18. To Pickering, No. 40, The Hague, April 14, 1798, Netherlands Despatches, I.

19. *Ibid.;* WVM to Bourne, April 15, Misc. Letters, WVM MSS, LC; WVM to JQA, April 17, *AHA Report of 1912*, 395; WVM to Pickering (private), May 5, Pickering MSS, 22, 148, MHS.

20. Georges Pallain, ed., *Le Ministère de Talleyrand sous le directoire* (Paris: E. Plon, Nourrit et Cie., 1891), 309, hereinafter cited as Pallain, *Le Ministère de Talleyrand;* WVM to Pickering, No. 40, Netherlands Despatches, I; JQA to WVM, Berlin, April 27, 1798, Adams MSS, MR 133.

depredations. The present time, he told Adams, was "a bad one for them and good for us," which explained why Gerry had been asked to stay.[21]

Ordinarily Murray disapproved of Congress' penchant for publishing "live" diplomatic correspondence, but on May 27 his delight approached ecstasy on receiving from Rufus King the published text of the XYZ dispatches. Pinckney, Marshall, and Gerry, he exulted, had made "a full display of the tendered prostitution of the F. Govt.—the 50,000 £ douceur &c &c—& its rejection." Two days later, when the *Leyden Gazette* picked up the story, he wrote in his diary that the exposé "makes great noise!" adding, "I help it all I can god knows." [22] King's news clipping he circulated among his friends whose satisfaction matched his own. How the French would react he could only imagine:

> It will be with astonishment that they will see scattered over Europe—& exultingly read & believed a publication like this. So inflated, so drunken are they with the novelty of tyranny—so unused to hear the truth—they will at first be stunned by this exposure which has laid fast hold on the public mind, & even magnify'd by the hatred that gave it an easy credit. Be assured . . . however, that they will also be roused and no effort will be left untry'd to revenge it.[23]

Mixing metaphors in his excitement, Murray wrote that Dutch officials with whom he had talked "scarcely at first believed that there existed spirit enough to say to *France's beard* that she was a prostitute." War, he felt, was now inevitable. Knowing that the President had authorized the arming of merchantmen, he urged that now "Congress must do the rest." Nor was Murray content at the prospect that his countrymen might settle for a defensive war. Anything short of an all-out effort, he was certain, would suffer at the hands of the economizers. Rather, he was ready to prescribe that "fear and avarice . . . be drowned . . . in the din of the more careless passions and the love of glory." [24] Thus, briefly, did the war hawk take wing.

Adams' was the steadying voice. The President's son did not agree that the United States should make the first move. Rather, defensive

---

21. WVM to JQA, The Hague, April 17, 1798, *AHA Report of 1912*, 396; same to Pickering, No. 40, Netherlands Despatches, I.
22. Entries of May 27 and 29, 1798, "Commonplace" of 1797, WVM MSS, LC.
23. To Pickering, No. 46, The Hague, June 1, 1798, Netherlands Despatches, I.
24. To JQA, The Hague, June 1, 1798, *AHA Report of 1912*, 412–13.

measures should be tried, Congress arming the nation while the administration continued to proffer the olive branch. A war declaration, Adams warned, must rest on a unanimity of popular support which he doubted existed. In this the younger Adams not only approximated his father's reaction, but also read aright the domestic political situation. On the home front, the Pickeronian extremists now found themselves caught between their own urgings that Congress declare war and their sure knowledge that neither the President nor the party moderates wanted to go that far.[25] Nonetheless, in early July, the war hawks presented the House with a resolution tantamount to a declaration of war, only to see it defeated. Thereafter they could only hope that France herself would force the administration's hand. In expectation of war, meanwhile, Congress moved swiftly. It created a Navy department, enlarged both Army and Navy, authorized the seizure of French armed vessels, and suspended commerce with both France and French possessions. What most complicated the later relations between the two countries, however, was the action Congress took on June 4 in abrogating all of the earlier Franco-American engagements: the treaties of alliance and commerce of 1778 and the consular convention of 1788. This complication became evident when France later denied the right of the United States to abrogate treaties without also making a formal declaration of war.

While the question of war hung in the balance, an event occurred at The Hague which helped to make Murray more receptive to French peace overtures when they began to come his way. On June 12 the French Directory watched benevolently as the Dutch Moderates staged a successful coup against the January regime. To Murray, the Moderates' return to power at The Hague reflected a resurgence of moderatism in Paris itself. The French executive, having suppressed its enemies on the Right the previous fall, had just succeeded in putting down a threat from the Left. Despite a Jacobin victory at the polls in April, enough elections had been invalidated to preserve majorities of directorial supporters in both French chambers.[26] Because the French regime was warring against its own Left, Dutch Moderates could logically expect support from Paris against the Radical government which had come to power in January.

25. JQA to WVM, Berlin, June 7, 1798, Adams MSS, MR 133. For the President's belligerent reaction to XYZ and his subsequent cooling, see DeConde, *Quasi-War*, 67–69; also Kurtz, *Presidency of John Adams*, 306.

26. Jacques Léon Godechot, *France and the Atlantic Revolution of the Eighteenth Century, 1779–1799* (New York: The Free Press, 1965), 198–99.

But more important, in Murray's view, was the possibility that the French Directory might be persuaded by its domestic difficulties to make a definitive settlement with the United States.[27]

It was this possibility that made Murray a keen though wary listener when, toward the end of June, Louis Pichon, a French Foreign Office factotum, turned up at The Hague bearing what looked like genuine peace offers. Initially, Pichon's appearance served only to stir Murray's suspicious curiosity. He had known Pichon earlier when the latter had been secretary to Genêt, and later to Fauchet, at Philadelphia, but the context of that earlier acquaintance was not one to inspire immediate confidence. Not until late summer would the Murray-Pichon conversations produce the basis for an actual negotiation.

More auspicious, meanwhile, was Murray's hope that, Paris politics permitting, he might be instrumental in effecting a peace settlement between The Hague and London. With the Dutch Moderates back in power, he hoped to convince Lord Grenville that here was a Batavian government that might be brought to the peace table. The advantage to his own country lay in the reasonable supposition that the Dutch, having made peace with England, would be less likely to join France should Franco-American hostilities be pushed to the ultimate.

By way of background, the Dutch Moderate faction had been brewing a counter-coup against the January Radicals ever since the latter had forced their way to power. Discontent found a focal point in May when the Radicals' constituent assembly, having disfranchised a large part of the electorate, won a stunningly lopsided victory for its newly drafted directorial constitution. Instead of disbanding, however, the constituent assembly divided itself into two chambers and declared itself to be "representative." In short, the men elected to draft the constitution seized the legislative power without benefit of elections—an impertinence which proved to be their undoing.[28]

Led by a Dutch general named Herman Daendels, a once convinced but now repentant Radical, the Moderates took maximum advantage of the regime's political misconduct. On May 16, in the wake of the constitutent assembly's outrage, Daendels dined with Charles Delacroix, accused the French minister and his friends of misuse of public funds, and denounced the puppet directory for its broken promises. Delacroix tried to have the general arrested, but the latter escaped to Paris where, it

27. WVM to Pickering, No. 51, The Hague, June 17, 1798, Netherlands Despatches, I.
28. Cf. Edmundson, *History of Holland*, 350; entries of April 25 and May 6, 1798, "Commonplace" of 1797, 364–65; WVM to Pickering, No. 42, The Hague, May 8, 1798, Netherlands Despatches, I.

turned out, the French Directory gave him a sympathetic hearing. When he returned to The Hague, Daendels was under official French protection. On the afternoon of June 12 the Dutch general actually dragged the January regime from power.[29]

Members of the Directory were arrested at 4:30 P.M.; two hours later the legislative councils were dispersed, and by seven o'clock a new government had taken charge. Murray, Charlotte, and Dandridge were all in the streets that afternoon, watching at first hand the highlights of the coup. With gleeful satisfaction Murray recorded the fall of Charles Delacroix who, though he had been ordered back to Paris, was still at The Hague on the day of revolution. Unable to prevent the seating of a new government, Murray wrote Adams, the Frenchman left the chambers and

> came out in a perfect fury. He roared in a voice so suffocated by rage that it was a scream of agony; he abused them all vehemently to his own house. I met him near that; he was with his son and a Colonel of Hussars, and a mob of boys and blackguards behind him—a mournful spectacle I assure you, and certainly too much humbled for any foreign minister.

As for Daendels, Murray had nothing but praise for the general who, he wrote, "behaved very handsomely indeed," adding, "I saw him almost at every step. He was cool . . . but firm & I rejoice SUCCESSFUL! . . . I begin to breathe again." Grateful, too, for the absence of bloodshed, Murray described the coup to Adams as being "easily written, easily endured, and read without convulsion." [30] Later disclosures of corrupt dealings by members of the ousted regime seemed to lay to rest any danger of a Radical resurgence for the near future.

Following the June coup, Murray revived a project which had long figured in his calculations: that of arranging a peace settlement between the British and the Dutch. Back in March, Rufus King had written from London that the British had "no settled hostility against the Dutch" and might be willing to arrange a separate peace. King, Murray, and John Quincy Adams had all agreed, however, that the January regime was not likely to seek peace. Nor was France likely to permit them to do so.[31] Nevertheless, Murray had pursued the subject with certain Mod-

29. See Murray's dispatches to Pickering, Nos. 42, 43, and 44, of May 18, 19, and 28, 1798, respectively, *ibid.*

30. To JQA, The Hague, June 12, 1798, *AHA Report of 1912*, 418, 420; also WVM to Bourne, June 13, 1798, Misc. Letters, WVM MSS, LC.

31. King to WVM, London, March 31, 1798, Misc Letters, WVM MSS, LC; entry of April 23, 1798, "Commonplace" of 1797, 372; JQA to WVM, Berlin, May 8, 1798, Adams MSS, MR 133.

erate leaders in May, when it appeared that the Moderates might return to power. Most notably, he had broached the question of a separate peace to Admiral Jan de Winter, commander of the Dutch fleet which had been defeated at Camperdown.

On May 24 de Winter had called on Murray, divulged the Moderates' plans for the forthcoming coup, and requested the American to propose (through Rufus King) that London give certain political assurances. Specifically, the admiral stipulated that London make an explicit but secret guarantee of noninterference in Dutch politics: the present Batavian constitution to remain intact, no attempt made to restore the Stadtholder. Murray was heartened by this conversation but all too aware of the political difficulties. Britain was unlikely to abandon the Stadtholder; Orangists would certainly be reluctant to support a directorial regime; and France would allow the Dutch to make a separate peace only if she were beset by a powerful coalition of enemies.[32]

Not until June 26 did Murray again broach the subject of Anglo-Dutch relations, this time to Isaac Gogel, one of the new Directors. Gogel gave him an opening when he asked Murray to suggest, through Rufus King, that the British forego their recently established practice of seizing Dutch fishing boats. Murray promised to intercede, and then began to talk about "what I thought G. B. ought to do," i.e., to refrain from meddling in Dutch internal politics so that all Dutchmen could then unite in their efforts to secure freedom from French domination. Gogel was warmly responsive. His government's policy, he told Murray, was to seek peace with England and to cut some of its ties with Paris.[33] Murray left this conference hopeful that the new regime at least intended to shift its political center of gravity. The fisheries question, meanwhile, gave him the opportunity to broach the more serious matter of British noninterference to Rufus King. By special courier he sent word to King that an Anglo-Dutch peace might be arranged if London would renounce "all pretensions, by solemn act, to interfere in this country—." As Murray told Pickering, much depended on the willingness of the British to give up their hopes of restoring the Dutch Stadtholder.[34]

On receiving Murray's letter of July 27, King met with Lord Grenville

32. Entry of May 24, 1798, "Commonplace" of 1797, n.p.; see also WVM to Pickering, No. 44, The Hague, May 28, 1798, Netherlands Despatches, I.

33. Entry of June 26, 1798, "Commonplace" of 1797, n.p.

34. WVM to Pickering, private, The Hague, July 2, 1798, Pickering MSS, 22, 258–65, MHS. Murray's letter to King, July 27, apparently not extant, is paraphrased in Murray's "Commonplace" entry of June 26, and in King to Pickering (private), No. 94, London, August 20, 1798, Pickering MSS, 23, folios 51–51v, MHS.

and was told that the British government would find it difficult "by any formal act to discard the Prince of Orange," even though earlier British ministries had occasionally overlooked the claims of the House of Orange in dealing with the Dutch. Grenville did, however, authorize Murray (through King) to inform the Batavian Directory that London would send an emissary "to any convenient place that they shall name confidentially to confer upon these important matters." Murray was warned, however, that Britain preferred to restore the Stadtholder, albeit with protections guaranteed to the revolutionaries and some provision for reform in the Stadtholderate itself.[35]

Knowing these terms to be unacceptable, Murray dropped the whole project. Any lingering hopes were crushed when Grenville subsequently rejected as being "wholly inadmissible" the Dutch requirement that Britain abandon the Stadtholder. For Britain to renounce officially its hope of restoring William V would so demoralize the Orangists, Grenville thought, as to render the Netherlands even more submissive to French domination.[36]

Murray totally disagreed with this view. Neither the Orangists nor their British partisans, he felt, had come to grips with reality. The Dutch royalists, he wrote, "have lost their gilded yacht, they are in the water, and ought to be happy if they can save themselves in the long boat." That is, they should rally to the new moderate regime and thus help it to throw off French patronage.[37] Britain's primary objective, too, should be to loosen Batavia from the French dominium; London could dicker later about the future of the Stadtholderate. To Adams he wrote:

> If Great Britain were not oak in the head as well as heart, she would settle affairs here by disavowing any interference in their affairs. A pledge like that once given, and *other things* concurring, I tell you, my dear sir, the Dutch would take Holland. That pledge not given, France will have it.[38]

John Quincy Adams' response was quietly negative. The Dutch, he felt, were too rich, fat, and lazy to shed any blood for independence; Murray should not take too seriously the Dutch talk of resistance. The British

35. King to WVM, London, August 16, 1798, King, *Correspondence*, II, 389–90; also King to Pickering, No. 94, Pickering MSS, 23, folios 51–51v, MHS.

36. Grenville to King, November 6, 1798, forwarded to Murray on November 17, 1798, King, *Correspondence*, II, 461–62.

37. To JQA, The Hague, June 12, 1798, *AHA Report of 1912*, 419.

38. The Hague, July 6, 1798, *ibid.*, 428; same to Pickering, No. 54, The Hague, July 13, 1798, Netherlands Despatches, I; see also WVM to John Adams, The Hague, July 1, 1798, Adams' *Works, VIII*, 697.

knew what they were about in foreseeing no hope of a truly independent Netherlands under any revolutionary regime. Nor would they abandon the Prince of Orange, whose supporters were the only friends the British had in that quarter. Despite London's protestations of sympathy for the Dutch, Adams concluded, Albion would probably not object if its former commercial rival were partitioned between Prussia and France.[39]

Though nothing of substance came from Murray's excursion into Anglo-Dutch relations, his efforts bespoke a greater readiness to engage the opportunities of diplomacy—a realization, perhaps, that diplomacy, even more than politics, is the art of the possible. As his apprenticeship drew to a close, there appeared in the more mature diplomat a man ready to seize the fortuitous moment, which may explain why Murray, during this same period of his mission, was listening intently to Louis Pichon, the self-proclaimed harbinger of Franco-American reconciliation.

39. Berlin, letters of July 14 and 31, 1798, Adams MSS, MR 133.

9

Conversations with Pichon

TALLEYRAND'S CHOICE of Louis-André Pichon as bearer of peace overtures and his singling out of William Vans Murray as their recipient were, no doubt, moves carefully calculated to bring about a renewal of Franco-American negotiations. One can imagine Talleyrand consciously weighing the backgrounds of the two men, balancing Murray's known capacity for independent action against the drag of his "devout" Federalism, weighing Pichon's first-hand knowledge of Americans and American politics against Murray's possibly adverse reaction to a minor official with whom he had been passingly acquainted when Pichon had been secretary to the French legation in Philadelphia. Too, Talleyrand could reasonably expect that whatever Pichon conveyed to Murray would ultimately reach the eye and catch the attention of John Adams through Murray's regular correspondence with the President's son. The possibility that Murray was chosen simply because his location at The Hague made him the nearest end of a pipeline through Berlin to Philadelphia does not stand up too well, however, in light of Talleyrand's simultaneous, though muted, approaches made directly to John Quincy Adams through an agent named Louis Guillaume Otto. In short, the French Foreign Minister was working the channels of diplomacy in both capitals, but Murray was his chosen instrument.[1]

Earlier historians analyzing Talleyrand's careful choice of emissary and recipient have tended to overlook certain elements that may have figured in the selection of these men. Pichon, for example, was a young

1. For DeConde's speculation of these points, see his *Quasi-War*, 147–48; also "The Role of William Vans Murray in the Peace Negotiations between France and the United States, 1800," *Huntington Library Quarterly*, XV (February 1952), 187–88; and his "William Vans Murray and the Diplomacy of Peace, 1797–1800," *Maryland Historical Magazine*, XLVIII (March 1953), 9. For Otto's approaches to John Quincy Adams, see JQA to WVM, Berlin, July 10, 1798, Adams MSS, MR 133.

man in his late twenties whose ambition for advancement made him by nature ingratiating. Never one to underrate the uses of flattery, Talleyrand must have seen the wisdom of sending to The Hague an agent who possessed a positive talent for pleasing. Once Pichon had passed the initial barrier of Murray's suspicions, the two men indeed developed a mutual trust that was to weather some serious crises. In Murray, Talleyrand must also have discerned by this time a diplomat whose recurrent devotion to his country's need for peace outweighed his own partisan distrust of France. What appeared to be mere flattery in Talleyrand's later observation that Murray was "neither French nor British" may well have reflected the Frenchman's realization that he was dealing with a patriot whose clear view of his country's national interest transcended the imperatives of Federalist demonology. Had it been otherwise, Talleyrand might have had to look elsewhere for a recipient of his overtures.[2]

Much has been written to explain the about-face which occurred in Directorial policy toward the United States in the early summer of 1798. Why, for example, should the warlike measures of an American Congress, provoked by the XYZ Affair, drive Talleyrand to become what one historian has called "an apostle of peace"?[3] The seed of an answer was sown in Talleyrand's much earlier advice to the Directory: that French interests would be ill served if the United States were pushed into an alliance with England. Now, in June of 1798, American indignation at XYZ had made an Anglo-American alliance a distinct possibility. Were the United States to enter the war on England's side, he warned, France would lose the services of American carriers in the French and French West Indian trade. At worst, the conjuncture of American manpower and British seapower would snatch Louisiana from Spain before Talleyrand could mature his plans for regaining that province for France; and the French Foreign Office could only speculate as to what other territorial losses might be the consequence of an active Anglo-American military operation in the New World.[4]

Any doubts lingering in Talleyrand's mind as to the advisability of conciliation were erased by a timely memorandum from Victor Du Pont. Sent earlier to Philadelphia to replace Consul General Létombe, Du Pont had promptly returned to Paris when the Adams administration

2. Talleyrand to Pichon, Paris, August 28, 1798, AAE EU, 50, folios 201–202v.
3. E. Wilson Lyon, "The Directory and the United States," *American Historical Review*, XLIII (April 1938), 524.
4. See Talleyrand's report to the Directory, Pluviôse, An 6 [January 20–February 18, 1798], AAE EU, 49, folios 184v–185; for Talleyrand's report to the Directory, June 1798, see Pallain, *Ministère de Talleyrand*, 309.

had refused to issue him an exequatur. Significantly, he brought back reports of excessive abuses being practiced against U.S. shipping by French West Indian prize courts. So far had these prize-court proceedings surpassed the intent of French maritime decrees, Du Pont wrote, that the warlike temper of the Adams administration lacked nothing to justify righteous indignation.[5]

Thus did Victor Du Pont hand Talleyrand a ready-made scapegoat for explaining the crisis in Franco-American affairs. XYZ could now be forgotten (and with it, Talleyrand's involvement), while the Foreign Minister expressed both surprise and chagrin at the official wrongdoing in the West Indies, and loaded Gerry with promises of reform in maritime regulations. Better still, Talleyrand acted on those promises with such dispatch that Gerry was able to take back with him a Directorial decree which ordered the revocation of all letters of marque and summoned home all prize judges suspected of having a vested interest in West Indian privateering.[6] Now, too, Talleyrand, like an anxious octopus, reached out for any American of consequence who might heed his pleas for conciliation. The hapless Gerry was held and squeezed until he had no other interest in life than to secure his passage papers. Dr. George Logan of Philadelphia, for whom the fraternal embrace was to be purely tentative, had not yet come within reach. The arm that was Pichon, therefore, groped most promisingly in the direction of The Hague.

At the time of Pichon's arrival, Murray was in a frame of mind to believe that if France sincerely wanted peace, it must be because she had recognized the righteousness of the American cause, or had become genuinely alarmed at American naval preparations. As to the latter, Murray did not naively exaggerate the capacity of a few American frigates to overawe France. But as a long-time believer in national respectability, he saw a supporting role for a United States Navy in which geography counted more than fire-power. When still a congressman he had equated three American warships with ten of any European power simply because "we lie near the high road of commerce to the West Indies."[7] Within this geopolitical framework, Murray was now predicting that America's naval entry into the war against France

5. See Du Pont's letters to Talleyrand of July 6, 21, and August 13, 1798, AAE EU, 50, folios 8–9, 99–106v, 163–163v.

6. "Extract from the Register of Decrees of the Executive Directory," July 31, 1798, AAE EU, *ibid.*, folios 138–138v; Talleyrand to Gerry, Paris, July 22, 1798, *ibid.*, folios 113–113v.

7. See Murray's speech, January 30, 1797, *Annals*, VI, 2125. DeConde finds Murray naïve on this point in his "Role of William Vans Murray," *loc. cit.*, 188.

would "shake every colony in the West into States, free & independent."
This was a possibility that even Talleyrand had reason to fear.[8]

Exultant to hear Pichon complain so "piteously" about the hostile
character of the XYZ disclosures, Murray wrote in his diary:

> How I rejoice to hear a frenchman—& one of the Bureau too—
> obliged to tackle to & placed on the Defensive towrds. a country
> wh. 6 months—nay 35. days since, they considered as feeble & a
> poor opponent—.[9]

Obviously, Murray did not suppose that a large American Navy had
been, or would be, created overnight. He did believe, however, that any
augmentation of American naval power would threaten France disproportionately in her exposed West Indian outposts. Were France
to show that she recognized that threat, any peace overtures emanating
from Paris might be taken as sincere.

Tuesday, June 26, 1798, found Murray and Pichon reporting to their
respective chiefs their first impressions of each other. That in the
persons of these two men France and the United States had at last set
their feet on the long road to peace was not at first apparent. Pichon described Murray as being approachable but deeply suspicious, convinced
in fact that France, far from wanting to accommodate, still planned to
work a revolution in American politics. Such a design could not now
succeed, Murray insisted, because the publication of the envoys' dispatches would draw the parties together to resist any further French
machinations. When Pichon had remarked on the hostility inherent
in a government's publishing diplomatic correspondence, Murray had
replied that it was the Congress, not the President, which had ordered
the publication. Murray had then carefully differentiated between what
Pichon labeled the "war party" in Congress and the relatively conciliatory stance of the administration; he had even given Pichon a copy
of the envoys' instructions so that the Frenchman might see for himself
how reasonable a position the administration had taken. In forwarding
this document to Talleyrand, Pichon revealed that he had been at least
partially persuaded when he observed that the instructions to Pinckney,
Marshall, and Gerry had not been calculated to give offense. The American mission had been asked to seek indemnity for maritime depreda-

8. Cf. entry of June 30, 1798, "Commonplace" of 1797, n.p.; E. Wilson Lyon,
Louisiana in French Diplomacy, 1759–1804 (Norman: University of Oklahoma
Press, 1934), 80–98.
9. Entry of June 28, 1798, "Commonplace" of 1797, n.p.

tions, but not as a *sine qua non.* Moreover, insofar as the envoys had been instructed to win French agreement to the maritime principles of Jay's treaty, this was merely a proposal to modify, not abrogate, the Franco-American commercial treaty of 1778.[10]

On the same day that Pichon reported to Talleyrand, Murray wrote to Pickering. The French agent's whole manner, Murray told the colonel, compelled him to conclude that Pichon's approaches had been ordered by Paris, that Pichon had been sent to The Hague expressly to sound him out. The Frenchman, he wrote,

> tries to soften every thing, and with a degree of persevering industry that leads me to believe he has been sent on purpose—entering as he does into various details—lamenting this, & softening that.

Despite the blandishments, Murray foresaw no root-change in French policy: Paris would continue to plunder American shipping, bully Europe, and "attempt to soothe the United States by writings." [11] The only new element was that Murray had suddenly become a party to informal conversations with a mysterious French agent. The pattern was familiar enough to put the American fully on his guard.

The sequel to this first meeting came two days later when the Murrays gave a dinner party, after which Pichon stayed behind to talk. Murray was sorely provoked when the Frenchman remarked that the American mission might have been successful, had it adhered to the spirit of its instructions. Pichon praised the instructions and by implication disparaged the envoys. Murray brought him up sharply, reminding him that Pinckney and company had dragged out four months in a patient "effort of Logic to open the ears of France" before they had finally loosed their accusatory memorial of January 31. At all events, Pichon grumbled, the outcome would have been different if Madison or Jefferson had been sent. Not so, Murray retorted; the envoys were "distinguished & profound & excellent men—as of *no party* & therefore the best also on that score." The warmth of Murray's rejoinder on this point was not lost on Pichon. Never again was Pichon to allude to his government's ideological conviction that Republicans would be easier to deal with than Federalists. The evening ended amicably enough, although Murray was still puzzled by Pichon's attentions, and still more skeptical at the Frenchman's denial that he was acting on orders from above.[12]

10. Pichon to Talleyrand, The Hague, June 26, 1798, AAE, EU, 49, folios 455–58.
11. WVM to Pickering, No. 52, The Hague, June 26, 1798, Netherlands Despatches, I.
12. Entry of June 28, 1798, "Commonplace" of 1797, n.p.

Murray's attitude toward Pichon underwent a subtle and perhaps significant change during the week following their initial conversations. When they had first talked on Tuesday and again on Thursday, Murray had been content to listen to Pichon and to refute certain of the Frenchman's misconceptions. By Saturday, June 30, however, the American minister was beginning to consider what precise concessions France might make that would warrant his continuing those conversations. This change of stance was almost certainly influenced by his encounter that day with Gustave Löwenhielm, the Swedish minister to The Hague. To his surprise, Löwenhielm had asked

> if I wd. not like to be the negotiator of Peace between the U.S. and F.—& that he shd. not be surprised if Mr. Robinjot [Claude Roberjot, Delacroix' successor] & I should come to an understanding on this subject through the mediation of Sweden.[13]

Murray, because he liked and trusted the Swedish nobleman, did not dismiss this proffer of mediation out of hand. He replied that the United States would, of course, welcome an honorable peace but that such a peace was unlikely because of the "shocking" way France had treated his country. When Löwenhielm persisted, Murray told him candidly that he would look on "offers unaccompany'd by ACTS on the part of F[rance] as intended . . . only to divert us from preparation," though he presumed that the Adams administration "would meet the hand of F[rance] half way." He went on to estimate that France already owed his countrymen some fifty million dollars in indemnity for illegal maritime seizures, and that until Paris gave some indication that it would honor those claims he would do nothing "to break down or weaken the spirit of America now so elevated." Again, however, he did not rule out his own possible role as peacemaker if the terms were consistent with "honour & justice." [14]

That evening, as he puzzled over the week's events, Murray wondered if Löwenhielm had been "misled by a desire to figure as a mediator." Or had the Swede become the guileless seconder of Pichon's overtures? Whatever the interplay of French and Swedish diplomacy, Murray was strongly impressed by the barrage of difficulties which had recently descended on France. He ticked them off:

> Rastadt looks black—Swissd. black—all Germany in a tremor of rage agt. her. . . . Engd. invulnerable—Holl'd not friendly—a

---

13. Entry of June 30, 1798, *ibid.*, n.p.
14. *Ibid.*

combination ahead—Buonaparte's fleet running before Nelson's. . . . I believe F[rance] is alarmed.[15]

But was France so beset, he wondered, as to make Paris sincere in its ostensible wish to reconcile the United States? Against this central question Murray made a decision: he would hereafter avoid even the appearance of formal conversations with Pichon; nor would he tell Philadelphia what Pichon said—unless France called in her privateers and acquiesced in the British convoying of American merchantmen.[16]

By July 2 it appeared that further conversations with Pichon had become unnecessary. Murray learned from Gerry that France would probably send a peace emissary directly to Philadelphia. While this event would relieve him of any potential embarrassment in his dealings with Pichon, Murray was not sanguine about the outcome. He doubted that any French emissary would be instructed to treat in good faith. A new envoy could be expected to follow the pattern of his predecessors, who had been unable to resist opportunities for meddling and subversion. France might be hard pressed in Europe, and even fearful of an open rupture with the United States, he wrote to his friend in Berlin, but "still they will go on, plunder as much and whine more." [17]

As if to confirm this prediction of more plundering, the Paris Directory on July 11 placed an embargo on all American vessels in French ports. That France should impose an embargo at the same time it was making overtures to Murray was not as inconsistent as might appear. The American Francophile, Joel Barlow, then in Paris, assessed the embargo as the mildest response that France could make to the news of the warlike measures of Congress. Barlow, of course, did not know that Murray had been approached, but he did believe that Talleyrand's last-minute assurances to Gerry signified an intention to avoid war. The embargo was simply a face-saving gesture.[18]

Murray, who was not so optimistic, conjectured briefly that the embargo might be the prelude to his own recall. Meanwhile, he moved swiftly to save as many American vessels as possible from being impounded. Foreseeing that the interdiction would be extended from

15. Night entry of June 30, 1798, *ibid.* For insights into the imperial conference at Rastatt, during which the Directory failed to secure certain Rhineland territories by diplomacy, and for the unsettled state of the Helvetian (Swiss) Republic, see Lefebvre, *The Themidorians,* 369–72.

16. Night entry of June 30, 1798, "Commonplace" of 1797, n.p.

17. WVM to Pickering (private), The Hague, July 2, 1798, Pickering MSS, 22, 258–62, MHS; WVM to JQA, The Hague, July 3, 1798, *AHA Report of 1912,* 426–27.

18. Barlow to James Watson, Paris, July 26, 1798, Gibbs, *Wolcott,* II, 111–12.

French to Dutch ports as soon as the Directory could make its will felt
at The Hague, he immediately sent warnings to American shipmasters
to make sail before the embargo hit them. To that end, Dandridge
hastened to Amsterdam while Murray sent a hurried note to U.S. Consul
John Beeldemaker at Rotterdam. Dutch authorities, meanwhile, pleaded
ignorance.

By July 14 the embargo had reached the port of Flushing, a jurisdiction shared by both France and Batavia, and the next day Murray
fixed on Flushing as a test case of Dutch good will. Although no American vessels were known to be in Flushing harbor, Murray nonetheless
prepared a protest against the levying of an embargo within what was
partially Batavian jurisdiction. Even before he wrote the formal note of
protest, however, he was able to get unofficial assurance from Jacob
Spoors, the Batavian Minister of Marine, that the Dutch commissary at
Flushing would be dismissed forthwith if he had actually ordered an
embargo. Having won this point Murray relented and urged Spoors
not to discharge the port official; it was enough, he said, that the
Batavian government simply publish a retraction of the embargo. On
July 19 he was gratified to learn from Spoors that Flushing was no
longer interdicted.[19]

Late July found Murray alternately perplexed, amused, and disgusted
at the march and countermarch of French diplomacy. On the seventeenth,
Pichon again sought him out, and showed him a letter from Talleyrand
in which the Foreign Minister not only "approved" of their earlier
conversations but also urged Pichon to continue his efforts to persuade
the American minister of France's sincere desire for an amicable settlement. Nor did this letter lack the whining tone which Murray accepted
as being typical of French policy pronouncements toward his country.
"You know," Talleyrand had written, "that an accommodation would
be effective immediately if the irritating measures of the United States
had not constantly posed an obstacle." Elbridge Gerry, he continued,
had refused all overtures, even the most sincere and detailed proposals;
nor had France taken umbrage at American hostility.[20]

Murray took a copy of Talleyrand's letter and that night scribbled his

19. Murray's correspondence with Spoors of July 19 and 20, 1798, was enclosed
in Murray's No. 56 to Pickering, The Hague, July 21, 1798, Netherlands Despatches, I. See also his dispatches Nos. 54 [55?] and 58, of July 17 and 28, 1798,
respectively, Netherlands Despatches, I; also entries of July 13 and 14, 1798,
"Commonplace" of 1797, n.p.; and WVM to John Adams (private), The Hague,
July 14, 1798, Pickering MSS, 22, 295, MHS.

20. Talleyrand to Pichon, Paris, July 9, 1798, Misc. Letters, WVM MSS, LC;
Pichon to Talleyrand, The Hague, July 18, 1798, AAE EU, 50, folios 81–88v.

reaction across the bottom of it. He knew that Talleyrand wanted him to forward the letter to Philadelphia, but, he wrote:

> Much as I wish for Peace I will not be the instrument of such uncertain advances to it. America has now taken her stand. It does not now become her to make advances after such ill-treated moderation.

Talleyrand's purpose was partially accomplished, however, when Murray that same day wrote a long letter to President Adams setting forth all that had passed between him and Pichon. He explained why, in the first instance, he had thought it necessary to speak to the Frenchman. His reason was simple and straightforward: Pichon was so grossly misinformed on American policy that Murray had seen an opportunity to enlighten him and perhaps, through him, to correct the misinformation of the French Foreign Office. He was quite sure that Talleyrand expected him to write openly of Pichon's blandishments in the hope that his letters to America would be published and that American opinion toward France would once more be divided. To minimize this risk, Murray continued, he planned to correspond only with President Adams and his son. He would not write to Pickering about Pichon because too many persons had access to State Department files. Above all, Pichon would never know that he had written to anyone about the overtures. Should Pichon come forward with specific proposals, Murray promised the President that he would listen but declare himself incompetent to treat, and would remind France that she herself was "competent to acts of justice and sincerity without negotiation." [21]

Pichon confirmed the fact of Murray's reticence during their long conversation of July 17. He wrote to his chief that he found the American minister as usual, "the most pronounced federalist," quick to parry his conciliatory thrusts with charges of bad faith and reminders of XYZ. Though discomfited, Pichon nonetheless learned that Murray had spoken daily with the President just before he left Philadelphia and was certain that Adams wanted to end the difficulties. Pichon fretted: the United States wanted peace, but the United States was offended. When would it stop being offended? To which Murray replied blandly that there would be no peace without honor; meanwhile, Congress' warlike preparations were merely defensive, and France had nothing to fear for her colonies. Americans, however, had no intention of prostrating themselves before France or yielding to her revolutionary designs.

21. WVM to JA, The Hague, July 17, 1798, Adams' *Works,* VIII, 680–84; see also WVM to JQA, The Hague, July 30, 1798, *AHA Report of 1912,* 437.

Pichon rejoined that such suspicions of France were fantastic. Did Murray seriously believe that men like Jefferson and Madison were capable of subverting their country's independence? This rejoinder led the two men to discuss the interesting changes which the political philosophy of James Madison had undergone since 1787, ending with Murray's assurance that Madison stood no chance of being sent on mission to Paris. Pichon then steered Murray toward the specifics of a Franco-American reconciliation, and suggested that peace would be a boon to American commerce.

If the Frenchman hoped to touch a sensitive nerve of merchant Federalism, he was disappointed. It was the nationalist in Murray that responded, not the Federalist. Entirely aside from the fact that American commerce was already flourishing, Murray drove home the point that it was not commerce, or vessels, or even principles of neutrality that his country was defending—it was its independence. And it was that independence which France had challenged.[22]

Having impressed on Pichon that "nothing now but acts of justice could restore harmony," Murray was interested to learn two days later that Talleyrand had asked the Council of Five Hundred to reform the judicial proceedings in prize cases. Was, perhaps, an appropriate "act of justice" now in the making? Murray thought not. The date of Talleyrand's request first puzzled, then amused, and finally alarmed him. Paris journals of July 10 reported that Talleyrand had asked for judicial reforms as early as May 10. Apparently there had been a two-month hiatus between the time of the request and its public disclosure. Then Murray saw the explanation. Two months earlier Talleyrand had not known the American response to XYZ. Now, news had arrived that American ships were being armed against French privateers. By falsifying the date of his reform proposals, Talleyrand undoubtedly hoped to save France "from the appearance of an act of repentance too late." Murray was not surprised when the Council, many of whose members were financially interested in the outcome of prize cases, rejected the notion of reforms. He was alarmed, however, lest France announce that the news of American hostility had now turned aside a conciliatory gesture that had been originated in May. By simply predating his proposals to the Council Talleyrand could now blame the United States for defeating proposals that had never been made.[23]

22. Pichon to Talleyrand, The Hague, July 18, 1798, AAE EU, 50, folios 81–88v.
23. Entry of July 19, 1798, "Commonplace" of 1797, n.p.; also WVM to Pickering, No. 56, The Hague, July 21, 1798, Netherlands Despatches, I.

Murray was only mildly impressed on learning that Talleyrand, unable to influence the Council of Five Hundred, had succeeded in persuading the Directory itself to revoke all current privateer commissions. An exuberant Pichon brought him the news that henceforth, under new commissions, French privateersmen would operate "within the LAWS." Privately, Murray scoffed at Pichon's supposition that herein lay the basis for Franco-American reconciliation. After all, the French maritime laws, in themselves, were bones of contention.[24] He also rebuffed Pichon's efforts to make substance out of the shadowy correspondence which Talleyrand had exchanged with Gerry.

At Pichon's insistence, the two men breakfasted together on July 31, so that Murray might see the contents of a letter which Talleyrand had sent to Gerry (probably that of July 12) in which Pichon said he saw "every basis for a new negotiation."[25] In the Frenchman's account of this breakfast meeting, Murray had appeared to be visibly affected by what he read. So pleased was he by Murray's favorable reaction that he ventured to his chief that the American minister did not seem at all the blind Federalist partisan he had imagined him to be. Moreover, Pichon reported happily that Murray had written to the State Department, a dispatch that would certainly reflect favorably on Talleyrand's dealings with Gerry.[26]

What Murray wrote to Pickering hardly explained Pichon's optimism. France seemed momentarily disposed to be conciliatory, he told the colonel, but that was to be expected in the light of the recently-evinced American hostility. Clearly evident in this dispatch was Murray's determination not to spark an optimism that might be exploited by the political opposition. "France would soon listen to reason," he supposed, unless the Republican faction in the United States gave her cause to believe that a reasonable settlement was unnecessary.[27]

What Murray had tried to convey most emphatically to Pichon—but Pichon neglected to report—was that Talleyrand's last-minute communications to Gerry did not meet Murray's specifications for another peace negotiation. Pichon unfortunately thought they did. Murray had told the Frenchman—or so he related to John Quincy Adams—that if France truly wanted a restoration of amity, "there was one way too

24. See Talleyrand's "Report to the Executive Directory," July 27, 1798, and the resultant "Decree" of July 31, 1798, in AAE EU, 50, folios 131–131v, 138–138v.

25. WVM to JQA, August 2, 1798, *AHA Report of 1912*, 443.

26. Pichon to Talleyrand, The Hague, August 1, 1798, AAE EU, 50, 139–42.

27. WVM to Pickering, The Hague, July 29, 1798, Pickering MSS, 22, folios 326–28v, MHS.

obvious to be mistaken, which was, a great spontaneous act of justice on the part of France; [and] that no envoys were necessary for that." No more embassies would emanate from Philadelphia "until some very solid *fact* showed, proved that there existed mutual wishes on equal terms." [28]

That Murray wanted some more concrete act of repentance than France had yet performed was lost on Pichon. No word of Murray's expectation reached Talleyrand from that quarter. Either Pichon did not wish his chief to know that his talks with Murray were foundering, or he saw no politic way of explaining to Talleyrand the need for that "very solid fact" that would prove France's good will. Murray, too, had reached an impasse. For all his talk of substantive justice, Murray could not, without instructions, name the price of a new negotiation. Only John Adams could do that.

The log-jam in the Murray-Pichon dialogue broke clear when news arrived that John Adams, unlike his emissary to The Hague, was willing to settle for less than "a great spontaneous act of justice." The President's terms, sent to Congress on June 21, were that he would "never send another minister to France without assurances that he will be received, respected, and honored as the representative of a great, free, powerful, and independent nation." [29] Though the phrasing was negative, the door was left ajar. Were France to offer the stipulated "assurances," Adams might send another mission to Paris. The meaning of this sentence was obscured for a time by the din of Adams' own warlike utterances, but it rang clearly in Murray's ears. To Murray, the diplomatic function was implicit: he must listen to and weigh any emanations from Paris which might constitute the assurances Adams required.[30]

Curiously, though he must have known the text of Adams' message by July 25, Murray did not press the French Foreign Office for "assurances." Nor did Talleyrand hasten to offer them. More than a month passed before the French Foreign Minister fully recognized the need for a specific compliance with Adams' terms. Murray, meanwhile, felt inhibited by a lack of instructions. He felt he could not actively seek "assurances" without seeming to treat officially, and therefore continued

28. To JQA, The Hague, August 2, 1798, *AHA Report of 1912,* 443, 445.
29. Richardson, *Messages,* II, 266.
30. The author agrees with Dauer that John Adams favored limited, not full-scale, war. See Dauer's "Preface to the Paperback Edition," *Adams Federalists,* xxi–xxii.

to insist that what passed between him and Pichon remain unofficial. Moreover, he was reluctant to begin a detente which, if called to public attention, might effect a slackening in the American preparedness movement. With consummate indirection, therefore, he turned to his friend Maarten van der Goes. Little time elapsed between his learning the President's requirement and his request to the Batavian Foreign Office that it might "try to get F[rance] to give *the assurances* to our govt. mentioned in Presidt. message 21. June last." Van der Goes replied that he would try.[31]

Talleyrand, meanwhile, persisted in ignoring the explicit terms of Adams' requirement. When, for example, France lifted her embargo in mid-August, the Frenchman relayed to Murray his view that this act was sufficient "assurance" of France's good will. Murray could only reply to Pichon that this and other conciliatory measures were no guarantee that a new mission would be properly received.[32] Part of the difficulty lay in Talleyrand's preoccupation with personal diplomacy. His "mediation" maneuvers with the Dutch envoy at Paris and his diffident wooing of George Logan, well-meant though they may have been, not only inhibited Murray's talks with Pichon, but also thrust the matter of "assurances" into the background. Perhaps most blighting of all, Talleyrand was relying on Elbridge Gerry to convey directly to John Adams all of the "assurances" that would be necessary for a fresh start.

31. Entry of July 25, 1798, "Commonplace" of 1797, n.p.
32. Entry of August 29, 1798, *ibid.*

10

Talleyrand Gives Assurances

MURRAY'S CONVERSATIONS with Pichon were overshadowed in August by the attention drawn to the peacemaking efforts of Rutger Jan Schimmelpenninck, Batavian envoy to Paris, and Dr. George Logan of Philadelphia.

Logan was a wealthy and well-meaning Quaker who, from motives that were purely "humanitarian and religious," undertook his own personal peace mission to Paris in the summer of 1798. He probably intended no more than to lend moral support to Elbridge Gerry. Arriving in Paris after Gerry had left, Logan contented himself with friendly but informal talks with high French officials. The pseudo-diplomatic character which the Paris press attached to Logan's mission, coupled with the Philadelphian's well-known Republican affiliations, evoked strong anger from Federalists.[1]

Murray was instantly alerted. On Sunday, July 29, Murray learned from van der Goes that an American named "Droghan" had landed at Hamburg, armed with messages for the French Directory from Thomas Jefferson. He might be overrating the new arrival's importance, Murray wrote Pickering, but he knew how prone the French were to entering into partisan intrigue. He surmised that Logan (whose identity was now established) had come to warn the Directory of the dire consequences that would befall the Republican party in America if France were to continue her present policy. Conversely, should Logan win any concessions, they would redound to the prestige of the Republican party and serve to embarrass the administration. At worst, the French might be encouraged to continue their meddling in American politics. Until

1. The fullest account of Logan's mission is contained in Chapter VIII of Frederick B. Tolles, *George Logan of Philadelphia* (New York: Oxford University Press, 1953), hereinafter cited as Tolles, *George Logan.*

Logan's arrival, Murray noted, the French "were staggered & getting into a state of reflexion—This may intoxicate them again." [2]

Believing that Logan would pass through Amsterdam, Murray asked a friend in that city to intercept him and find out what credentials he bore. From this source, Murray's agent having been successful, Murray learned that Logan had at least one passport from the French minister at Hamburg. Within two hours of receiving word that Logan was in Amsterdam, Murray made a series of attempts to reach van der Goes. Not until late that evening, however, did he find the Dutchman and persuade him to send an order to the Amsterdam authorities to detain Logan for questioning. By midnight Murray had heard that Logan's purpose was to summon Gerry and Pinckney back to Paris to resume the negotiation. Pinckney, he predicted, "if not gone will give him a warm reception." [3]

Next day it became apparent that Dutch newspapers had mistaken Logan for an official envoy. This was too much. That night Murray and Major James Mountflorence took a coach-and-four to Rotterdam, ostensibly Logan's next way station. They arrived at two in the morning, found the city gates shut, and spent the remainder of the night at nearby Turenne. At dawn, while Mountflorence scoured the taverns for news of Logan's whereabouts, Murray went to tell the president of the Rotterdam city council that he wished to talk to Logan if the latter could be apprehended. High Sheriff Hubert was called in for consultation. This reluctant official patiently explained that Logan's passports could not be demanded unless Logan were suspected of a crime, or unless the government ordered it.

Murray argued that Logan was known to have a French passport, but not an American one. If it could be shown that Logan had a passport from either Jefferson or from a Pennsylvania judge named Thomas McKean, he might reasonably be detained on grounds that only the United States Government could issue one.[4] Murray also tried to impress the sheriff with the harm that might be done by such an unofficial emissary. Finally, Hubert agreed that when and if Logan passed through Rotterdam he would be detained as an enemy alien—as an

---

2. See Murray's private letters to Pickering of July 29 and August 6, 1798, Pickering MSS, 22, folios 326–28v; 23, 10–11v, MHS: also WVM to JQA, August 2, 1798, *AHA Report of 1912*, 444.

3. WVM to Pickering, The Hague, August 6, 1798, *loc. cit.;* entries of August 6, 1798, "Commonplace" of 1797, n.p.

4. Logan brought two dispatches from Consul General Joseph Létombe addressed to Talleyrand and Merlin, and letters of introduction from Jefferson and Chief Justice McKean of Pennsylvania. See Tolles, *George Logan*, 155–156.

Englishman! This would give Murray time to talk to him. Hubert
warned, however, that Logan could not be held long without explicit
authorization from The Hague. With this, Murray and Mountflorence
returned to the capital that afternoon, reasonably certain, however, that
Logan had eluded them. Back at The Hague, Murray had no difficulty in
obtaining a detention order and, as late as August 10, continued to hope
that he could have this "authorized fanatic" arrested. Next day, however,
he received a letter from Sheriff Hubert confirming that Logan had left
the country.[5]

Though he failed to intercept Logan, Murray hoped to draw the sting
from the Quaker's mission with a stiff warning to Pichon. He told the
Frenchman that Logan's mission was no secret, that Philadelphia would
hear of it within thirty days, and that if the French tried to treat with
Logan they would "only tend to widen the breach." [6] This warning,
when relayed to Paris, may well have discouraged Talleyrand from intrigue. The French Foreign Minister hastened to reassure Murray that
Logan's reception had been wholly proper. The doctor had given some
treatises on agriculture—nothing else—Talleyrand wrote, although he
admitted believing at first that Logan had been sent by the American
government to start a secret negotiation. No, Logan had no letters for
him; nor had he been announced as the American chargé d'affaires.
Moreover, it was absurd to suppose that the Directory would negotiate
with anyone but the President of the United States. His own hopes for a
settlement, Talleyrand explained, rode with the letters that had been
sent with Gerry.

When Pichon relayed all this, Murray replied heavily that any official
dealings with Logan would justify Americans in their suspicions that
France still had "revolutionary pretensions" toward the United States.[7]
Privately, Murray did not believe a word of it. He wrote Pickering that
the French had made their denials "with infinite solicitude . . . but I
know better," adding wryly, "it is *something* however to bring them to
forswear their friends." [8] Despite the reassurances from Paris, he heard
from other sources that Logan was meeting secretly with Talleyrand,

5. This account is pieced together from Murray's entries of August 6, 8, and
10, 1798, "Commonplace" of 1797, n.p.; his private letters to Pickering of August
7 and 13, 1798, in the Pickering MSS, 22, 450–52; 23, 37–40, MHS; and his
letters to JQA of August 6 and 10, 1798, *AHA Report of 1912*, 448–50, 452–53.
His letters to and from Dutch officials are in WVM MSS, Misc. Letters, LC.

6. As recounted to JQA in Murray's letter of August 10, 1798, *AHA Report of
1912*, 452.

7. Talleyrand to Pichon, Paris, August 16, 1798, AAE EU, 50, folio 169;
Pichon to Talleyrand, The Hague, August 24, 1798, *ibid.*, folios 188–91v.

8. The Hague, August 23, 1798, *AHA Report of 1912*, 460.

and was "abusing" the government of the United States. In an outburst that presaged the Logan Act, Murray exclaimed to John Quincy Adams: "Here is a traitor without legal treason. Such language ought to be treason, if held in any foreign country." [9]

His worst suspicions appeared to be borne out when on August 17 the Paris press announced the lifting of the French embargo and gave the credit to Logan. Pichon, of course, was quick to deny that Logan had had any part in the Directory's decision. Whether Logan's appearance in Paris was the cause, or merely the occasion, for raising the embargo, Murray's own explanation of the act was that France was feeling the pinch of commercial nonintercourse. Whatever may have transpired between Talleyrand and Logan, Murray gradually credited the French with sincerity in their subsequent disavowals. He even accepted the notion that Logan had appeared in a private capacity and not as a party emissary—this after a long conversation with Rutger Schimmelpenninck. Be that as it might, he grumbled to Adams, the line must be drawn somewhere between what was treasonable and what was not.[10]

In retrospect, Murray was not quite sure that he had acted properly in trying to waylay Logan. He justified himself to Pickering, but to John Quincy Adams he betrayed a feeling of uncertainty as to whether he had overstepped his ministerial authority. Adams wrote back approvingly that Murray's effort to intercept Logan could be classed among a great many matters, large and small, on which he and Murray invariably concurred; and for the sake of their friendship, he promised to tell Murray candidly if he ever disagreed with him.[11] Unhappily mindful of possible partisan repercussions, Murray wrote in his diary: "I see they know of Logan in america," adding defiantly, "Jefferson and the rest will be my mortal enemies—this I expected—but I did right—." But things were not as bad as they might have been. In failing to have the Quaker arrested, he quipped to Adams that "he, and perhaps *I*, too, escaped!!" But even in the attempt, he later confessed to Adams, he had fully expected to be crucified in the Jeffersonian press.[12]

9. The Hague, August 24, 1798, *ibid.*

10. WVM to JQA, The Hague, September 11, 1798, *ibid.*, 469–70; also WVM to Pickering (private), The Hague, September 1, 1798, Pickering MSS, 23, 98, MHS; same to same, No. 61, The Hague, September 3, 1798, Netherlands Despatches, I. For evidence that the Directory had decided to lift the embargo prior to Logan's arrival, see Tolles, *George Logan*, 167.

11. WVM to JQA, The Hague, August 15, 1798, *AHA Report of 1912*, 456; JQA to WVM, Berlin, August 21, 1798, Adams MSS, MR 133.

12. Entry of August 21, 1798, "Commonplace" of 1797, n.p.; letters to JQA of August 28 and December 18, 1798, *AHA Report of 1912*, 460, 497–98.

When Congress met in December its first and only important business was to enact a law forbidding Logan's type of "diplomatic" activity. When he heard of it Murray wondered if anyone knew that he had attempted to detain this "emissary of sedition." If they had, he supposed that he would have heard of an impeachment proceeding against him. Again, the younger Adams was reassuring: Murray was not likely to be impeached merely for *trying* to detain Logan. Moreover, Adams observed, had Logan never reached Paris, there would have been no Logan Act. All in all, the end result was a salutary one.[13] Neither man could foresee the ironic aftermath of the Logan Affair in which John Adams many years later would designate Logan, together with Murray, Gerry, and his own son, as the persons on whose collective advice he had determined to send another mission to France.[14]

Murray felt nothing but revulsion for Logan's mission. When the Dutch government offered to mediate, however, his reaction was not wholly negative. He knew the Dutch to be amicably motivated insofar as they had no wish to become involved in the cross fire of a commerce-destroying war between France and the United States. Their well-known wish to avoid war lent sincerity to their offer. Murray nonetheless suspected a second and less creditable motive: that The Hague hoped in this way to publicize its independence from Paris. In that guise, the puppet might gratify its *amour propre,* but it could hardly assume the posture of a disinterested mediator. Still, Murray saw the Dutch overture as potentially useful. For one thing, he preferred The Hague to Philadelphia as a locale for any new negotiation. If past experience was an indicator, any French envoy sent to Philadelphia "would rally every sort of Devil from the Mississippi to the Delaware, and his house would be the scene of all sorts of seditious deputations." Even barring an active mediatory role for the Dutch, Murray thought they might become an appropriate channel for French "assurances" that a new mission would be honorably received.[15]

August was scarcely a week old when Murray learned that the Batavian minister to Paris, Rutger Schimmelpenninck, had actually found Talleyrand receptive. He wrote Pickering that if a Dutch mediation proposal came to him officially he would "avert" it but listen. Not only would the Dutch make poor mediators, but France had not yet

13. WVM to JQA, The Hague, March 12, 1799, *ibid.,* 525–26; JQA to WVM, Berlin, March 19, 1799, Adams MSS, MR 133.
14. See John Adams' letters to the *Boston Patriot,* 1809, reprinted in Adams' *Works,* IX, 243–46.
15. WVM to JQA, The Hague, August 3, 1798, *AHA Report of 1912,* 447; WVM to Pickering, letters of August 7 and 18, 1798, Pickering MSS, 23, 14–17, 49–50, MHS.

relaxed her maritime decrees. Besides, he had no authority to receive such proposals. On August 9 Murray heard that Talleyrand would avail himself of the Dutch proposal only if his overtures, being conveyed by Gerry, failed to bring an amicable settlement. During the third week in August, amid thickening rumors, Paris newspapers reported that mediation had been offered and accepted.[16] Eventually, it came out that The Hague, fearing a rebuff from the United States, had offered the Directory its "good offices" rather than mediation. Seizing the moment, Talleyrand published an official acceptance, a copy of which Murray forwarded to the State Department on the 23rd. Two days later, however, Murray concluded that Talleyrand had not actually accepted the Batavian offer; he had simply "received it with satisfaction." At all events, he had already told van der Goes that there would be nothing official in his referral of Talleyrand's note to Philadelphia.[17] Degrees of informality having been observed, the French "acceptance" of the Dutch "mediation" could be relegated to the trash heap of Talleyrandian gestures. Before the end of August the Frenchman himself was to characterize the Dutch proposal as "absolutely useless." Thereafter, the Dutch confined themselves to telling Murray that French "assurances" respecting a new mission would be forthcoming shortly.[18]

Small wonder that Talleyrand, threading his way between the blandishments of Schimmelpenninck and Logan, lost sight of the all-important matter of "assurances." Moreover, in the Frenchman's view, the necessary "assurances" had already been given to Gerry. Not only had Gerry been repeatedly told of France's desire for reconciliation, but he had also been sent a copy of the July 31 decree regulating privateers, just before he sailed. Talleyrand counted on Gerry's homecoming, replete with messages of peace, to set the stage for a new negotiation. What the Frenchman could not foresee was that neither Murray, nor the President, nor the President's son, would regard the fulsome letters to Gerry as an adequate substitute for explicit "assurances that [another minister] will be received, respected, and honored as the representative of a great, free, powerful and independent nation." [19]

16. WVM to Pickering (private), letters of August 7 and 18, 1798, *loc. cit.;* and entries of August 19 and 20, 1798, "Commonplace" of 1797, n.p.

17. WVM to Pickering (private), letters of August 23 and 25, 1798, Pickering MSS, 23, 61–63v, 75–82, MHS.

18. Talleyrand to Pichon, Paris, August 28, 1798, Thomas B. Wait, ed., *State Papers and Publick Documents of the United States* (Boston, 1819), IV, 295; Entry of September 12, 1798, "Commonplace" of 1797, n.p.

19. Cf. WVM to JQA, The Hague, September 6, 1798, *AHA Report of 1912*,

Murray, although he knew what was required, hesitated to play an active part in securing those "assurances." To begin with, he doubted the wisdom of Adams' sending another mission even if it were assured of proper reception. He believed that a new negotiation could be safely tried only if American public opinion were kept as firm toward France as it had been the previous spring, and only if Congress sustained its preparedness effort during the period of negotiation. Moreover, his sense of propriety dictated that he exhaust his Dutch connections where the channels were official rather than deal with Pichon, whom he could not officially recognize. Finally, should Talleyrand actually present him with the necessary "assurances," Murray set himself the difficult task of receiving them "in such a way as not to commit the American government on the point of sending [another mission]." [20]

In view of Talleyrand's ignorance of precisely what was expected of him and Murray's reluctance to press him, it is not surprising that the Murray-Pichon conversations languished during most of August. Talleyrand continued to give encouragement to Pichon, and Pichon still reported that he had Murray's confidence. On August 20, however, a subtle change overtook the Hague conversations when Murray directed Pichon's attention to the exact nature of the "assurances." He told Pichon that Adams probably would not nominate another envoy on the basis of the "assurances" entrusted to Gerry. This was because France, in choosing to deal with Gerry while rejecting Pinckney and Marshall, had given offense by seeming to dictate the kind of envoy she would receive. He warned Pichon that any attempt by Paris to stipulate the character or political coloration of American emissaries would be worse than useless. Such stipulations touched on the vital issue of American independence. That Gerry had been singled out from his colleagues for political reasons would surely cast doubt on his credentials as a bearer of conciliatory proposals. Pichon replied that "only an extreme irritation could misinterpret so simple a thing." He nonetheless reported that Murray was unmoved on this point.[21] When Murray further defined the future role of the Dutch as simply that of intermediaries and not arbiters, his signal to the French Foreign Office was clear. Talleyrand should give

---

467; JQA to WVM, Berlin, October 6, 1798, Adams MSS, MR 133; John Adams' letter to the *Boston Patriot* in 1809 as reprinted in Adams' *Works*, IX, 244.

20. WVM to Pickering (private), The Hague, August 13, 1798, *AHA Report of 1912*, 454; also WVM to JQA, The Hague, letters of September 14 and 25, 1798, *ibid.*, 470–71, 473.

21. Pichon to Talleyrand, The Hague, August 21, 1798, AAE EU, 50, folios 188–91v.

up his hopes for Gerry; and if he wished to give further "assurances," The Hague was the proper channel.

Brushing aside the "offices" of the Dutch, Talleyrand wrote a letter to Pichon on August 28 which marked a long step forward along the road to peace. In words intended for Murray's eyes, Talleyrand depicted the Marylander as an estimable man, perhaps unduly influenced by British propaganda, but "neither French nor English; he is ingenuously an American." Talleyrand then traced the sources of Franco-American misunderstanding: Americans had suspected France of wanting to "revolutionize" them, and France had believed that the American government "wanted to throw itself into the arms of England." Neither suspicion was true. Now was the time for calmness and dispassionate confidence. Gerry, whose refusal to negotiate still puzzled the Frenchman, had been given "the most solemn assurances concerning the reception that a new plenipotentiary would receive." Thereupon, Talleyrand simultaneously denied and confirmed Murray's belief that France would try to influence the choice of an American envoy. "I should be very badly understood," he wrote, "if there should be found, in my expressions, a restriction on the nature of the choice, which the President might make." Before the end of the paragraph, however, he was wondering how any envoy "who should profess a hatred or contempt of the French Republic . . . can inspire the directory with a favorable opinion of the dispositions of the government of the United States?" [22] In short, France would not dictate the choice, but she would prefer an envoy whose ideology was not repugnant to the principles of the French Revolution.

At any stage of his talks with Pichon, Murray would have found this letter unsatisfactory. It was the more so on September 7, when it arrived, because Murray had already tried to sharpen the focus of Pichon's attention on the very explicit nature of the "assurances." At a conference on August 29, Pichon had handed him a copy of the decree lifting the embargo, together with circulars to various French port officials ordering the release of American seamen interned since July 11. That night Murray wrote in his "Commonplace": "He thinks *the assurances* are given. I told him I did not—that if they are sincere they will put it in our power to treat." [23] Specifically, he had told Pichon that day that no new negotiations could be expected

> unless assurances were given of a treatment worthy the minister of a great free and independent nation, and that even then I did

22. Talleyrand to Pichon, Paris, August 28, 1798, Pickering MSS, 23, 183–91, MHS.
23. Entry of August 29, 1798, "Commonplace" of 1797, n.p.

not know at all what might be now the intention of my government
. . . and that the assurances mentioned ought to be as formal and
solemn as the declaration of the President had been.[24]

Pichon, who had no authority to give formal "assurances," worked with
what he had at hand. He cited the lifting of the embargo, the release of
American seamen, and the forswearing of Logan and others "who
meddled on both sides of the water." Finally, he remarked that American
affairs at the Foreign Office had been taken out of the hands of former
Consul General La Forest and were now being handled directly by
Talleyrand. Pichon even admitted having been sent to The Hague for
the express purpose of effecting a reconciliation, adding plaintively that
if he failed, he, La Forest, and Talleyrand might all be ruined.[25]

Privately, Murray was jubilant at his country's ability to discomfit
France. "It would dilate every artery in you," he wrote James McHenry,

> to see the glory which is spreading over the United States at this
> moment in the eyes of Europe. She comes on the stage at an instant
> highly propitious to eclat. When the heart of the continent had
> sunk—she plants her foot with firmness—France recoils—and
> every body is revived—& in triumph—for France does recoil.[26]

Murray's own arteries dilated at Pichon's increasingly frenetic appeals
for a new negotiation. He wrote John Quincy Adams that the Frenchman
was insisting "over and over" that France shrank from a war that might
face her with "loss of colonies," and an American "juncture with
England." Though nearly convinced that Paris was sincere, Murray remained uncertain that France would agree to humble herself to the point
of giving the explicit "assurances" which he thought necessary, and
which, he must remind Pichon, would of themselves be no guarantee of
a new negotiation. Also, he wondered, would France actually end the
negotiation with a treaty, or would her ultimate decision for war or
peace be governed by collateral events? So profoundly did Murray suspect Directorial France that he readily envisioned her as undertaking a
negotiation with no intention of completing it. "If they get a negotiation," he wrote John Quincy Adams, "I am convinced that they will still
work at our roots . . . and if they saw their party increase from that

24. WVM to Pickering (private), The Hague, September 1, 1798, *AHA Report
of 1912*, 464–65.
25. *Ibid.*, 464. See also entries of August 29 and 31, 1798, "Commonplace," of
1797, n.p.
26. The Hague, August 30, 1798, Steiner, *McHenry*, 341–44.

critical interval . . . they would again be intoxicated and again be insolent." [27]

On September 6 Pichon returned to The Hague from an unexplained visit to northern Holland, where Talleyrand's letter of August 28 had overtaken him. Murray saw Pichon and the letter that evening at seven. Next day he received a copy of it.[28] Now began a delicate task of explaining to Pichon that no matter how sincere France was in her wish for a new negotiation, the "assurances" must follow precisely the form of Adams' message of June 21. Mindful that he was suggesting the ultimate abasement, Murray proposed that the "assurances" be accompanied by a face-saving explanation. He hinted to Pichon that Paris might reasonably plead ignorance of the recent envoys' instructions as the cause of earlier misunderstandings. Now that those instructions had been made public, France could announce her gratifying discovery of American good will and "thus give the assurances wh[ich] became necessary to repair the breach occasioned by her not being acquainted with the instructions." Explicit "assurances" need not be regarded as a special favor to the United States, nor looked on as being a "matter of delicacy," because France was too great a nation to be embarrassed by admitting to an earlier error.[29]

To impress on Pichon the importance of phrasing the "assurances" word for word as Adams had stipulated, Murray informed him that this latest letter from Talleyrand was defective in at least two respects. Its allusion to Murray's being British-influenced would, in the first instance, preclude him from sending it to Philadelphia. The subsequent "spice for Mr. Murray" that he was "neither French nor British" did little to remedy the defect. In all, Talleyrand had left the impression that American policy-makers were the minions of Great Britain. The other defect appeared in Talleyrand's lingering assumption that France could properly express a preference for the political hue of the envoy whom Philadelphia might choose to send. Murray was unmoved by Talleyrand's argument that the Directory would find it difficult to treat with an emissary who professed hatred of the French Republic. He left

27. The Hague, September 21, 1798, *AHA Report of 1912*, 473; also Murray's letter to JQA of August 31, 1798, *ibid.*, 463.
28. Pichon to Talleyrand, The Hague, September 1, 1798, AAE EU, 50, folios 206–207; Pichon to WVM, The Hague, September 6, 1798, Misc. Letters, WVM MSS, LC.
29. Entry of September 7, 1798, "Commonplace" of 1797, n.p.; WVM to Pickering, private, The Hague, September 8, 1798, Pickering MSS, 23, 125–32, MHS.

no doubt in Pichon's mind that the Adams administration must be absolutely free in its choice of envoys.[30]

While Murray waited for Talleyrand to make the next move, he explained to John Quincy Adams how tortuous the path of diplomacy had become. Pichon kept seeing "assurances" in various conciliatory acts of the French government, and seemed to resist the notion of explicit "assurances," ceremonially rendered. Against this obduracy Murray had insisted that Franco-American relations were so badly out of joint— the American right of embassy having been twice refused—that nothing short of the required formalities would suffice. At the same time, Murray felt the need to convince both Paris and Philadelphia that he, personally, had no authority, nor would he presume, to commit the United States to further negotiation no matter what form the "assurances" took. He assured Pickering that he did not judge the expediency of renewing diplomatic relations. Only the fact that the United States was unrepresented at Paris, together with the implied overture of Adams' June 21 message, had led him "to act as I have done." He characterized that action as leading the French *"to a point favorable in all shapes to our Govt.—but not committing it to anything."* [31]

While Pichon steadily corresponded with Paris, it was not until September 23 that he made a major effort to convince Talleyrand of the need for explicit "assurances." He might never have done so had Murray not taken the initiative of "throwing on paper" an explanation of why they were indispensable. During a breakfast meeting on September 22, Pichon asked Murray to set down "what might be the *form* for him to obtain Mr. Talleyrand's consent to, respecting the 'assurances.' " No, Murray replied, he would not specify the "form," but he would elaborate the need.[32] Next day Murray put in writing what he had been telling Pichon for a fortnight: that the extraordinary rebuff which France had given to two embassies required an extraordinary pledge of good faith before a third would be sent. Then, although he had told Pichon he would not spell out the "form" of the "assurances," Murray quoted directly from Adams' message of June 21. "This I guarded top and bottom," he wrote later, "with the solemn declaration

30. *Ibid.;* also WVM to JQA, The Hague, September 25, 1798, *AHA Report of 1912,* 473–74.
31. See Murray's private letters to Pickering of September 8 and 19, 1798, Pickering MSS, 23, 125–32, 148–51v, MHS; and his letters to JQA of September 14 and 28, 1798, *AHA Report of 1912,* 470–71, 476.
32. Entry of September 22, 1798, "Commonplace" of 1797, n.p.

that all our conversations had been on my part unauthorized, and as an individual, and that that paper was also unauthorized." [33]

Murray's memorandum of September 23 cleared the way for Pichon to broach to his chief the subject of explicit "assurances," without seeming to inject this embarrassing requirement on his own initiative. Further, it told Talleyrand exactly what was expected of him. And finally, it kept Murray clear of the imputation of meddling.

Forwarding Murray's memorandum to Paris that same day, Pichon covered it with a letter warning Talleyrand that he had reached a critical point in his talks with the American minister. "Assurances," he wrote, were the *sine qua non* of any further dealings either with Murray or the Adams administration. He also conveyed Murray's admonition that France would be ill advised to rest her future policy on the outcome of the congressional elections. No matter how the Federalists fared in the fall elections, Adams would have the support of the present Congress through the lame-duck session. In sum, Pichon spared no effort to impress on Talleyrand the need for explicit "assurances," and the need for haste in delivering them—even to the point of noting ominously that Murray had leased his house only until the following May.[34]

On September 28, 1798, Murray's memorandum elicited from Talleyrand a letter which was possibly the most significant landmark in the history of the Federalist party. Of this letter John Adams later remarked:

> I own I am not acquainted with any words, either in the French or English language, which could have expressed in a more solemn, a more explicit, or a more decided manner, assurances of all that I had demanded as conditions of negotiation. . . . If ever there was a regular diplomatic communication, this was one. The diplomatic organs were all perfect and complete.[35]

By the time Talleyrand's letter reached Philadelphia, Adams had received from other sources ample evidence that France was now willing to treat. Reassuring letters from his various correspondents, however, did not move the President to take his next decisive action. "Though they might convince my mind," he wrote later, his other informants

---

33. WVM to JQA, The Hague, September 28, 1798, *AHA Report of 1912*, 476; Murray enclosed a copy of his memorandum to Pichon in his letter to Pickering, October 12, 1798, Pickering MSS, 25, 219a–221a, MHS.

34. The Hague, September 23, 1798, AAE EU, 50, folios 227–30.

35. From Adams' letters to the *Boston Patriot*, 1809, Adams' *Works*, IX, 247.

would not have influenced him to nominate another mission to Paris had he not received from Murray these "authentic, regular, official, diplomatic assurances."

Talleyrand's letter of September 28 was, then, the firmest documentary basis for rapprochement. It opened to Adams a course of action that he was already contemplating. It did not, however, force the President's hand. There was something spurious in Adams' later complaint that he could not "get rid" of this letter "with honor, or even without infamy." Ten years later, when he was defending himself against Hamilton's charge, posthumously revived, that he had been wrong to seek any reconciliation with France, it may have made good argument for Adams to insist that once confronted with Talleyrand's letter he had no choice but to respond. In the context of 1798–99, the President could scarcely have misread Murray's insistent assertion that no commitment to negotiate had been undertaken. In truth, Murray had handed the President a useful weapon in his struggle with the High Federalists over the control of foreign policy. But the weapon was in Adams' hand, not over his head.[36]

The "assurances," such as they were, were contained in this passage which Talleyrand had written to Pichon:

> According to these bases, you were right to assert [to Murray] that whatever plenipotentiary the government of the United States might send to France in order to terminate the existing differences between the two countries, he would be undoubtedly received with the respect due to the representative of a free, independent, and powerful nation.[37]

Despite the President's satisfaction with this passage, Murray was doubtful as to its form and content. The "assurances" were not, after all, addressed to Adams directly. The letter merely sanctioned what Pichon had said to Murray. And, on closer scrutiny, the Talleyrand letter disturbed Murray by the use of that phrase which read "according to these bases," a reference to the earlier and unsatisfactory "assurances" accorded to Gerry and to himself. Murray recalled that those earlier effusions had also alluded to the desirability of an American envoy's being pro-French.

36. *Ibid.*, 245–46.
37. For an English translation of the Talleyrand-to-Pichon letter of September 28, see Wait, *State Papers*, IV, 297.

At still another point Murray puzzled over the Frenchman's remark that once the two cabinets had explained their respective positions, "the Ties of Friendship would be more firmly united, by the Knowledge each party will acquire of the Hand that attempted to disunite them." If by "Ties of Friendship" Talleyrand was forecasting a revival of the alliance, Murray wanted no part of it. Congress had "fairly got rid of" both of the old French treaties, and he was depressed to think that Talleyrand might predicate a peace settlement on the renewal of the alliance. Less disconcerting because it was predictable was the reference to "the Hand that attempted to disunite them"—an obvious reference to British influence in American councils. Murray could only remark to Pickering that the letter as a whole was "more free of that insult than any I have seen from the same hand." [38]

In disparaging what was, in part, his own handiwork, Murray was patently apprehensive of having his own motives misconstrued. He made this clear when he wrote John Adams that "unless the purity and disinterestedness of my motives are appreciated by you, Sir, I shall consider these informal endeavours to coöperate in what I thought to be your plan . . . as the greatest errors of my life!" [39] Pickering, too, was given a careful catalog of motives. Mindful of the colonel's uncompromising Francophobia, Murray explained that he never would have listened to Pichon had he not been convinced that Americans had the fortitude to continue their resistance to France while negotiating. Moreover, he was firmly convinced that the Directory wished to avoid an open rupture, else he would not have pursued what he believed to be the President's willingness to receive overtures in keeping with the June 21 message. To Pickering, Murray soft-pedaled his talks with Pichon. What had transpired, he wrote, was unofficial and totally without commitment. Yet the resultant "assurances" might prove useful in that they gave the administration the initiative "to act on it or not" as it might choose.[40] Whether or not Pickering would agree on these points, Murray was uncertain. The State Department, he wrote John Quincy Adams, "take things in a very straight forward, right down and down right way." [41]

Murray's misgivings deepened as he awoke to other possible consequences of his action. Suppose Talleyrand were to send a copy of his

38. WVM to Pickering (private), The Hague, October 12, 1798, Pickering MSS, 25, 219a–221a, MHS; also WVM to JQA, letters of October 9 and 18, 1798, *AHA Report of 1912*, 480, 483.
39. The Hague, October 7, 1798, Adams' *Works*, VIII, 689.
40. To Pickering, The Hague, October 12, 1798, Pickering MSS, 25, 219a–221a, MHS.
41. The Hague, October 12, 1798, *AHA Report of 1912*, 483.

"assurances" to the Philadelphia press before Murray's explanations arrived. His correspondence with Pichon would then become "a handle for the opposition," a false hope for peace seized eagerly by Republicans to justify a slackening of preparedness measures. Worse, his own friends might suspect him of seeking a mission to Paris. Talleyrand's honeyed characterization of him as being neither French nor English might well mislead Murray's fellow Federalists into believing that he had been seduced and was now conniving for a Paris appointment. "If you ever believed a diplomat in your life," he wrote the President's son, "believe my declaration, my dear sir, that indeed I had no such thing in view." To make a similar disclaimer to John Adams himself was more awkward. Murray could hardly refuse an appointment that had not been offered. As a delicate way of disqualifying himself from a Paris mission, however, he brought to the President's notice how poorly he spoke French. It was Pichon's fluency in English, he suggested, that had brought Franco-American diplomacy to The Hague in the first place.[42]

Throughout September, John Quincy Adams acted as sounding board at one end of the Murray-Pichon conversations. Yes, he agreed with Murray that "assurances" from Talleyrand might reopen the door to negotiation. Yes, the wisdom of pursuing a negotiation would hinge on the willingness of Congress to continue a spirited defense policy. As for France, her difficulties in Europe (most recently, Nelson's victory over the Toulon fleet) and American hostility, they both agreed, had seemed to render the French more conciliatory. Yet, neither believed that any real change in French policy could be certified short of concrete acts of good will.[43] Such wide-ranging agreement may have lessened Murray's anxieties when he forwarded the Talleyrand letter to the President. Without implicating the son in what he himself had undertaken, Murray nonetheless wrote the father that he enjoyed John Quincy Adams' "concurrence of opinions on the points which I have stated to him on this subject."[44]

Unknown to Murray, the younger Adams was simultaneously urging the State Department to put Franco-American affairs in Murray's hands. On October 6 he wrote Pickering that Talleyrand seemed better disposed toward Murray than he had been toward Gerry, and that Murray should be given explicit authority to continue "this intercourse."[45] What both

42. *Ibid.*, 481.
43. See Murray's letters to JQA of September 11, 18, and 21, 1798, *AHA Report of 1912*, 470–73; and JQA to WVM, Berlin, September 18, 1798, Adams MSS, MR 133.
44. WVM to JA, The Hague, October 7, 1798, Adams' *Works*, VIII, 690.
45. Despatch No. 137, Berlin, October 6, 1798, in Ford, *Writings of JQA*, II,

diplomats had in mind was that Murray might be able to constrain Paris to give a more direct and explicit assurance that new envoys would be received, the maritime law of 29 Nivôse repealed, and a promise that American shipowners would be indemnified. Eager to have Murray take up these points, Adams was not quite candid with his friend at The Hague. "The course I should advise," he wrote Murray, omitting entirely that he had already pressed it on Pickering, "would be, that you should receive authority to confer with any person properly authorized by the French government, and agree on some basis for negotiation." Murray's response gave no hint that he knew Adams to be grooming him for further prenegotiation maneuvering.[46] Had Murray been ambitious for the job, however, he could have had no stronger supporter than John Quincy Adams.

Talleyrand's letter of assurances probably did not reach Philadelphia until early February of 1799.[47] By that time John Adams had already taken the first step toward rapprochement. On January 15 the President's son, Thomas Boylston Adams, bringing letters from Murray and John Quincy Adams, arrived in Philadelphia fresh from his elder brother's legation in Berlin. Had Thomas B. Adams delayed his departure from Hamburg by a day or two, he might have brought the Talleyrand letter with him.[48] As it was, the conciliatory pattern of French conduct set forth in the letters which he now received from Murray and John Quincy convinced the President that the time had come to move toward peace. On that same day, January 15, Adams called on Secretary of State Pickering to anticipate a new negotiation by preparing drafts of a treaty and a consular convention.[49] Little more than a month later—with the Talleyrand letter now in hand—Adams tossed his bombshell into the Senate. On February 18 he requested the confirmation of William Vans Murray as minister plenipotentiary to the French Republic.

372–73. That Pickering may have withheld this dispatch from the President is suggested by Samuel F. Bemis in *John Quincy Adams and the Foundations of American Foreign Policy* (New York: Alfred A. Knopf, 1949), 100.

46. JQA to WVM, Berlin, October 20, 1798, Ford, *Writings of JQA*, II, 375; WVM to JQA, The Hague, October 26, 1798, *AHA Report of 1912*, 485.

47. See C.F. Adams' footnote, Adams' *Works*, VIII, 688n.

48. For Murray's unsuccessful effort to put the Talleyrand letter in the hands of Thomas B. Adams before the latter sailed, see WVM to JQA, The Hague, October 9, 1798, *AHA Report of 1912*, 481; and JQA to WVM, Berlin, October 2, 1798, Ford, *Writing of JQA*, II, 371.

49. JA to Pickering, Philadelphia, January 15, 1799, Adams' *Works*, VIII, 621; also DeConde, *Quasi-War*, 172–74.

11

Adams' Decision for Peace

MURRAY'S INFORMAL diplomacy gave John Adams the opportunity, but certainly not the motive, to set in motion a reconciliation with France. Because Adams' decision for peace had such a ruinous effect on the unity of the Federalist party, historians have been fascinated by this question of presidential motives. Though not unanimous, they tend to agree that Adams, having amply notified the High Federalist wing of his party that he would renew negotiations with France on receipt of the required "assurances," did just that.[1] Those same High Federalists who were "thunderstruck" at the Murray nomination in February merely revealed the measure of their disappointment. Given Adams' repeatedly expressed hopes for an accommodation, they had no cause to be astonished except insofar as the President had flouted their own designs to make a war. Had they listened more carefully to the President and paid less heed to the extreme Francophobia of his Hamiltonian cabinet members, they might have foreseen the pattern of Adams' diplomacy.

What the war hawks should have noted, as the crisis unfolded, was that the President did not countenance either the hysteria or the latent adventurism which characterized High Federalist thinking. He fell in with neither the project for a British alliance nor the Miranda-Hamilton intrigue for liberating South America.[2] Nor did he welcome the notion

---

1. See, for example, John C. Miller, *The Federalist Era, 1789–1801* (New York: Harper & Bros., 1960), 243–45; Arthur B. Darling, *Our Rising Empire, 1763–1803* (New Haven: Yale University Press, 1940), Ch. XIII; Dauer, *Adams Federalists,* 230–31. On the crucial question of whether Adams wanted a formal declaration of war by Congress, recent historians are divided. DeConde in his *Quasi-War* (note 66, p. 411) and Page Smith in *John Adams* (p. 979) lean to the affirmative. Dauer, however, in his "Preface to the Paperback Edition" of *Adams Federalists* (pp. xxi–xxii), feels that DeConde and Smith rely too heavily on the contemporaneous letters of Abigail Adams and give too little weight to the "bulk" of Adams' own writings which suggest that the President was content with "limited war."

2. Dauer, *Adams Federalists,* 183–86.

that war with France would so far discredit the Republicans as to confirm the ascendency of the Federalists. True, Adams did sign into law
the Alien and Sedition bills; moreover, he unquestionably lent himself
to the High Federalist cause by making warlike replies to the importunings of various patriotic groups in the summer of 1798. The tone
of his public utterances, however, showed that he was more concerned
for the national security than he was for partisan justification. And when
the High Federalists proposed to intimidate the opposition by enlarging
the military establishment, it was Adams who warned that the taxes
necessary to raise a large army "will make the government more unpopular than all their other acts." [3] Nor did Adams, like some High
Federalists, exaggerate the ability of France to damage the United States
in an all-out war. American shipping, certainly, would need additional
naval protection, but the idea that a large army was needed to repel a
French invasion struck the President as mildly ludicrous. He wrote
McHenry in October that "at present there is no more prospect of
seeing a French army here, than there is in heaven." [4] Clearly, John
Adams was out of tune with the High Federalist orchestration.

Too, unlike the war hawks in his entourage, the President never
forgot that he had made an indirect commitment to peace on June 21.
As the summer passed, Adams frequently expressed doubt that France
would tender the necessary "assurances," but he never renounced his
willingness to send another envoy to Paris if such "assurances" came to
him.[5]

Evidence that the Directory had lowered its tone began to reach the
President in early October. Elbridge Gerry, landing at Boston on October 1, brought word to Adams in Quincy that Talleyrand had earnestly
besought him to negotiate. On the 9th, two letters arrived from Murray.
That of July 1 merely described Murray's efforts to put the Dutch
Moderates in touch with the British Foreign Office. That of July 17,
however, recounted the early conversations with Pichon and contained
Talleyrand's assertion, made to Pichon, that "our intention is always
to put an end to a state of things so contrary to the interests of the two
countries." Murray remarked in his covering letter that the Directory
was "deeply alarmed," even stunned by the American reaction to XYZ.
Adams sent the two letters to Philadelphia to be deciphered; the de-

3. Theodore Sedgwick to Hamilton, Philadelphia, February 7, 1799, Hamilton,
Works, VI, 293–94.

4. Quincy, October 22, 1798, Adams' *Works*, VIII, 613.

5. See Adams' "replies" to the patriotic addresses of various groups of citizens
around the country in Vol. IX of Adams' *Works*, 203–19 *passim*, 228, 232,
written between June 1798 and April 1799.

coded versions were returned to him on October 18. Two days later the President wrote Pickering to consult the cabinet on what should be included in the annual message to Congress. Should he recommend that Congress declare war, if France had not already declared it? Or would the cabinet advise "any further proposals of negotiation" that could be made "with safety"? [6]

Adams' own preference showed unmistakably in his reminder to Pickering that he had left the door open to negotiation in his message of June 21. The President even suggested that he should name an envoy on a standby basis, ready to sail as soon as the required "assurances" were received. Whereupon Adams listed the names of ten persons, including Murray, who might be so designated. This readiness to respond was attributable, in part, to Murray's letters ("The first has made a great impression on me," he wrote), and certainly to his conversations with Gerry.[7] What other influences may have spurred Adams' optimism during the month of October is not recorded, although November found the President exposed to many sources of intelligence tending to confirm the Directory's wish to avoid war.

The cabinet's response, drafted by Oliver Wolcott, probably with suggestions from Hamilton, left no doubt that Adams' High Federalist advisers intended to oppose any meaningful gesture of accommodation. It pictured France as being unwilling to make either war or peace, weighed the advantages and disadvantages of continuing the quasi-war, and concluded that neither should Congress be asked to declare war nor should another mission be sent to France. The cabinet then put a twist on Adams' own declared position. Let France send a minister, they suggested, and "he will be received with honour and treated with candour." [8]

While this proposal to let France show her good will in this way smacked of reasonableness, Adams was not for a moment beguiled. Long after, from the vantage point of the year 1809, the former President still expressed doubt that his Hamiltonian advisers ever seriously believed that France would send an emissary. They had proposed it, he believed, in order to keep Hamilton at the head of the Army until, by an accumulation of "provocations and irritations," either France or the United States would have no alternative but to declare war.[9] Lest this hindsighted judgment seem colored by the bitter memories of an old

6. For these letters to and from Adams, see *ibid.*, I, 532–33; VIII, 600, 677–84.

7. JA to Pickering, Quincy, Mass., letters of October 20 and 29, 1798, *ibid.*, 609, 614–15.

8. Gibbs, *Wolcott*, II, 169–71.

9. Adams' *Works*, IX, 294.

man, there was the fact that Adams pointedly rejected his cabinet's proposal, and reasserted his own policy in his message to Congress of December 8, 1798. To be sure, this message followed rather closely the points which Wolcott had enumerated. Adams recounted, one by one, the futile efforts of the administration to make amicable adjustments, the Directory's apparent wish to avoid war laced with insulting "qualifications" as to what sort of American envoy it would receive, the French announcement that privateers had been restrained within the bounds of French law which overlooked the American dissatisfaction with the laws themselves; and finally, finding nothing "in the conduct of France which ought to change or relax our measures of defense," Adams urged that preparedness measures be continued. Thus far the President hewed to the hard line. Then came the break, contained once more in negative phrasing. It was the President's opinion that

> to send another minister without more determinate assurances that he would be received would be an act of humiliation to which the United States ought not to submit. It must therefore be left with France (if she is indeed desirous of accommodation) to take the requisite steps.[10]

If High Federalists did not hear the echo of the June 21 message, it may have been because the reference to "more determinate assurances" was drowned out by the President's over-all tone of hostility to France. Those same High Federalists were no doubt further misled by Adams' subsequent replies to addresses from the House and Senate. To the Senate he wrote, "I have seen no real evidence of any change of system or disposition in the French Republic toward the United States." To the House he replied that "while those who direct the affairs of France persist in the enforcement of decrees so hostile to our essential rights their conduct forbids us to confide in any of their professions of amity.[11] In short, Adams did not sound like a man who was contemplating a new negotiation.

Adams later explained his decision for peace as being predicated on Talleyrand's "assurances," plus the need which he saw to undo a Hamiltonian war plot, and on his own reading of the peaceable disposition of American public opinion. He might have added that until February 18, 1799, his own policy toward France had increasingly shown itself to be procedurally vulnerable and politically unfeasible.

From the first, Adams had not required of France any substantive

10. Cf. Wolcott to JA, Gibbs, *Wolcott,* II, 168–71; Adams' "Second Annual Address," December 8, 1798, Richardson, *Messages,* I, 271–75.
11. *Ibid.,* 277, 280.

concession (as, for example, a French promise to indemnify American shippers), but demanded merely the formal "assurances" that a new envoy would be properly received. As a practiced diplomat he knew that negotiations must be preceded by a mutual understanding as to the rights of embassy. The form must be observed before the substance could be obtained. The hurdle which he placed before the Directory was neither high nor unreasonable. But it left Adams open to the charge that he had no justification—other than Talleyrand's compliance with a formality—for sending another mission. He could not, however, point to any substantive concession which France had made to American grievances. The High Federalists who wanted war denounced Adams, therefore, for accepting what they believed to be insufficient evidence that peace could be obtained. The President could answer to such critics only that he had followed his own procedure consistently.[12]

Adams' policy was also weak in its political underpinnings. Throughout the crisis the President insisted that Congress go forward with defense preparations, regardless of the issue. Such insistence ran counter to partisan aims on both sides. Whereas the Hamiltonians saw preparedness as a prerequisite to a declared war, Republicans wanted neither the war nor the expenditures for defense. Adams' middle course, summed up in his own phrase that "an efficient preparation for war can alone insure peace," fell, politically, between two stools. In the United States of 1799, one either prepared for war or one relaxed toward peace. Congress since its inception had raised or lowered its military guard, from session to session, according to the dangers of the moment. The notion of arming for peace was beyond it. Thus, when Adams nominated Murray envoy to France he was undoubtedly moved by the knowledge that Congress was not sophisticated enough to implement a policy of vigilant defense. What then appeared to High Federalists to be an inexplicable reversal of policy may simply have been the measure of Adams' realization that there remained no middle course.[13]

Across the Atlantic, Murray had foreseen both the procedural and political difficulties. A theme often repeated in his correspondence was that French peace overtures could be believed only if they were accompanied by "acts of justice." On learning that Adams would settle for the mere formality of "assurances," Murray fell in loyally with what he believed to be the President's "plan." [14] But even as he put in Adams'

12. Adams' *Works*, IX, 308.
13. See Adams' messages to Congress of May 16, November 22, 28, and 29, 1797, and March 19 and December 8, 1798, in Richardson, *Messages*, I, 236–73, *passim*.
14. WVM to Pickering, private, The Hague, October 12, 1798, Pickering MSS, 25, 219–21, MHS.

hands the means of effecting a reconciliation, he never mistook France's protestations of amity for the substance of good will. Similarly, he had no illusions about the ease of persuading Congress to make defense appropriations in prospect of peace, and was sure that congressional Republicans would dismantle the preparedness program at the first sign of it. For the sake of the national interest, Murray was anxious to see Adams move American policy off dead center. "The government," he wrote,

> is undoubtedly stronger and more solid than it was a year since. An honorable accommodation, or a brisk war, will settle it into a tone of proper energy. This half-way state is the greatest danger it can run, and ought to be ended immediately.[15]

Murray's nomination evoked three distinct political responses. Most vociferous was that of the High Federalists who, disappointed at the peaceable turn of events, lashed out indiscriminately at the President, the decision, and the chosen agent. No less important, however, was the reaction of moderate Federalists who, though fearful of party schism, rallied loyally to the chief executive. Republicans, for their part, were smugly pleased, convinced that French overtures had by their sincerity forced Adams belatedly to recognize the futility of war.

While most of the High Federalists' outrage was vented on Adams, Murray was not spared. Hamiltonian critics took the line that Murray was too inconsequential a figure to be charged with so delicate a negotiation. For a time, Murray's supposed incompetence was the chief target of the Hamiltonian counterattack. Adams noted this when he met with a group of High Federalist senators on February 23, and later recorded that they "made no remonstrance to me against the mission, or the diplomatic communications on which it was founded, but only against the missionary, Mr. Murray." When the senatorial deputation wanted to know why Adams had not selected some other member of the diplomatic corps, the President replied defensively that he thought Mr. Murray to be

> a gentleman of talents, address, and literature, as well as of great worth and honor, every way well qualified for the service, and fully adequate to all that I should require of him. . . . That my motives for nominating him in preference to others, were simply because the invitation from the French government had been transmitted through him, and because he was so near to Paris that he might

15. To JQA, The Hague, November 5, 1798, *AHA Report of 1912,* 486.

be there in three or four days, and because his appointment would
cause a very trifling additional expense.

When pressed to enlarge the embassy Adams replied from his own experience that "business could be better done by one than by many." The
President yielded, however, to the High Federalist insistence on a three-
man commission when it became apparent that the Senate might reject
Murray's nomination altogether.[16]

How much of the "dissatisfaction" with Murray was genuine and how
much of it stemmed from Murray's agency in securing the "assurances"
from Talleyrand is impossible to determine. Certainly Murray was guilty
by association; his had been the instrumentality. Men like Sedgwick,
Hamilton, Cabot, and Cobbett doubtless recalled the former congressman's occasional lapses from party regularity as reasons enough to
disqualify him. It was not Murray's politics, however, but rather his
personality that came under heaviest fire. Senator Sedgwick, for example,
who turned instinctively to Hamilton for consolation, looked aghast at
the incalculable "evils" of reopening negotiations with Paris even if
Murray were "the ablest negotiator in Christendom," adding that "with
all his virtues, he is feeble, unguarded, credulous, and unimpressive." [17]
Hamilton agreed: "Murray is certainly not strong enough for so im-
mensely important a mission," and urged Sedgwick to insist on a commission of three.[18] From Brookline, Massachusetts, Junto leader George
Cabot also registered disapproval. On learning that the embassy had
been enlarged to include Patrick Henry and Oliver Ellsworth, Cabot
remarked that this modification "removes the objection of incompetency
in the negotiator." [19]

Among the journals of opinion, *Porcupine's Gazette* was the most
outspoken in denouncing both Adams and Murray. Its editor, William
Cobbett, at first affected to disbelieve the report of the nomination.
Suggesting a Republican hoax, Cobbett asked editorially on February
20 if anyone could believe that Adams would respond to "one soothing
letter from the pen of Mr. Talleyrand to the sentimental Mr. Murray."
The Marylander was depicted as a man of "slender political abilities."
Another Federalist chieftain, Fisher Ames, though less explicit, was

16. Adams' *Works,* IX, 249–50, 251. See also Sedgwick to Hamilton, Philadelphia, February 25, 1799, Hamilton, *Works,* VI, 399–400.
17. Philadelphia, February 19, 1799, *ibid.,* 397.
18. New York, February 21, 1799, *ibid.*
19. To Pickering (private), Brookline, March 7, 1799, Henry Cabot Lodge, ed.,
Life and Letters of George Cabot (Boston: Little, Brown and Company, 1877),
224, hereinafter cited as Lodge, *Cabot.*

equally damning when he wrote that "had the President acted only half as wonderfully, the defense of his conduct would have been harder to the few who vindicate the nomination of Mr. Murray." [20] Secretary Pickering, meanwhile, while raising no specific objection to Murray, left no doubt that he regarded the nomination as an "evil" which had been "palliated" by joining Murray with two others and by stipulating that further assurances would be required as to the proper reception of all three envoys.

Postponement, not palliation, was, of course, the real purpose of the High Federalist clique. Much could happen in the lengthy interim before those further assurances arrived. Moreover, the presence of Oliver Ellsworth on the commission reassured the war hawks that France would make peace only with difficulty. As Pickering put it, "my motto is 'Nil Desperandum.' " George Cabot, too, saw the enlargement of the embassy as "a real relinquishment of the original measure," although he still bridled at the idea of pursuing any negotiation at all.[21]

Other High Federalists revealed their disapproval of Adams' peace policy with varying degrees of restraint. Rufus King presumed that Pickering so well knew how strongly he regretted the nomination of Murray that "I will not give you the trouble to read, nor myself the pain of saying, a word respecting it." [22] Congressman Robert Goodloe Harper in a lengthy letter to his South Carolina constituents suggested obliquely that Murray had been hoodwinked by Talleyrand's "professions of friendship" since, obviously, France had shown no signs of abating its maritime depredations. Harper was willing, however, that Adams should try a sword-and-olive-branch policy, provided the sword be kept sharp.[23]

Perhaps the most carefully refined objection came from John Jay, the dean of Federalist diplomats, who took issue with what he believed to be the faulty mechanics of the administration's diplomacy. Adams, he felt, should never have asked merely for "assurances"; nor should Murray have exceeded his instructions (and his office) by engaging in conversations with Pichon. The result of this bungling was an equivocal peace overture from Paris. All this was made worse, wrote Jay, by "the manner in which Mr. Murray transmitted these overtures to the President [which] is such a deviation from the official and customary course as

20. To Pickering, March 12, 1799, Pickering MSS, 24, 171–72, MHS.

21. Pickering to King (private), Philadelphia, March 6, 1799, King, *Correspondence*, II, 548–49; Cabot to King, March 10, 1799, *ibid.*, 552.

22. June 5, 1799, Pickering MSS, 24, 297–98, MHS.

23. Harper to his Constituents, Philadelphia, March 20, 1799, "Papers of James A. Bayard, 1796–1815," *Annual Report of the American Historical Association for the year 1913* (Washington, D.C., 1915), II, 88–89.

. . . is certainly exceptionable." Jay concluded that while Adams might
have made the right decision, he had acted prematurely. The French
overtures themselves had been too tentative to warrant "any formal,
national act." [24] The same sort of criticism came from Mount Vernon.
Washington was no war hawk, but he was nonetheless surprised to learn
that Adams had nominated Murray to a Paris mission in the absence of
a *"direct* overture" from the French government.[25]

Ranged against the vocal objections of the Hamiltonians and the
puzzled reactions of others in the Federalist hierarchy, John Adams'
decision for peace did not lack for supporters. Moderates of both parties
rallied to the President, the popularity of whose new tack in French
policy was amply demonstrated by Federalist gains in the 1799 elections
—gains which, significantly, tended to make the House of Representatives simultaneously more Federalist but more moderate.[26]

The press and editorial reactions to John Adams' decision reflected,
perhaps most clearly, the spent quality of war-hawk Federalism and the
regrouping of moderate political forces. Some newspapers, like *Porcupine's Gazette,* whose editor, William Cobbett, was too fully committed
to virulent Francophobia to do otherwise, remained openly hostile to
the mission. So, too, did the powerful *Gazette of the United States,*
although its editor, John Fenno, was more offended by the mission itself
than by the choice of the emissary. More significantly, perhaps, the
Republican newspaper, *Aurora,* announced editorially on February
20 its "highest satisfaction" with the peace policy. Editor Benjamin F.
Bache could not refrain, however, from voicing the suspicion that Adams
had had it in his power to treat with France at a much earlier date.
Bache, nonetheless, had kind words even for Oliver Ellsworth, asking
only that the Chief Justice "divest himself of the narrow principles of a
Connecticut politician." As for Murray, the *Aurora* merely noted on
February 27 that he had been the conveyor of bona fide assurances.

Press reaction outside the capital was less partisan. In New York, the
Commercial Advertiser—a Federalist organ—responded on March 2
that it was "happy to have it in our power to state" that Adams had
received the requisite assurances. Five days later the *Advertiser* cautioned
Adams against sending another mission to Paris until France had

24. To Benjamin Goodhue, Albany, March 29, 1799, Henry P. Johnston, ed.,
The Correspondence and Public Papers of John Jay (London and New York:
G.P. Putnam's Sons, 1890–1893), IV, 256–57.

25. To Pickering (confidential), Mount Vernon, March 3, 1799, Fitzpatrick,
Writings, XXXVII, 141–42.

26. Cf. Kurtz, *Presidency of John Adams,* Ch. 16; Dauer, *Adams Federalists,*
233–37.

stopped preying on American shipping; its general tone, however, expressed confidence in the President. Its rival, the *New York Daily Advertiser,* indulged in editorial comment on February 28 only to the extent of warning readers not to judge hastily of the President, whose measures were as yet "not generally understood."

The New England press, as George Cabot angrily discovered, either supported Adams or kept silent.[27] From Boston, for example, the *Massachusetts Mercury* (March 1 and 8) hailed the President for having followed the logic of his "public declarations," while denouncing Cobbett for having twisted the facts of presidential policy. It was the duty of all true Federalists, *Mercury* editorialized, to give "ready approbation" to Adams' decision. On the Republican side, the *Boston Independent Chronicle* of February 25 grudgingly found the President to be "better late than never," and then went on to bemoan Gerry's lost opportunity to save "millions." Three days later one of the *Chronicle's* contributors remarked happily that Adams' decision had so discomfited the Federalists that their "drooping spirits" were revived only by the rumor that Bonaparte was dead. In a friendlier vein was the pseudonymous defense made by "American Independence," reprinted in no fewer than four Northern newspapers during the month of March. The writer found no incongruity in simultaneously arming and negotiating, although he had to go back to 1779 to find a precedent. At that earlier time, the writer recalled, the Congress had appointed John Adams as peace commissioner while "war was continued as before." It made sense, he concluded, for the United States to have an agent ready to negotiate no matter how the crisis ended.[28]

North and South, at least a half-dozen major Federalist organs kept editorial silence. One explanation of this relative quiet undoubtedly lay in the reluctance of the Federalist press to exacerbate the party schism. Too, the President himself had reduced the potency of his decision as a public issue by stipulating that Paris must give further assurances—a qualification that was printed in italics in most of the press accounts. Finally, by mid-March, the outbreak of Fries' Rebellion—an eastern Pennsylvania protest against the so-called "window tax"—tended to claim the attention of the press as an event more newsworthy than the President's still-conditional embassy to France.

Press references to Murray were even less frequent. Against Cobbett's

27. To Pickering (private), Brookline, March 7, 1799, Lodge, *Cabot,* 225.
28. Reprinted in the *New York Commercial Advertiser,* March 7, 1799; *New Hampshire Gazette,* March 6, 1799; *Newport Mercury* (Rhode Island), March 19, 1799.

stricture that Murray was a man of "slender political abilities," the *Baltimore Daily Advertiser* on February 25 voiced the opposing view that Murray's appointment "has given general satisfaction." The *Advertiser* continued:

> His very amiable manners, joined to his known abilities and genuine patriotism, afford us strong hopes, that (if an accommodation be possible) we shall contract a new and lasting obligation with Mr. Murray, for having added an exemption from the horrors of war to his faithful services, as a dignified representative of his country in peace.

Moderate Federalists probably agreed with this estimate. At least those who supported Adams, and endorsed the mission, did not publicly disparage the qualifications of the emissary. Their views remain obscure, however, because as a group the Adams men were not as closely knit, politically, as were the Hamiltonians; nor were they as prone to seek partisan consensus in their letters to one another or to the press. Had there been any organized opposition to Murray's nomination, it would almost certainly have surfaced in House debate. In fact, the day after the nomination, during debate on a bill to encourage the capture of French privateers, House members repeatedly mentioned Murray by name—but in no instance unfavorably. Some speakers did, of course, express doubt as to the wisdom of pursuing the policy which he had helped to make possible.[29]

Gallatin's was the most damning judgment from the Jeffersonian camp. Writing privately to his wife, Gallatin may have expressed a view widely held in some quarters when he wrote: "Murray, I guess, wanted to make himself a greater man than he is by going to France." In so writing, Gallatin merely put on paper what Murray had earlier foreseen would be his enemies' misconstruction of his motives. Considering their former rivalry in debate, Gallatin's peevish remark was but a spark from old fires.[30]

Jefferson wasted no concern for either Murray's motives or his qualifications. To the Republican chief, the "event of events" was the astonishing fact that the administration's policy toward France had taken an irreversible course. Adams' decision, he wrote, "silences all

29. *Annals*, VIII, 2935–54 *passim*. For evidence that moderate Federalists supported the President, see the letters to Adams for Charles Lee, John Marshall, Henry Knox, and Uriah Forrest in Adams' *Works*, VIII, 626–38.
30. Philadelphia, March 1, 1799, Henry Adams, *Life of Albert Gallatin* (Philadelphia, 1879), 227–28.

arguments against the sincerity of France, and renders desperate every further effort toward war." This cry of triumph was closely followed, however, by anxious mutterings. Like the editor of the *Aurora,* Jefferson suspected that Adams could have announced the French peace overtures earlier, and wondered why he had not. Also, he was disturbed that Adams should now require personal assurances from Paris for Ellsworth and Patrick Henry. The intervening delay, he foresaw, would allow the High Federalists "more time for new projects of provocation." [31]

At The Hague, meanwhile, Murray could only guess at the possible consequences of his diplomacy. Rumors clattered abundantly, but facts were hard to come by. During the last three months of 1798 only one dispatch reached him from the State Department, although a letter from James McHenry suggested that the administration was waiting for France to come forward with "plain and unequivocal offers." Paris was a far more fertile source of rumors. From thence came word that Philadelphia would send out a new minister on the basis of proposals made to Elbridge Gerry. Murray was doubtful. From what he had seen of the Gerry-Talleyrand correspondence, he felt that Gerry had been entrusted with "professions," not "proposals," and the former would better serve the Republicans than they would the administration.[32]

Amidst the froth of speculation Murray looked in vain for France to perform some substantial act of good will. Instead, he found an unsettling article in the Paris *Redacteur* of September 21, which accused the United States of wanting war and proposed, therefore, that France treat Americans as Englishmen and pay no respect to their flag. Because the *Redacteur* often mouthed official policy and because Pichon had returned to Paris, Murray worriedly sought an explanation from the French chargé, Champigny-Aubin. The latter's inability to say whether or not the article constituted official policy was not reassuring. Nor did Pichon, on his return to The Hague, settle all of Murray's doubts. Murray remarked gloomily to Pickering that "in general the Redacteur foreruns the *acts* of Government by its paragraphs." Three days later, however, Murray had managed to put the antics of Paris journalism in clearer perspective. Parisian newspapers were merely reacting, after some inexplicable delay, to the reality that American vessels were being armed and that the old treaties had been nullified. For all this, he wrote

31. Letters to Madison, Philadelphia, February 19 and 26, 1799, Ford, *Writings,* IX, 52–53, 60.
32. See letters to JQA of November 5, December 11 and 18, 1798, *AHA Report of 1912,* 485, 493, 497, respectively.

Pickering, he could discern no real turn for the worse in French policy toward the United States.[33]

Murray's sense of uncertainty that winter was matched only by his disappointment in France's enemies. Although he no longer speculated on what effect a French military disaster might have on Franco-American relations, he continued to hope the worst for France. Surely now, as never before, France was a vulnerable target for any well-organized grouping against her. Nelson's victory at Abukir Bay followed by Bonaparte's tortuous campaign in Egypt, the imminence of Turkish hostility, and the rumor that a Russian fleet had passed the Dardanelles —these, combined with American hostilities and actual uprisings in Flanders and in the Swiss canton of Grisons—all seemed to Murray to present "golden opportunities." If Prussia and Austria failed to take advantage of them, they deserved to be revolutionized. Unfortunately, France's enemies were in disarray. Despairingly, Murray confided to John Quincy Adams that

> these things have produced such a stagnation in my mind that I
> have not written to the Secretary of State for more than a month!
> as it seemed nonsense in me to hazard opinions upon a state of
> things that appeared regulated by no natural mode of proceeding,
> and where probabilities were eternally overcome by the greatest
> improbabilities.[34]

If Europe seemed sick that winter, Murray definitely was. He suspected he had jaundice, made worse by the extreme cold and certainly not helped by the long hours he put in on the *Wilmington Packet* case. "Either by cold or candle light," his eyesight became so weak during this period that at least once the prospect of becoming blind passed terrifyingly through his mind. Though Murray seldom wrote of personal matters, his letters to John Quincy Adams that winter unconsciously conveyed the details of a self-portrait. He depicted himself as a sedentary man, often bedridden or wrapped in flannel. When he went out, it was to buy drugs from a friendly apothecary, or to visit his club where, he admitted, he smoked too much. But the pipe-smoke, so like the fog outside, he mused, "prepares the skin to resist the moist air." And then, between wry quips, appeared his genuine concerns: for Charlotte who suffered from the climate more than he, for the thousands of Dutchmen

33. No. 61, The Hague, October 5, 1798, Netherlands Despatches, I; also same to same, private, October 2, 1798, Pickering MSS, 23, 181–82, MHS.

34. Cf. letters to JQA of November 13 and December 11, 1798, *AHA Report of 1912*, 487, 493.

made homeless by the late winter floods, and for the fuel shortage which was so acute by early February that if the cold weather lasted another month, he wrote, "I do not know what we shall do." [35]

Along with physical illness Murray also showed signs of suffering from isolation of the intellect. He later admitted that in order to break the "deathlike silence" of his sickroom, he had welcomed long conversations with an American colonel named Benjamin Hichborn, a previously enthusiastic but now apparently repentant Republican. As his health improved, Murray regretted having "wasted powder" on the man when he discovered that Hichborn was "still with dangerous and fretful principles." More to his liking was the company of Major James Mountflorence, who replaced Dandridge as his private secretary. Mountflorence had been earlier posted at Paris as chancellor to Consul General Fulwar Skipwith. Murray was particularly gratified when Mountflorence agreed to stay on as his "honorary secretary" when his official secretarial office expired in December. It was not, however, until late February that Murray felt he could "look back on the blue devils of this hard winter as on a dream." Though his health remained uncertain, Murray's spirits began to improve with the advent of milder weather and the arrival of ships bearing news from the United States.[36]

On April 13, 1799, news reached Murray that he, together with Ellsworth and Henry, had been named to the Paris mission. He reacted with characteristic self-effacement, glad, and genuinely so, that the responsibility was not to be his alone. Ellsworth he knew and respected. He would feel "safe," he told John Quincy Adams, working with a man so justly regarded as a person of judgment and character. On the other hand, the appointment of Patrick Henry merely stimulated his curiosity. And when Henry refused the appointment Murray was not altogether pleased to see him replaced by the Federalist governor of North Carolina, William R. Davie. What particularly irked him was that Davie was named second in the commission while he (Murray) was named last.[37] At the outset, however, Murray was plainly gratified that John Adams had seen fit to name him at all. Between the dry lines of the newspaper accounts the experienced politician in Murray sensed the uproar that

35. See letters to JQA of December 28, 1798, and January 1, 15, 25, and February 8, 1799, *ibid.*, 501–17 *passim*.
36. Letters of January 22, February 18 and 26, March 14 and 26, 1799, *ibid.*, 512, 520, 522, 526, 531–33, respectively.
37. WVM to Pickering, private, The Hague, April 13, 1799, *ibid.*, 538; WVM to JQA, April 16, 1799, *ibid.*, 539.

had centered on John Adams between February 18 and 25. He readily
guessed what sorts of political pressures had been put on the President
to force him to enlarge the embassy. Murray was deeply moved that
Adams had even tried to put the mission in his hands alone. "Dear Sir,"
he wrote to John Quincy,

> Inclosed you have a message and a new nomination of envoys to
> France, among which the kindness and long settled partiality of the
> President have led him to give me a place. But this is not all. He
> had on 18 February sent a first message in which he did me the
> honor of nominating me solely for this business. You know me
> sufficiently I trust to believe that I am, as I ought to be, indeed
> profoundly grateful for this peculiar mark by which his confidence
> has distinguished me! He always, indeed, treated me with peculiar
> kindness, always at all times and in all places. I was from the first
> sensible of this, and independent of his high stations have always
> been sincerely and faithfully attached to him! I have not in political
> life those friends that help to keep alive the recollection of the
> absent, and I therefore know that all this honor which he bestowed
> upon my name and family by his nomination of me, came from
> himself! For though I know that many of the gentlemen near him
> are my friends, yet I do not think that they think so highly of me as
> I know he does. From 1785 I have been, as it were, his pupil,
> always indeed at the same time enjoying a great freedom of
> argumentation with him on hundreds of questions. I am very sen-
> sibly affected by this affair, for I had no pretensions to it in my
> own opinion.
>
> A great and respectable voice among the few or the many must
> have said the same when it was found that I was to go alone, for
> you see he now modifies the nomination. Perhaps I love the
> President more for his disappointment, because his second proves
> to me that he hazarded a little by the first nomination. I dare say
> that between the 18 and 25th a great stir took place.[38]

However specific its references, this letter also revealed how keenly
Murray understood his place in the political universe. He was an Adams
man, and his place was in the second rank. These were the orbits within
which he would spin out the remainder of his political life.

38. The Hague, April 16, 1799, *ibid.*, 538–39.

12

Echoes from Philadelphia and Paris

NEARLY EIGHT MONTHS elapsed between John Adams' decision to send another mission to Paris and the actual departure of two of his three emissaries. Although the evidence seems overwhelming that his war-hawk enemies sought during this interim to delay, even to prevent, the mission altogether, it is also evident that Adams himself failed to press the negotiation until the early fall of 1799. In all likelihood, both the President *and* his enemies contributed to the delay: Adams, because he believed that the three naval squadrons then nearing completion would measurably strengthen this country's negotiating position; and his enemies, because they saw neither profit nor promise of success in any negotiation.[1]

Out of loyalty to Adams and perhaps, too, from an awareness of his own responsibility for the President's decision, Murray now strained to find evidence that peace could, in fact, be obtained. The most hopeful sign, he felt, was France's seeming recognition that in the United States she faced a redoubtable enemy. Proof lay in the mildness of the French reaction to Truxtun's capture of the *Insurgente*. Nor was Paris openly resentful at the "public gibbeting" to which American officials had exposed French policy. In short, France seemed chastened, her feeble responses to insult and injury "conclusive evidence of the ac-knowledged strength of the United States." It was his opinion—and Europe's, too—he told Pickering, that the administration could now afford to meet the French at the bargaining table. "A good arrangement would be most likely," he concluded, provided, of course, that Americans continued to show their mettle and barring some unlikely revival of French military prospects.[2]

1. Stephen G. Kurtz, "The French Mission of 1799–1800: Concluding Chapter in the Statecraft of John Adams," *Political Science Quarterly*, LXXX (December 1965), 555–56.
2. The Hague, April 23, 1799, Pickering MSS, 24, 236–37, MHS.

Pickering, however, would hear none of it. The Secretary's reply crackled with contempt for Murray's optimism. "The French government," he snapped, "tamely bears our defiance . . . not because they acknowledge the strength of the U. States, but because they have too much other work on their hands to trouble themselves about us, at present." And if, as Murray had reported, the Dutch were surprised to learn of Adams' decision, Murray should know that Philadelphia was astounded. With something less than loyalty, Pickering regaled Murray with the pungent observation that

> every man whom you knew and respected, every *real patriot,* every man who has steadily and faithfully supported his and his predecessor's administration was *thunderstruck,* it was *done* without any *consultation with any member of the* government, and for a reason *truly remarkable—because he knew we should all be opposed to the measure!*

Pickering went on to relate how the Senate had forced Adams to multiply the number of envoys, though to what end he could not imagine, short of a complete change in the French government which might, then, make a new negotiation feasible.[3]

Faced with such evidence of the hard bitterness that was dividing the Federalist ranks, Murray and the President's son turned to each other for reassurance. "More than ever I need your friendship!" wrote Murray. He had not much more than "zeal" to offer his country, he added, and "you know that that zeal often wants a *friend.*" Even before this letter reached Berlin, Adams had written that although he was glad to hear of the triple appointment, he had never doubted that Murray could handle the mission alone. For Murray, however, it was not the addition of Ellsworth and Davie that stung him; it was the questioning of his motives. Writing of the nomination, he noted that

> Porcupine abuses it, and me in particular, a "damned good natured friend" so writes me. I dare say the world will say, and some of it really think, that I worked and wriggled myself into this appointment. I did not. I did not even wish to be in it. I saw all its perils to whoever has it!

Pay no attention to Cobbett, Adams wrote back; the "Peter Porcupine" of Philadelphia was, after all, one of the British faction and sure to oppose both the appointment and the idea of peace. As for Murray's

---

3. Philadelphia, July 10, 1799, *AHA Report of 1912,* 573–74.

arranging his own appointment, wrote Adams, he would be far less likely to believe Murray if he had said that he did want it.[4]

Another strip of skin came off when Murray learned that Cobbett had called him "sentimental." He wrote Adams that he would examine himself to see if he *was* sentimental, although he was prepared to conclude tentatively that

> if hating *Universal Benevolence!* "despising *philosophy"* and narrowing down *Philanthropy* to a nutshell, is to be sentimental, I am a "beefeater!" I am weak, but I deny Peter's charge. The rascal knows when to touch a man's pride!

Because Cobbett was an English immigrant, Murray suggested facetiously that men of his sort might best be dealt with by requiring thirty or forty years' residence before naturalizing them.[5]

Both Murray and Adams were somewhat mystified by the High Federalist reaction. Far from the mainstream of domestic politics, they could only conclude that the party leadership had decided that peace was too uncertain a prospect to warrant the sending of a new mission. And yet, what other choice did the administration have? Congress had not declared war, and only Congress could. If, as it seemed, the party's leaders were unable to push a war declaration through Congress, the President could scarcely be blamed for putting out peace feelers.

What neither diplomat realized was the intensity of intraparty animosities. Murray little suspected, as he reached for the raveled ends of Franco-American relations, how pervasive those animosities were. Even the innocent matter of his conveying to Talleyrand the news of Adams' appointments and the need for further assurances embroiled him once again with Timothy Pickering. The incident began on May 4 when Murray received instructions from the State Department to notify Talleyrand that three envoys had been appointed with "full powers to discuss and settle by a treaty, all controversies between the United States and France." [6] In setting down the terms, Pickering had employed certain phrases which struck Murray as being awkward, but he nonetheless copied them out meticulously. Talleyrand was warned that the envoys

4. For this exchange see Murray's letters to JQA of April 19 and May 7, 1799, *ibid.,* 541, 549; and JQA to WVM, Berlin, letters of April 23 and May 14, 1799, Adams MSS, MR 133.

5. Letters of July 1 and 16, 1799, *AHA Report of 1912,* 569, 576.

6. Pickering to WVM, No. 22, Philadelphia, March 6, 1799, Instructions to U.S. Ministers, V, Record Group 59, National Archives.

will not embark for Europe until they shall have received from the Executive Directory direct and unequivocal assurances . . . that the envoys shall be received in character to an audience of the Directory, [here Murray would have preferred the phrase "shall be publickly received or have a public reception in character"] and that they shall enjoy all the prerogatives attached to that character by the law of nations, and that a minister or ministers of equal powers shall be appointed and commissioned to treat with them.[7]

This paragraph seemed to cover all possible contingencies—all but one, an omission that passed unnoticed until the actual negotiation was about to begin. This was the requirement that France agree to end the negotiation with a treaty. Not until a year later did it dawn on anyone that the possibility of a negotiation-without-end had not been guarded against. Murray did not foresee it. What troubled Murray in the spring of 1799 was that Pickering had not insisted that the reception of the American envoys be public.

Murray's concern at this minor oversight, however, was as nothing compared with the colonel's outrage at the phrases which Murray chose to decorate his first and second letters to Talleyrand. His note of May 5 had begun: "It is with the greatest pleasure that I hasten to fulfill the instructions, which I have just had the honor to receive . . . ," and closed with the phrase: "Accept, Citizen Minister, the assurances of my perfect high esteem." Pickering nearly collapsed with disapproval when he read these lines. That Murray should "hasten" to fulfill his instructions must have given Talleyrand the impression that "we are impatient under their displeasure and willing to make any sacrifices to regain their goodwill." Moreover, Murray should never have used the phrase "perfect respect and high esteem" toward a man who, in Pickering's view, was "a shameless villain." He should have used the "customary, cold 'consideration'" instead. Thereupon the Secretary instructed Murray at length on the definitions of the words "respect" and "esteem," noting how grossly Murray had misused them. How was he to construe the meaning of those same words, Pickering wanted to know, when Murray addressed them to him as even-handedly as he did to Talleyrand who, as Murray should know, was "one of the most false, hypocritical, and corrupt villains of whom France has produced so plentiful a crop"? [8]

Murray was aghast that his seemingly harmless pleasantries to Talley-

7. WVM to Talleyrand, May 5, 1799, copy enclosed in Murray's No. 75 to Pickering, The Hague, Netherlands Despatches, I.
8. Trenton, October 4, 1799, *AHA Report of 1912*, 600–602.

rand had caused such a furor. Not only was he the butt of Pickering's wrath, but also, thanks to Pickering's allowing his letters to Talleyrand to be published, the number of his critics had been multiplied. Here Murray touched on a chronically sore point. Long had the Federalist penchant for publishing "live" diplomatic correspondence been a hazard to American diplomats-on-mission. As a sort of pre-Wilsonian "open diplomacy," its practice was usually explained at Philadelphia as being needful for good public information. Its real purpose, just as often, was to win public support for an administration policy. In the case of his letters to Talleyrand, however, Murray felt that Pickering had gone beyond the requirements of public instruction. Only in a limited sense, he felt, could those letters be classified as "official," even though he had written them at the direction of the State Department.[9] Moreover, he was not about to admit that his courtesies to the French Foreign Minister had been improper. Angrily he wrote McHenry that if his addresses to Talleyrand were thought to be "fulsome," it was because "I was to presume that success would be *agreeable*." The occasion had called for courtesy, and inasmuch as he was not yet accredited to the Paris government, he had seen nothing improper in departing from the coldness of formalities. Even should McHenry disagree, Murray urged his old friend to convey this explanation to Adams and Washington.[10]

That so small a gaffe could be blown to the size of a major indiscretion puzzled Murray and pained him, too, until he realized that the cause lay not in himself but in the magnifications wrought by High Federalist hostility to even the most meager approaches to Franco-American reconciliation. His critics were simply persons who did not want peace and who, in this instance, wilfully misunderstood his uses of "mere civility." What hurt him most was the prospect of losing old friends. This he had not foreseen. He still had a friend in Berlin, however, who once more buoyed him up. John Quincy Adams wrote that those erstwhile friends who carped at Murray did so solely because they opposed the mission. Their barbs were aimed in that direction and not at him personally. Murray was urged to be less sensitive and more objective.[11]

Murray, meanwhile, did not leave Pickering's rebuke unanswered. He wrote Philadelphia that he knew as well as did the Secretary how "vicious" the government of France was, but he had seen no reason to forego the niceties of diplomacy. He had "presumed" that the administration wanted to negotiate; his letters to Talleyrand had been

9. To JQA, The Hague, December 3, 1799, *ibid.*, 627–28.
10. The Hague, December 2, 1799, Steiner, *McHenry*, 429–30.
11. Berlin, January 6, 1800, Adams MSS, MR 134.

written in that spirit. "Words of roughness," he lectured Pickering, "never add dignity to weakness; words of mere civility no more detract from substantial strength . . . than an embossed scabbard does from the polished and strong blade which it surrounds." He was satisfied that a haughty French government had been compelled to offer humiliating assurances which "will add to *the glory* of my country when the manner of my letters and of your critique shall be in oblivion." Murray expressed no doubt as to Pickering's motives. "You have been angry at the thing itself," he wrote, "and no *manner* of success could have pleased you." Then came the break, syntactically choked but nonetheless forthright: "I cannot help regretting sincerely the loss of your friendship; [but] the terms, the harsh and ungenerous terms, on which you have withdrawn it from such a man as I am conscious I am as an American, have helped me to bear it." [12]

Two months later Murray confided to John Quincy Adams that he felt he had been "too warm" with the colonel. Still, he was impatient with those Federalists whose loyalty to the President was less than his own. His term for them was "Jacobinical federalists," meaning partisan extremists who insisted on having their own way at their country's expense. The President's son agreed: a "federal jacobinism" had appeared among those Federalists who were so convinced by British influences as to object to any measure of the administration which did not coincide with British cabinet policy. It was a deplorable development, both men agreed.[13]

The irony of Pickering's rebuke is found in the extreme caution with which Murray went about his diplomatic business in the spring of 1799. No sooner had word of the appointments reached Paris than Pichon wrote, urging Murray to hasten to the French capital so that Talleyrand could give him a full hearing on all the points at controversy. To this invitation Murray returned a friendly but noncommittal answer, thus anticipating that part of his instructions which forbade him to communicate further with any French representative respecting substantive issues. The irony was compounded when Murray's instructions arrived on May 4. The "haste" with which he told Talleyrand he was writing was carefully calculated not to be too hasty. He framed his first note to Talleyrand on May 5, but deliberately held it back until the regular post left for Paris on the 7th. He might have sent the letter by an ex-

---

12. The Hague, December 1, 1799, *AHA Report of 1912*, 623–27.
13. See WVM to JQA, letters of December 6, 1799, and February 7, 1800, *ibid.*, 629, 641; JQA to WVM, Berlin, December 15, 1799, Adams MSS MR 134.

press—the idea occurred to him—but he was as anxious to avoid the imputation of "solicitude" as was Pickering later on.[14]

Talleyrand's reply came swiftly. It was explicit and, to Murray, entirely satisfactory: it complied with all the conditions of "assurances" that Pickering had asked for. Murray was jubilant. The Frenchman's word-for-word compliance, he wrote, was

> perhaps one of the most explicit things that the French Republic has ever been reduced, by the spirit and hostility of any foreign nation, to perform. It must have been a bitter pill, for the *case put* by my letter, was plain as a pike staff, and they give a response to every important member of the case put.[15]

Talleyrand, to be sure, complained mildly of the time that would be wasted in conveying further assurances, but Murray took no notice. Nor would the President have done so, had not Pickering tried to argue that the French Foreign Minister had insulted the administration by accusing it of wasting time. John Adams, however, took the long view: only time could reveal whether France intended war or peace. If Talleyrand was fretful, Adams at least no longer feared the machinations of French diplomacy on the domestic scene. The public mind was sound, and preparations for the worst would still go forward.[16]

Murray, meanwhile, thanked Talleyrand for his promptness and told him that his supplementary "assurances" were on their way to Philadelphia. When told that he might apply at once to Paris for his passports, Murray replied cautiously that he would do so when instructed. The final formalities observed, Talleyrand thanked Murray for expediting the "assurances" and again intimated that France was eager to begin negotiations. Murray, too, was eager to begin. Pickering's injunction against further conversations came none too soon. Just before that warning reached him, Murray had begun to sound out Pichon on the various ways by which France might satisfy the damage claims put forward by the American victims of her maritime policy. Pickering's caveat broke off this exchange.[17]

14. WVM to Pickering, The Hague, April 16, 1799, Pickering MSS, 24, 228–31, MHS; and to JQA, The Hague, May 10, 1799, *AHA Report of 1912*, 550.

15. To JQA, The Hague, May 21, 1799, *ibid.*, 554; For Talleyrand's reply see WVM to Pickering (private), May 18, 1799, Pickering MSS, 24, 249–50, 261, MHS.

16. Pickering to JA, Philadelphia, July 31, 1799; JA to Pickering, Quincy, Mass., August 6, 1799, Adams' *Works*, IX, 10–11.

17. Pickering to WVM, No. 22, March 6, 1799, Instructions to Ministers, V, RG 59, NA. See also WVM to Talleyrand, The Hague, May 18, 1799; and Talleyrand to WVM, Paris, May 31, 1799, AAE EU, 51, folios 158–158v, 160.

John Adams' decision for peace and the efforts of the war hawks to defeat it would have given Murray excitement enough in the spring of 1799. The unsettling noises of partisan strife that reached him from Philadelphia, however, were more than matched in loudness and proximity by the renewal of coalition warfare against France. For a time that spring the armies of the French Republic seemed to be in full, perhaps final, retreat. On the German front, an Austrian army under the Archduke Charles met and defeated Jourdan at Stockach on March 25. Soon afterwards, it became apparent that a Russian campaign in Italy, led by Alexander Suvarov, was enjoying similar successes against the French generals MacDonald and Moreau.

While the military situation remained uncertain, American diplomats in Europe reacted as variously and as often as they had reason to hope or fear. John Quincy Adams was consistently pessimistic: at first doubtful that Austria would fight at all, then skeptical of the allies' ability to win, and finally deprecatory of their victories when they came. Also dispirited were the reports from Rufus King in London. Of the three, only Murray gave way to optimism. "Why," he wrote Adams chidingly, "my Austrians are at Schaffhausen, victorious in Italy and Tyrol. Your French [are] at Strasburgh and at Colmar in Alsace!" John Quincy Adams replied by twitting Murray for his "rapidity of imagination." The French were far from being expelled from Italy, although Adams admitted that they might be; and the Russians had made a strategic error in bypassing the French stronghold at Mantua. Murray took these checks to his enthusiasm with good humor, continuing to hope, nonetheless, that the Austro-Russian offensive would prove to be irresistible.[18]

A political upheaval in Paris, Murray felt, would be the certain result of military reverses. His first thought was that the Republic itself would be swept away by invading armies, in which event the United States would be well advised to commence negotiations while the government still lasted and while France's military defeats seemed more conducive to a "good arrangement." When, in early June, the fighting was still at the French periphery, Murray was "not so sure" that the Republic would end with an allied invasion. More likely, now, would be an internal political shifting. On that score, Murray duly noted that the spring elections had brought into the French legislative councils dis-

18. See JQA to WVM, letters of February 2 and 12, March 23, April 27, May 18, 25 and 28, 1799, Adams MSS, MR 133; WVM to JQA, letters of April 19, June 7 and 10, 1799, *AHA Report of 1912*, 541, 559–60; also WVM to Pickering, The Hague, April 8, 1799, Pickering MSS, 24, 217, MHS; and King to Pickering, London, dispatches of January 27, March 23, and June 5, 1799, King, *Correspondence*, II, 528–29, 584–85; III, 31, respectively.

sidents of both Right and Left, whose charges of Directorial incompetence and corruption heralded another power struggle between executive and legislative branches. Opposition to the Directory seemed to be gathering behind the oracular figure of Joseph Sieyès, former priest and *conventionnel*. By the end of May, Murray was half-convinced that Sieyès would become the agent for a Bourbon restoration, an expectation that was strengthened when the abbé gained a seat on the Directory. With a Warwick now on the stage, Murray was fascinated by the prospect of revolutionary France returning to monarchy. Adams, who had met Sieyès in Berlin, foresaw nothing of the kind: the new French Director was an ill-natured, gloomy man who did not impress him as a mover of great events. Sieyès, he noted, had no political ties with the royal family; moreover the abbé had struck Adams as being more concerned with making peace than making kings.[19]

Murray persisted in forecasting great changes. In another "fructidorian" contest between the Councils and the Directory, he guessed the outcome would be another triumph for the executive, although the final dispensation might depend on the part taken by the military. He wrote Pickering that "could the armies come to a complete certainty of amnesty and of being kept in grade, I should expect to hear that Louis Eighteenth were on the throne in a few months." [20] This prediction had unfortunate consequences when Pickering later used it to argue that the Ellsworth mission be delayed until the Bourbons had been restored. Pickering even went so far as to thank Murray for confirming what he had long suspected would be the outcome of the French political drama.[21]

Meanwhile, Murray's expectations were sharpened when Boulay de la Meurthe, a prominent member of the Council of Five Hundred, published a pamphlet comparing England on the eve of the Stuart restoration to France in the spring of 1799. Murray read Boulay's tract with astonishment. It was "more a beckoning along the path," he wrote Adams, "than a warning to avoid it." Why would the government allow its publication, he wondered, unless a restoration was already in train? Then came the news that the Councils had ousted all of the incumbent

19. See, for example, WVM to Pickering, The Hague, April 23, 1799, *AHA Report of 1912*, 544; same to same, No. 78, June 13, 1799, Netherlands Despatches, I; and WVM to JQA, letters May 17 and 24, and June 17, 1799, *AHA Report of 1912*, 555, 562–63. For JQA's rejoinders see his letters to Murray of June 1 and 8, 1799, Adams MSS, MR 133.
20. No. 78, The Hague, June 13, 1799, Netherlands Despatches, I.
21. Pickering to WVM, letters of October 4 and 14, 1799, Instructions to Ministers, V, RG 59, NA.

Directors except Barras. "Prairial," as this coup was called, undid Murray's prediction of Directorial victory, but it strengthened his opinion that a monarchical restoration would follow shortly. Whether a Bourbon or an Orléanist would take the throne remained to be seen. Again, it was Adams' voice from Berlin that sounded a muted demurrer. Paris might be showing "symptoms of monarchy," Adams wrote, but all the talk of restoring the monarchy might mean just the opposite of wanting it.[22]

Prairial inevitably cast the prospect of a Franco-American peace negotiation into uncertainty. The neo-Jacobins and reforming moderates who had overthrown the old Directory were an unknown quantity in foreign policy calculations. Certainly Talleyrand, whose authorship of peace overtures had held out the best hope for a peaceful denouement, could not long survive a political housecleaning of the executive branch. As one who reeked of corruption, he was sure to be found expendable by the reformers who now held the upper hand. Murray, though he knew that Talleyrand was on the way out, saw reason to expect that the new regime would continue Talleyrand's peace efforts. They would denounce their predecessors for having roiled Franco-American relations and quite logically thrust themselves forward as the appropriate instruments of reconciliation.[23]

On July 20, about a month after the Prairial coup, Talleyrand fell from power, and the French Foreign Office was taken over by a little-known diplomat named Charles Frédéric Reinhard. Murray could only speculate as to what direction French policy would take. He saw little improvement—in fact, no "alteration in practice"—in French policy toward American shipping. There still existed the "same system of gross violation" of U.S. maritime rights. Nor did the new regime appear eager to press for negotiation. The word from Paris in mid-August was that the French did not expect the Ellsworth mission to put in an appearance. Press reports from Philadelphia seemed to confirm the probability of delay. Murray had to admit that the instability of the French government lent weight to the argument for postponing a peace negotiation. If he were denounced for his own part in the earlier peace preliminaries, he wanted his critics to recall how much brighter the

22. WVM to JQA, letters of June 21, 25 and 28, 1799, *AHA Report of 1912*, 565–67; JQA to WVM, Berlin, July 6, 1799, Adams MSS, MR 133. Sieyès' intrigue with royalist elements remains "very much in the shadow," Glyndon G. Van Deusen, *Sieyès: His Life and His Nationalism* (New York: Columbia University Press, 1932), 70n.

23. WVM to Pickering, No. 83, The Hague, July 20, 1799, Netherlands Despatches, I.

prospect for a successful negotiation had been at the time of his talks with Pichon. Men's actions should be judged in the context of events, he remarked to Pickering, "else it is not a fair trial." [24]

Had Murray known what Charles Reinhard intended for the United States, he would have despaired absolutely. Reinhard's ministry was brief, lasting only from July to November, 1799, and he left in the French archives only two important state papers relating to France's American policy. One, dated October 1, proposed a peace treaty with the United States, coupled with a French effort to liberate Canada, Nova Scotia, and Newfoundland "under the protection of France." Because he believed that the members of the Ellsworth Commission were politically "British," Reinhard recommended sending a French envoy directly to Philadelphia, where—shades of Genêt—he was to rouse the American people against their government as the preliminary to disclosing that he had come to make a treaty. Americans would accept the treaty because it would accord indemnity for maritime losses. Then French Canadians, fired by the spectacle of a Franco-American peace settlement at Philadelphia, would rise in arms against England. Americans would logically fly to the aid of the Canadians and thus become France's partner in the war against England.[25]

Reinhard's other state paper contained explicit instructions to the French envoy whom he planned to send to Philadelphia. The latter, once he had dispelled the notion that the new Directory might be short-lived, was to demand a revision of Jay's treaty, call for full execution of the Franco-American treaties of 1778, and negotiate an even closer alliance. Should the United States balk, the French emissary was to hint that France might reacquire Louisiana from Spain, and thus come to exercise great influence over "the peace and prosperity" of the American West.[26]

Fortunately for John Adams' diplomacy, the Prairial Directory *was* short-lived.

If Murray gave less thought to the prospects of peacemaking, it was partly because the sounds of battle that summer were almost within earshot. In late August 12,000 British troops led by the Duke of York

24. The Hague, August 28, 1799, *AHA Report of 1912*, 586–88; also WVM to Pickering, No. 87, The Hague, August 14, 1799, Netherlands Despatches, I; and same to same (private), August 12, 1799, Pickering MSS, 25, folios 91–92v, MHS.

25. "Observations sur la position actuelle de la République francaise envers les Etats unis de l'Amérique," October 1, 1799, AAE EU, 51, folios 240–240v.

26. "Projet d'instructions Pour le Ministre de la Rep. auprès des Etats Unis," Vendémiaire, An 6 [September 23–October 22, 1799], *ibid.*, 244–47.

and Sir Ralph Abercrombie joined some 17,000 Russians under General Hermann in a long-projected invasion of northern Holland. There followed nearly two months of desultory fighting before the invasion force ignominiously withdrew. Murray followed the course of the invasion from its first rumor to its final retreat, hoping at least that the Anglo-Russian offensive would take Batavia out of the French orbit. While he never for a moment expected, as did London, that the Dutch Orangists would rise in support of the invaders, he was sorely disappointed at the failure of the British and Russian commanders to coordinate their operations. At no time, he believed, were the coalition forces outnumbered by the French and Dutch troops led by Generals Brune and Daendels. Still, the invaders were unable to break out of their peninsular position. Finally, hemmed in by flooded terrain and beset by sickness, the expeditionary force was recalled, its departure permitted by the Convention of Alkmaar, signed by the Duke of York on October 18.[27]

Murray was not convinced that the withdrawal was the result of sheer incompetence. Perhaps the invasion had been recalled because London had despaired of reinforcement from the Austrians—a possibility that faded when the Austrian Archduke Charles turned southward to support Suvarov. John Quincy Adams grimly cautioned Murray not to look for such mysterious causes of the Anglo-Russian debacle: the explanation lay in poor leadership and poor planning. Adams recalled that Frederick the Great had once predicted that the Duke of York would someday be a great general, to which Adams now rejoined that if the Prussian monarch had been as poor a soldier as he was a prophet, "Prussia would have been this day, nothing but a tradition." [28]

Though an excited watcher during the cross-Channel invasion, Murray played a passive role in the events of September and October. Late November, however, found him tipped once more into frothy backwash of the Federalist party's maelstrom. The letter in which Pickering rebuked him for his pleasantries to Talleyrand took note of another indiscretion. Back in 1798 Pichon had handed Murray a letter from Talleyrand dated August 28 and containing a slurring allusion to the Adams' administration's being under "British impressions." Pichon had been required to explain the slur, and Murray, to guard himself, had also made the Frenchman promise never to allow the

27. For Murray's detailed reports on the invasion see his dispatches to Pickering, Nos. 85–99, written between August 3 and October 21, 1799, Netherlands Despatches, I; and his letters to JQA of the same period in *AHA Report of 1912,* 580–610 *passim.*

28. Berlin, October 29, 1799, Adams MSS, MR 134. Adams' diagnosis is upheld by *Cambridge Modern History,* VIII, 662.

letter to be published or his receipt of it disclosed. Pichon had duly promised.

Now, on November 27, 1799, Murray discovered from Pickering that the Talleyrand letter had appeared earlier that autumn in the Richmond *Examiner,* accompanied by Pichon's verification that the letter had been shown to Murray "to be communicated to the President of the United States." Because the date of the letter—August 28— showed that French overtures had been tendered a full month earlier than was publicly known, Republicans were now claiming confirmation of their suspicion that the administration had delayed overlong its response to the French peace feelers. Pickering furiously concluded that France was again seeking to undermine the government's authority. Moreover, the colonel gave no sign that he recalled the conditions under which Murray had agreed to receive the letter. Those references to British influence, Pickering wrote scornfully, "would have justified you in dashing the letter in Citizen Pichon's face." [29]

While Murray could only repeat to Pickering what Pichon had promised, he wrote what he later called a "tolerably bitter" letter to Pichon, accusing the latter of violating his pledge of secrecy—and more than that, of having failed to explain that he (Pichon) had "softened the offensive and ridiculous passages about 'British impressions.' " Of the *Examiner*'s incomplete picture of what had transpired Murray wrote: "If you are the author of this act, Sir, or have been the instrument of it, that was the omission which you perfidiously made." [30]

When Murray's letter reached him, Pichon was serving as legation secretary in Berne. Hurt and frankly puzzled at the charges of bad faith, the Frenchman wrote immediately to Talleyrand (who was once more in the Foreign Office), imploring his chief to "tell me how I can answer him." Pointedly mindful of the XYZ Affair, Pichon remarked sorrowfully that Franco-American relations seemed "continuously fated to be a field of scandals." He could only suppose that the Prairial regime had been "betrayed by certain persons who pretend to be our friends and who wish to satisfy their passions." It spoke well of his regard for Murray that Pichon should be upset at the thought "that Mr. Murray was ready to believe me capable of such a villainous role."

When Talleyrand neglected to answer the plea from Berne, Pichon

29. Pickering to WVM, Trenton, October 4, 1799, *AHA Report of 1912*, 602; the Talleyrand-to-Pichon letter of August 28, 1798, is in the Pickering MSS, 23, 183–91, MHS; and Murray's explanation in his No. 106 to Pickering, November 28, 1799, Netherlands Despatches, I; and in his private letter to Pickering of December 1, 1799, Pickering MSS, 25, 296–300, MHS.
30. WVM to Pichon, The Hague, November 28, 1799, AAE EU, 51, folios 281–281v.

wrote Paris that since the ministry seemed to have left the matter in his hands he had written to Murray directly. Not to answer the American's charges, he felt, might jeopardize the forthcoming negotiations. He was "greatly disturbed," he told Murray, to hear of the publication and had made fruitless inquiries at Paris into this "strange and inexplicable incident." He sympathized with Murray's discomfiture but could offer no explanation except that he himself had had no part in the publication.[31] Murray remained neither convinced nor mollified. To Jean Luzac, publisher of the *Leyden Gazette,* he grumbled, "you see how these low devils act *man to man.*" [32]

Nearly a year later Murray recounted the sequel to John Quincy Adams. When he joined Ellsworth and Davie in Paris in March of 1800, Murray recorded that he had greeted Pichon coldly, only to find that Pichon had a plausible explanation of how the Talleyrand letter had happened to appear in the *Examiner.* He told Murray that on his return to Paris from The Hague in the fall of 1798 he had been asked to verify his summer-long correspondence with Talleyrand before submitting that correspondence to the Directory. On receiving these verified letters, the Directory had foolishly entrusted them to an American (whom Pichon referred to as *"a damned Jacobin"*) to be delivered to Adams. According to Pichon, this American intermediary had sent the letters to "Jacobins in Virginia" instead. Despite this explanation, Pichon was so sensitive to Murray's distrust when the two men met in Paris that he offered not to serve as secretary to the French negotiators if Murray objected to his presence. Pichon's explanation, however, satisfied Murray that there had been no personal breach of faith, whereupon the Frenchman undertook his secretarial duties with a zeal and a fidelity to all parties that earned Murray's respect. Looking back on the incident, he told Adams he was glad that Pichon had been able to exonerate himself because he believed that the secretary had not only served his own delegation well, but had also advanced the whole course of the negotiation.[33]

As the year 1799 drew to a close, however, the question that continued to daunt Murray in his waking hours was: would there be a negotiation?

31. Pichon to Talleyrand, Berne, letters of December 11, 1799, and January 14, 1800, *ibid.,* folios 279, 301.
32. The Hague, January 23, 1800, Misc. Letters, WVM MSS, LC.
33. The Hague, January 3, 1801, *AHA Report of 1912,* 671–72.

13

Adams, Bonaparte, and the Will to Peace

Two EVENTS, which involved Murray indirectly, brought an end to the uncertainty which had hung for nearly a year and a half over the prospect of a Franco-American peace settlement. One was John Adams' showdown—no other word describes it—with his High Federalist advisers at a stormy but decisive cabinet meeting at Trenton in October of 1799. The other was the advent of Napoleon Bonaparte, cast briefly but surely as the pacificator of France's enemies. These two events dispelled doubts on both sides of the Atlantic as to whether the Ellsworth Commission would be sent and received. Both Adams and Bonaparte were determined that it should.

The Trenton cabinet meeting was dramatically climaxed by Adams' command to Ellsworth and Davie that they sail at once. At his home in Quincy the previous summer the President had waited patiently for Pickering to complete the instructions which had been outlined at a cabinet meeting held in March. When Adams finally received the draft instructions he found them coupled with Pickering's recommendation, endorsed by Wolcott and McHenry, that the mission be postponed until the political situation in France had stabilized. From the outset Adams suspected that his cabinet's dilatory behavior had a political explanation, a suspicion that grew when he arrived at Trenton to find Alexander Hamilton there before him.[1] Had Murray been able to foresee the exact nature of the power struggle that was about to take place between the President and his Hamiltonian cabinet, he might have phrased his dispatches more guardedly. As it was, his highly suppositional forecasts of a monarchical restoration played directly into the hands of the Hamilton-Pickering coterie.

1. Adams' *Works,* IX, 23–25, 251–56.

As early as July 2, Pickering had begun to posit a Bourbon restoration on the prospect that allied armies would soon occupy Paris. News that Paris had been convulsed by the coup of Prairial did nothing to dampen the hope. Thus, when Murray lent his own authority to the prediction that the directorial structure would give way within six months to a restored monarchy, Pickering's case for postponing the mission was measurably strengthened. Although Pickering may have had still other sources for such speculation, he quoted Murray's dispatches in putting the case for postponement to Adams. Ironically, the Secretary of State, who had earlier scoffed at Murray's intelligence reports, now placed a high value on the Marylander's random speculation that the French Republic would not survive another six months. In his effort to stop the mission, Pickering had suddenly found Murray to be a more reliable source of information than, for example, Rufus King, who, Hamiltonian stalwart though he was, was contemporaneously dismissing any and all rumors of great changes at Paris. Or perhaps Pickering deliberately savored the irony that Murray, on whose agency Adams had relied in originating the mission, could now be quoted in support of arguments to postpone it.[2]

Adams at first seemed to agree with his cabinet that the mission be delayed, not because he expected a Bourbon restoration, but rather because he felt it might be desirable to learn more of what was transpiring at Paris before sending the envoys. Nor was the President convinced by Pickering's subtle use of Murray's predictions; he saw in them "no solid indications of a restoration." When he arrived in Trenton, however, Adams found the city agog with rumors that a restoration was imminent. "I could scarcely believe my own senses, when I heard such reveries," he wrote later. On finding that not only his cabinet but also Ellsworth and Hamilton were arguing for a postponement on such flimsy grounds, Adams turned abruptly to the business at hand. He told Ellsworth that if the Bourbons were ever restored the event would be at least seven years in the future; meanwhile, the Directory itself had conveyed the necessary "assurances" that the mission would be received. If the commissioners arrived to find Louis XVIII on his throne, they might congratulate His Majesty and write to Phil-

2. See, for example, Pickering to William L. Smith, No. 17, Philadelphia, July 2, 1799, Instructions to Ministers, V, RG 59, NA; Pickering to WVM, Trenton, October 25, 1799, *AHA Report of 1912*, 611; Pickering to JA, Trenton, September 11, 1799, enclosing Murray's letter of June 28, 1799, Adams' *Works*, IX, 24. See also King's letters to Pickering of June 5 and July 20, 1799, King, *Correspondence*, III, 31 and 67, respectively.

adelphia for new credentials. Thereupon Adams ordered the envoys' instructions to be put in final draft and instructed the envoys themselves to sail for France as soon as possible. Ellsworth and Davie left Newport, Rhode Island, on board the frigate *United States* on November 3, 1799.[3]

Scarcely had John Adams set in motion his policy of reconciliation than an event took place at St. Cloud which assured the success of that policy. On November 9—with Ellsworth and Davie only six days at sea—the conspiratorial threesome of Bonaparte, Sieyès, and Roger-Ducos arranged the demise of the Directory and became "temporary consuls" of a new regime whose central figure was Bonaparte. For Franco-American relations, the most auspicious augury for a peace settlement was the return of Talleyrand to the post of Foreign Minister. As one historian has remarked, "from the despised Directory, Bonaparte inherited both a minister and a policy." [4] Talleyrand was the minister, peace the policy; and Murray was one of the first to sense the hopeful direction which the new order would take.

Although Murray's prophecies for Prairial had missed the mark, most of his early assessments of "Brumaire" have stood the test of time. His first report of Bonaparte's coup warned against hasty conclusions. No one was sure what it portended, he wrote, but it was probable that the new regime had saved France from a resurgence of jacobinism. With Jacobins clamoring in the Councils for a more vigorous prosecution of the war, the emergence of Sieyès and Roger-Ducos, both known to be advocates of peace, led Murray to conclude that the political balance had now shifted in favor of a general peace settlement. The subsequent treaties of Lunéville, Mortefontaine, and Amiens were to confirm, though briefly, that Murray was not mistaken. He also foresaw a shifting of the political spectrum to the right.

This shift was dramatically illustrated in the capital of satellite Batavia, where a Jacobin coup scheduled for Thursday, November 14, 1799, was called off when the news arrived from Paris that jacobinism

3. For Adams' account of the Trenton cabinet meeting see Adams' *Works,* IX, 253–56; also JA to Pickering, Quincy, letters of September 16 and 19, 1799, *ibid.,* 30, 32. A more complete account of this tumultuous meeting is contained in DeConde, *Quasi-War,* 217–22.
4. E. Wilson Lyon, "The Franco-American Convention of 1800," *Journal of Modern History,* XII (September 1940), 308. Talleyrand's instrumentality in the peacemaking is most recently recognized by DeConde, *Quasi-War,* 334, 339.

was no longer in style. A reign of terror, Murray believed, was nar-
rowly avoided when General Brune, to whom the Dutch radicals looked
for leadership, apparently decided that Bonaparte represented a *force
majeure* and administered to his troops the oath of allegiance which
Paris had required.[5]

Some of Murray's musings expressed no more than his own uncertainty and wishful thinking. He continued to hope for either a
Bourbon restoration or France's adoption of a constitution modeled on
that of the United States. Before the Consulate was two months old,
however, he had settled on several points. First, the new regime could
not claim to be "republican" in the accepted meaning of the word.
France under Bonaparte would remain militant, but it could never again
make war in the name of republican principles. Henceforth the contest
in Europe would be "for POWER and territory; it can not be *republicanism* against *monarchy*." [6] At the same time, he foresaw a less militant
scene in France itself. From Paris came word that the law of hostages
had been repealed; other leniencies toward royalists and former émigrés
were expected. In Murray's view, France seemed to be moving into a
"milder & more generous order of things" in which Frenchmen might
hope to become more tolerant of one another. Finally, Murray was
convinced that France had reached a major turning point in her
history. Undeceived by the legislative and judicial trappings which
decorated the new executive, he saw clearly that the new era belonged
to Bonaparte. And this fact, he wrote, was "more favorable to the solution of all these questions which have made the world fanatic than had
Louis the 18 been brought back to Paris by force." [7]

All things considered (including a royalist uprising in the Vendée),
the short-range prospect for peacemaking was bright. Murray reasoned
that Bonaparte, in his eagerness to consolidate his position, would make
peace with the United States—if only to win favor from French
mercantile houses. The privateersmen would suffer, of course, but with
the dissolution of the Council of Five Hundred those French legislators
who had profited personally from privateering ventures could no longer
block reforms in the prize law. And within the new regime no less a
personage than Cambacérès, the Second Consul, had spoken out in favor
of such reforms. To Murray, it was a hopeful sign that Cambacérès

5. WVM to Pickering, Nos. 102 and 105, The Hague, November 15 and 23,
1799, Netherlands Despatches, I; also WVM to JQA, The Hague, November 22,
1799, *AHA Report of 1912*, 620.
6. To JQA, The Hague, December 24, 1799, *ibid.*, 634.
7. WVM to Pickering, No. 109, The Hague, December 20, 1799, Netherlands
Despatches, I; see also No. 103 of November 18, 1799, *ibid.*

should give privateering its proper name and call it "brigandage," describe French prize law as either "inadequate or bad," and single out the law of 29 Nivôse as being "vague and arbitrary." [8]

Talleyrand's return to the Foreign Office was also a good omen. Murray's confidence in Talleyrand was not so great, however, that he would forego an opportunity to remind the Frenchman that John Adams, not Thomas Jefferson, was the man to deal with. That opportunity occurred when the Duc de Liancourt, an erstwhile observer of the American scene, visited Murray on his way to Paris in late 1799. The two men had met the previous summer when Liancourt had traveled to The Hague expressly to hear Murray's critique of his latest volume on America. Knowing that Liancourt would confer with Talleyrand, Murray impressed on him that the American war hawks had been kept in check only by Adams' bold decision to send another mission. To Liancourt, Murray depicted the President as one who because he was "most moderate" in his attitude toward France would be the most logical formulator of a peace settlement. Should France embarrass Adams by postponing the negotiation until after the next presidential election, war would almost certainly follow.[9]

Murray's suspicions proved groundless. Talleyrand no sooner resumed office than he renewed his peace policy toward the United States. In a report to the Consuls on November 30 the French Foreign Minister set forth a somber but not wholly pessimistic view of Franco-American relations. Noting gloomily that Ellsworth and Davie had not yet arrived in France, Talleyrand blamed the delay on Sir Robert Liston's supposed influence over Adams. He speculated that Liston had doubtless tried to woo the United States into a British alliance by dangling the lure of joint aggressions against French and Spanish colonies. In a more optimistic vein, Talleyrand foresaw a diminution of British influence as the Jeffersonian party grew in strength. The next session of Congress, he predicted, would reflect this Jeffersonian resurgence by assuming a more neutral posture toward France and Britain.

Thus far, Murray might have recognized the old Talleyrand, carefully calculating the impact of partisan politics on the diplomatic scene, perhaps even urging the Consuls to "take up again our natural ties with the United States." Still, though the language was ominously familiar, it

8. To Pickering, No. 111, The Hague, December 26, 1799; also WVM to McHenry, The Hague, December 2, 1799, Steiner, *McHenry*, 429–30.

9. WVM to JQA, The Hague, letters of December 10 and 13, 1799, *AHA Report of 1912*, 630–32. Liancourt's four-volume work, entitled *Voyages dans les Etats Unis d'Amérique*, was first published in Paris in 1799.

no longer rang with revolutionary overtones. Nor was there any mistaking Talleyrand's commitment to an immediate negotiation. He urged the Consuls to welcome the American envoys with "friendly dignity" and to "abstain from all reproach." Specifically, the forthcoming negotiation should result in reaching agreement on the meaning of the three Franco-American treaties and "to find a way to compensate each other for damages done." Perhaps mindful of his earlier dealings with Murray, Talleyrand warned the Consuls not to expect that the settlement would be speedy. France would be dealing with "men who are essentially argumentative." [10]

Suspicious though he was of Talleyrand (whose past conduct no Federalist could approve), Murray fed hungrily on the optimism of a new year and a new century. His letters and dispatches took on the tempo of rising hopes. The release of an American vessel from French custody (confirmed) gave substance to the rumor (unconfirmed) that the law of 29 Nivôse had been set aside. The release of fifty American seamen at Nantes, though contingent on the release by the United States of an equal number of interned Frenchmen, was another hopeful sign. Most of all, however, it was Bonaparte's need for a respite in which to consolidate his regime that augured best. Neither Murray, nor John Quincy Adams, nor even Rufus King, was prepared to deny that the insecurity of Bonaparte's Consulate had created at Paris an atmosphere highly propitious for an accord.[11]

The worst that Murray foresaw for the immediate future was that Britain, now preparing to renew the war, would strike France so hard a blow as to topple the new regime. With Bonaparte, he felt, France had triumphed over her "worst enemies." His downfall would once again deliver France into the hands of the Jacobins, and throw Franco-American relations into disarray.[12]

Just before Christmas, 1799, Murray learned that his two colleagues had arrived in Lisbon on November 27. Not until the end of January, 1800, however, was the report confirmed. In the interval he waited impatiently, even anxiously, as weeks passed with no further news.

10. "Report aux Consules de la République," November 30, 1799, AAE EU, 51, folios 260–62.

11. WVM to Pickering, Nos. 113 and 115, The Hague, January 12 and February 2, 1800, respectively, Netherlands Despatches, I; JQA to King, Berlin, December 5, 1799, Adams MSS, MR 134; King to Pickering, No. 59, London, February 3, 1800, King, *Correspondence*, III, 188.

12. See, for example, WVM to JQA, The Hague, letters of January 31 and February 4, 1800, *AHA Report of 1912*, 639, 640–41.

He could only assume that cold weather had delayed the post or that the envoys were waiting in Lisbon until the new French regime had signified that their credentials would be accepted.[13] Finally, on January 30, he heard from William Smith, the American minister to Portugal, that Ellsworth and Davie had indeed landed at Lisbon. From other sources he learned that they had subsequently reembarked for the French west-coast port of Lorient. A letter from the envoys themselves arrived February 4; it explained the mysterious delay. They had touched first at Lisbon in order to take stock of the French political situation before proceeding to Paris. Confused as to the meaning of Brumaire, the two commissioners initially thought to sail from Lisbon to The Hague where they might profit from Murray's counsel. This plan was dropped when Captain John Barry balked at navigating the English Channel so late in the season. It was decided, therefore, that Barry should take them as far as Lorient from whence they would go on to Paris if their credentials were accepted.[14]

There now ensued a frustrating sequel to the quick passage from Newport. For nearly four weeks the *United States* was tossed by gale-force headwinds off the Bay of Biscay in seas so rough that Barry dared not attempt a landing anywhere on the west coast of France. The northerlies which had made the trans-Atlantic crossing so swift now forced the envoys to put back to the village of Puentedeume near the northwest tip of Spain. Safely ashore on January 16, the two men went at once to the nearby town of Corunna where next day they wrote letters to Pickering, Murray, and Talleyrand, explaining what had happened.[15] Talleyrand was asked to send passports for all three commissioners, provided he found their credentials to the old Directory to be acceptable to the new regime. While they waited for a reply, Ellsworth and Davie moved on to the Spanish city of Burgos, nearer the French frontier. Talleyrand's answering letter brushed aside the credentials question, extended sympathy to the storm-battered envoys, and told them they were "expected with impatience" and would be "received with eagerness." This welcoming letter arrived at Burgos by special courier on

13. WVM to Pickering, Nos. 110 and 113, The Hague, December 23, 1799, and January 31, 1800, respectively, Netherlands Despatches, I.

14. Smith to WVM, Lisbon, December 15, 1799, mentioned in Murray's No. 115, February 2, 1800, *ibid.;* Ellsworth and Davie to WVM, January 17, 1800, Despatches from France, VII, Department of State, RG 59, NA. Talleyrand forwarded the envoys' letter to Murray on January 31, 1800, AAE EU, 51, 307. For an account of the Lisbon stop-over see Ellsworth and Davie to Pickering, Lisbon, December 7, 1799, Despatches from France, VII, RG 59, NA; *ASP FR,* II, 307; and Rogers, *Evolution of a Federalist,* 328–29.

15. All three letters, dated January 17, 1800, plus the envoys' letter to Pickering (Burgos, February 10) may be found in *ASP FR,* II, 307–308.

February 9. Two days later the envoys set out for Paris where they
arrived March 2, to find that Murray had preceded them by a day.[16]

Murray had meanwhile put his affairs in order for the trip to Paris.
He also began to show signs of strain. While congratulating his colleagues on their safe arrival at Corunna, he explained that the "absolute
uncertainty" of their whereabouts had delayed his preparations for meeting them. The rebuke was plain: Ellsworth and Davie had neglected
to write him from Lisbon when they first landed. Murray also reminded
Pickering that "it would have been very grateful & not unprofitable to
have possessed some intimations by which I could have regulated my
domestic affairs & sale of furniture &c &c &c—." Either bad humor or a
wish for precision also led him to call Talleyrand's attention to the mis-
spelling of his name on the passport he had received from Paris. It was
a "small mistake of little importance," he wrote, but his middle name
was "Vans," not "Van." [17]

Leave-taking required that he sell his furniture, put his personal
library in storage along with John Quincy Adams' "bales" of books, and,
finally, that he attend an audience of leave from the Batavian Directory.
The latter, he felt, seemed sincere in their good wishes for a successful
negotiation. As for the mission itself, he confided to Adams that he was
awed at its importance and consoled only by the belief that Oliver
Ellsworth would "supply . . . that prudence which I doubt in myself,
and which even my friends doubt. My intentions," he added, "are between God and myself, and I earnestly hope that we shall do the best
possible." [18]

If Murray seemed querulous in the face of new responsibilities, it was
partly because he was shaken by the news that Washington had died.
That he felt a great personal loss is evidenced by a scrap of paper signed
and dated February 2, 1800, on which he wrote:

> Fame round his Bust her richest wreath had twin'd
> As Eden sweet—immortal as his mind!

for the melancholy news this day comes that this great & illustrious
man died on the 15th Decr. of a putrid Sore Throat. He is gone to a

16. Talleyrand to Ellsworth and Davie, Paris, January 31, 1800, AAE EU,
51, folio 306–306v; same to WVM, Paris, January 31, *ibid.*, folio 307.

17. WVM to Ellsworth and Davie, The Hague, February 4, 1800, Misc. Letters,
WVM MSS, LC; WVM to Pickering, No. 110, The Hague, December 23, 1799,
Netherlands Despatches, I; and WVM to Talleyrand, The Hague, February 4,
1800, Misc. Letters, WVM MSS, LC.

18. WVM to JQA, The Hague, February 14, and Rotterdam, February 17,
1800, *AHA Report of 1912*, 642–43.

sure immortality of true greatness—the Hero, Sage—friend, husband—the most illustrious man of any known times.[19]

In his grief, Murray was gratified that all Europe seemed to be mourning with him. Even in Paris the eulogies flowed freely, although with an ulterior design which completely escaped Murray's notice. Because he himself idolized Washington he thought it entirely logical for the man's fame to have silenced his former detractors. What he missed was the signal from Paris that this homage to Washington was the new regime's way of saying that France intended to let bygones be. In fact, it was Talleyrand, firmly bent on peace, who suggested to Bonaparte that by honoring Washington the First Consul could improve the climate for the forthcoming negotiations. At the Foreign Minister's suggestion, Bonaparte ordered a statue raised in Washington's honor. And with the First Consul's blessing, a returned *émigré* named Louis Fontanes gave a long funeral oration in the Temple of Mars. (Fontanes contrived to win favor for himself on this occasion by alluding to Bonaparte as often as he did to Washington.) The political overtones of all this memorializing were lost on Murray.[20]

Leaving The Hague on February 17, the American minister and his party spent their first night at Rotterdam after an uncomfortable day of "pushing our way across marshes, sloughs, and wide waters." Here that evening Murray wrote a farewell letter to John Quincy Adams in which he predicted that Bonaparte would make the mission a success, if only to win favor among the neutral powers. Not until March 7 did Murray again write to his friend in Berlin. By that time he could report that the First Consul had received the American ministers with "courtly frankness" and that "as yet I see no insurmountable things." [21] Thereafter, the Murray-Adams correspondence dwindled as Murray became increasingly preoccupied with treaty-making.

Murray's party rode into Paris on March 1, 1800, a day ahead of Ellsworth and Davie. Whatever warm greetings may have been exchanged during these near-coincidental arrivals, Murray soon found

19. Misc. Letters, WVM MSS, LC.
20. See Talleyrand's "Raport au 1ʳᵉ Consule" [*sic*], 13 Ventôse (March 4), AAE EU, 51, 357; also Bonaparte's undated "Minute d"Arrêté," *ibid.*, folios 311–12. See also Fay, *Revolutionary Spirit*, 430–38, for a more complete study of the ceremonial aspect of reconciliation. Murray's reactions were largely contained in his letters to JQA of February 4, 7, 14, and 17, 1800, *AHA Report of 1912*, 639–43.
21. *Ibid.*, 642–43, 644.

himself cordially disliking his fellow commissioners. Though unacquainted with Davie, he had known Ellsworth in Philadelphia and had long held him in high respect. As the months of negotiation unfolded, however, Murray came to regard both men with something akin to contempt, an emotion that sprang from what he believed was their feeling toward him. A year later, looking back on this period, Murray was to write in his diary that

> it is true my two colleagues I believe even disliked me—they were men of sense—but exceedingly rude and raw—with whom I was but on terms of decent civility—not *one* liked the *other!*—They came I believe under prejudice agt. me—I had originated the whole —in june July Augt. Sept. 1798—with Pichon—They thought lightly of me clearly—& I had too much pride to please them! as I had cause to believe that they had not a good nor respectful opinion of me! They were ignorant of the world & its manners & were too conceited, particularly Davie, to borrow any idea w[it]h complacency from me, the third named, & youngest of the mission— As to Mr. E—he thought little about anything but the Logic of the points—as if Logic had much to do with the courts of Europe! good man!—excellent & another *Judge!*— [22]

Although the personalities of the two men have been blurred by laudatory biographies, Ellsworth and Davie may have deserved Murray's characterization. Neither man had any diplomatic experience, any first-hand familiarity with Europe, nor even a knowledge of the French language. Against the statement made by one of Davie's later biographers that the North Carolina governor found Paris altogether congenial because of his accomplishments as a linguist, Murray recorded that he himself arranged the delegates' first meeting with their French counterparts because he alone "spoke a little French." [23] And what Murray called "conceit" another biographer describes as Davie's "beauty of person and graceful manner, rendered more attractive perhaps by a slight *hauteur* which was natural to him." The governor's personal secre-

22. Entry of April 24, 1801, Photostat Diary, 178–79, WVM MSS, LC. DeConde was the first historian to refute E. Wilson Lyon's earlier judgment that "the three men cooperated splendidly." DeConde explains Lyon's misconception by the fact that the latter wrote from official rather than personal papers. Cf. Lyon, "The Franco-American Convention of 1800," *op. cit.,* 306; DeConde, "The Role of William Vans Murray," *op. cit.,* 20.

23. Cf. Joseph Grégoire de Roulhac Hamilton, *William Richardson Davie,* James Sprunt Historical Publications (Raleigh, N.C.: North Carolina Historical Society, 1907), No. 7, 19; WVM to JQA, Paris, March 7 [March 8?], 1800, *AHA Report of 1912,* 644.

tary, apparently eager to dispel the notion that his employer was a person of no consequence, recorded that during an audience with Bonaparte the First Consul "seemed for a time to forget that Governor Davie was *second* in the commission, his attention being more particularly directed to him." [24]

Davie had come to the governorship of North Carolina by way of a law career, notably advanced by his having been wounded at the Battle of Camden. Wartime distinction seems to have begotten the aristocratic demeanor and its concomitant, a Federalist party affiliation. It was Ellsworth himself who testified to Davie's solid Federalist credentials. The Chief Justice visited the governor at Halifax in March of 1799, and subsequently commended him to Pickering for his "dignified manners, extent of political information, and correctness of opinions." Pickering was persuaded, hesitating only at the political inexpediency of pulling Davie prematurely from an important Federalist governorship before the mission to France had been finally decided upon.[25]

A paucity of personal papers has left Oliver Ellsworth an even cloudier figure than Davie. Ellsworth's public career had begun in the days of the Continental Congress, where he had represented his native state of Connecticut. For twenty years thereafter he had never lacked for the honors which Connecticut was able to confer on his abilities. He was one of his state's delegates to the Federal Convention and, with William S. Johnson, one of its first United States Senators. He came to national prominence in 1796, when Washington appointed him to succeed John Jay as Chief Justice. Even in this post the aura of anonymity persisted. Few cases came before the Supreme Court while Ellsworth presided; his own decisions were few and brief.

The Chief Justice was "decidedly cautious" in his attitude toward the French mission, even to the point of joining the High Federalist clique in their efforts to persuade Adams to postpone it. The President had visited Ellsworth at his home in Windsor on his way to Trenton and had found him "perfectly candid," ready to sail "at an hour's warning" or to postpone the mission if Adams saw fit. Adams' suspicions were roused, therefore, when Ellsworth followed him to Trenton. Despite the latter's explanation that he had come to Trenton in order to be in fuller com-

24. Fordyce M. Hubbard, "Life of William R. Davie" in Jared Sparks, ed., *The Library of American Biography* (Boston: Hilliard, Gray and Company, 1848), 2nd series, Vol. XV, 124–25.

25. Ellsworth to Pickering, Halifax, N.C., March 25, 1799, Davie MSS, North Carolina Department of Archives and History; see also Blackwell P. Robinson, *William R. Davie* (Chapel Hill, N.C.: University of North Carolina Press, 1957), for a full-length biography.

munication with the President, Adams suspected—and rightly so—that the Chief Justice had been summoned by members of the cabinet who wished him to lend weight to the argument that the mission be delayed pending a Bourbon restoration.[26] When this argument failed, and the envoys were ordered to sail, Ellsworth's presence in the embassy was at least an assurance to High Federalists that France would not be let off easily.

Even his political enemies reckoned Ellsworth a most powerful reasoner. His former Senate colleague, William Maclay, found him so tenacious in debate as to dub him "Endless Ellsworth," and Aaron Burr once remarked that if Ellsworth had ever chanced to spell the name of the Deity with two D's, it would have taken the Senate three weeks to expunge the superfluous letter.[27] Although Maclay and Burr were unfriendly witnesses, Murray's criticism that Ellsworth was more lawyer than diplomat seems not unwarranted. Still, it was not merely Davie's condescension or Ellsworth's preoccupation with legal points that Murray found distasteful. He was rankled, too, at having been named third in the ministerial commission when in the first instance he had been nominated to do the job alone. He also suspected that his colleagues were cool to the whole prospect of peacemaking. Davie appeared to be keen for the mission, but Murray knew that Ellsworth (in Pickering's words) had come only "to prevent something worse." [28]

All three Americans were lawyers, but there the similarity of background ended. A law career had brought Ellsworth to the bench, Davie to preeminence in state politics, and Murray to diplomacy. In accordance with the fairly well-established precedent of selecting diplomatic emissaries with an eye to geographic balance, each hailed from a different section: Ellsworth from New England, Davie from the South, Murray from a Border state. Even the span of their ages, though not great, impressed Murray with a sense of his own juniority. Ellsworth was nearing his fifty-fifth birthday; Davie was forty-three; Murray had just passed his fortieth. Murray's aloofness from his colleagues was further

26. For Ellsworth's dealings with Pickering and Wolcott see Pickering to Washington, Trenton, October 24, 1799, Gibbs, *Wolcott*, II, 280; Pickering to Cabot, Trenton, October 22, 1799, Lodge, *Cabot*, 248. For Ellsworth's assurances to Adams and the President's subsequent suspicions, see Adams' *Works*, IX, 37–38, 252.

27. *Journal of William Maclay, U.S. Senator from Pennsylvania, 1789–1791* (New York: D. Appleton and Company, 1890), 133; see also John Blair Linn, *Old Time Notables,* as cited by William Garrott Brown, *The Life of Oliver Ellsworth* (New York: The Macmillan Company, 1905), 224.

28. Pickering to WVM, Trenton, October 25, 1799, *AHA Report of 1912,* 611. See also WVM to JQA, Paris, March 7, 1800, *ibid.,* 644.

underlined by his separate place of residence. Ellsworth and Davie lodged together at the Hôtel des Oiseaux on the rue de Sèvres. The Murrays, after passing an expensive week at the Hôtel de l'Empire, moved into a private house on the rue St.-Dominique.[29]

Though "mere civility" continued to characterize the relations among the three envoys, the Paris interlude was a welcome change for Murray and Charlotte. After the cold damp of the Dutch climate the clear, warm air of Paris was like a tonic. Gone were the complaints of ill health and, in their place, intimations of renewed vitality.

29. *Ibid.,* 644–45; also entry of April 24, 1801, Photostat Diary, 179.

14

From Deadlock to Deadlock

THE ENVOYS' encounter with the French Consulate began briskly. Within a week of their arrival, Bonaparte himself received them at a ceremonial audience in the Salle des Ambassadeurs, and assured them that three French negotiators would be appointed forthwith. Surprisingly, Talleyrand had given little forethought to the selection of the French representatives. Not until March 4, 1800, did he propose the name of Joseph Bonaparte and five others. Whether or not Talleyrand's list of nominees ever reached the First Consul, Bonaparte acted that same day, appointing Joseph to head the French delegation but naming no others from the list. Instead he selected two men of Brumaire, Charles-Pierre Claret Fleurieu and Pierre-Louis Roederer. Fleurieu was sixty-two, a native of Lyons who had served briefly in 1790 as Minister of the Navy and Colonies. He had been jailed during the Terror and had not reappeared as a public figure until the advent of Bonaparte. Pierre Roederer (who subsequently proved to be the workhorse of the French delegation) was forty-six, an Alsatian who had once been a member of the National Assembly. Roederer was intensely loyal to Bonaparte, his fidelity extending even to the ill-fated Hundred Days. At the time of his appointment, Roederer had already been rewarded by recently having been made a member of that Consular appendage known as the Conseil d'Etat. Bonaparte, in selecting his own brother to head the delegation, had made a choice that he was not to regret. Joseph Bonaparte was to be a key figure in the First Consul's general pacification policy; his talent for diplomatic negotiation was later put to good use at Lunéville and Amiens.[1]

1. U.S. Ministers to Talleyrand (two notes), March 3, 1800; and Talleyrand to U.S. Ministers, March 4 and 5, 1800, *ASP FR*, II, 309. For the French appointments see Talleyrand's "Raport au Premier Consul de la République," 13 Ventôse, An 8 (March 4, 1800), AAE EU, 51, folios 357–58v, and "Extrait des Registres des Arrêtés du Premier Consul," same date, *ibid.*, folio 359. For biographical in-

Although the Americans notified the French delegation on March 10 that they were ready to begin, a delay ensued while Joseph Bonaparte recuperated from an unspecified illness of several weeks' duration. Apprised on March 27 that the chief of the French delegation was no longer indisposed, the Americans again asked for a meeting. With no further delay the delegations held their first joint meeting on April 2.[2]

The American envoys seized the initiative by announcing that they would shortly present a set of proposals. To this the French replied that they themselves had nothing to convey at that time and would eagerly await the American overture. Either during or shortly after this meeting of April 2, the envoys discovered what they believed was a flaw in the Frenchmen's credentials. Next day the long shadow of XYZ fell across their letter to the French negotiators, wherein they remarked that nowhere in the French delegates' "powers" were they explicitly authorized to conclude a treaty. Mindful of possible delay, the Americans agreed to accept, in lieu of new credentials, "a ministerial declaration" of the French government's intention to conclude the negotiating process with a treaty.[3] On April 7 the Ellsworth Commission got a taste of Napoleonic speed. By special decree the First Consul authorized his agents "to negotiate . . . as well as to sign and conclude . . . whatever shall appear to them necessary to bring about the perfect re-establishment of good harmony." Talleyrand also read the Americans a lesson in French diplomatic practice: that, since the Revolution, French diplomats had always had the power to conclude whenever they had the power to treat.[4]

Their suspicions set at rest, the Americans sent a note to their French counterparts that same day, setting forth the two principal aims of Adams' diplomacy: to agree to treaty articles that would satisfy private

formation see *Nouvelle Biographie Générale* (Paris: Firman Didot Frères, 1862) and *Les Ministères français, 1789–1911,* Publication de la Société d'Histoire Moderne (Paris: Edouard Cornély et Cie., 1911).

2. For the six preliminary notes exchanged between the U.S. Ministers and Talleyrand, March 9 to 30, see AAE EU, 51, folios 371–73v; and *ASP FR,* II, 310–11.

3. "Extrait du Journal de la Négociation avec les Ministres Plénipotentiaires et envoyés extraordinaires des Etats unis," 13 Germinal, An 8 (April 3, 1800), AAE EU, 51, folios 413v–414; also U.S. Ministers to French Ministers, April 3, 1800, *ASP FR,* II, 312; French Ministers to Talleyrand, 14 Germinal, An 8 (April 4, 1800), AAE EU, 51, 417.

4. "Extrait du Registre des Décrets du Premier Consul," 15 Germinal, An 8 (April 5, 1800), *ibid.,* folio 418; Talleyrand to French Ministers, 16 Germinal, An 8 (April 6), *ibid.;* French Ministers to U.S. Ministers, 17 Germinal, An 8 (April 7), *ASP FR,* II, 313.

claims for maritime indemnity, and to make a new commercial treaty.[5]
The envoys hoped to move quickly now, lest France become reluctant
to make concessions in the wake of military successes. All Europe knew
that Bonaparte was already preparing an Italian campaign; and if his
earlier performance in that theater were a gauge of his probable success,
the envoys were anxious to have a treaty signed before the news of victories hardened the French position. In pressing the initiative the envoys
also acted deliberately for, as Murray observed, "it is easier to press
what we originate . . . than to object to theirs & overturn them & yet
obtain substitutes of our own."

No less important was the sequence in which negotiable matters were
presented. American interests would be served best if at the outset
France agreed to pay indemnity for her maritime depredations. With
this concession in hand, the Americans planned next to "soften" the
indemnities agreement with a generous commercial treaty. Once these
two matters were disposed of, the Americans would stand ready to
repulse any French effort to revive the hated alliance of 1778.[6]

If the Americans wanted to talk about indemnities first, the French
ministers insisted that *national,* as well as private, claims be introduced into the discussion. The French reply of April 9 called attention to the existence of indemnifiable damages claimed by the French
government, arising ostensibly from the failure of the United States to
adhere to earlier treaty obligations. Secretary Pickering had foreseen
that France might press such national claims, and had instructed the
envoys to try to consign them to arbitration. In fact, both Pickering and
Talleyrand had envisioned an arbitral settlement of all claims, private
and national. While Talleyrand saw in the arbitral method a means of
delaying actual payments, the Frenchman was honest enough to calcu-
late, as did Pickering, that even with France's national claims thrown
on the scales a final accounting would tip heavily in favor of private
American claimants. The envoys readily agreed to admit the question
of national claims. Only the difficulty of estimating their value, they
explained, had led them to omit mention of national damages in their
first note.[7]

5. U.S. Ministers to French Ministers, April 7, 1800, *ibid.,* 314.
6. Entry of April 9, 1800, "Some Remarks on the Negotiation at Paris, 1800,"
WVM MSS, LC, hereinafter referred to as "Some Remarks"; see also U.S. Ministers to French Ministers, April 17, 1800, AAE EU, 51, folios 460–64.
7. Cf. Instructions to U.S. Ministers, October 22, 1799, *ASP FR,* II, 301–306;
Instructions to French Ministers, Germinal, An 8 (March 22–April 20, 1800),
AAE EU, 51, folio 394–394v. For the French reply of April 9 and the U.S. rejoinder of April 11, 1800, see *ibid.,* folio 454–454v; and *ASP FR,* II, 315, respectively.

The Americans' call for a new commercial treaty met a more solid opposition. France, they were told, preferred to execute "the treaties of friendship and commerce now existing." This insistence on old treaties provoked heated controversy as to whether the American ministers had the authority to undo that piece of legislation by which Congress had unilaterally abrogated all the old French treaties during the peak of the XYZ crisis. For the moment, Ellsworth and his colleagues avoided this basic issue, and simply restated their belief that a *new* treaty of commerce would "present fewer difficulties in construction and execution." [8]

Had each delegation been privy to the other's instructions, the forthcoming impasse on the treaty question would have been instantly visible. The French agents were bound to recover for France all of the treaty advantages which she had enjoyed before the rupture of diplomatic relations. These included the excessively privileged powers wielded by French consuls in U.S. ports. Beyond the earlier status quo, the French commissioners were to secure for France all of the treaty privileges which the United States had conferred on Britain in Jay's treaty. On each of these points the American ministers were instructed to resist. They were not to allow the resurrection of the treaties of commerce and alliance of 1778 or the consular convention of 1788. They were warned explicitly against any reinstatement of French consular authority that might be incompatible with United States sovereignty. With respect to Jay's treaty, which had gained priority with the abrogation of the French treaties, the envoys were to avoid any engagement "inconsistent with the obligations of any prior treaty." [9]

While imposing their own formulas on the indemnities and treaties questions, the French ministers also sought to embarrass the Americans by asking what steps President Adams had "undoubtedly" taken to terminate U.S. naval operations. Now that France had ceased her attacks on American shipping, what reciprocal action could be expected from the United States? The envoys, unable to give an explicit answer, responded awkwardly that since American naval actions were "defensive," they would recede in keeping with the lessening of French aggressions. On April 13, pressed again on this point, the Americans turned their initial embarrassment to better account. If France would sign a new commercial treaty, they replied, American naval operations would certainly come to an end. They had no authority to promise that this

8. *Ibid.*
9. Cf. Instructions to French Ministers, AAE EU, 51, folios 388, 390, 391–94; Instructions to U.S. Ministers, *ASP FR,* II, 301–306.

would happen, but they foresaw it as a natural consequence of treaty-making. The implication was that only a *new* treaty of commerce would have this pacifying effect. Thus, Ellsworth and his colleagues sought to put the treaty question back where they wanted it—near the top of their own agenda. This skirmish proved to be abortive, for although Murray admitted that they were all "a little uneasy" at being questioned about the immediate future of naval hostilities, the French delegation apparently realized that the American commissioners could promise nothing. At a dinner meeting on April 16, Louis Pichon, now acting as secretary to the French ministers, took Ellsworth aside and told him that France "did not mean to press the assurances any further." [10] Next day the negotiators turned to what they hoped would be more negotiable matters.

From April 17 to July 20 the treaty-makers floundered from one deadlock to another. The first day, Ellsworth and company presented six treaty articles, five having to do with indemnification. While waiting for a response, Murray began to anticipate a strenuous French demurrer to Article 2, which stipulated that maritime claims antedating July 7, 1798 (the day Congress abrogated the treaties), be awarded for violations of the old treaties, while the post-July 7 claims would be adjusted under the principles of international law. The envoys were relieved, therefore, when at a dinner meeting the next day, "nothing was said respecting the . . . different periods of Injury & Claims." [11]

Because Article 2 would make France liable for claims both before and after the treaties had been voided, a temporary silence from the French quarter did not mean consent. On May 6 the French signified that they would not differentiate between claims arising before and after July 7, 1798. First, the "true meaning" of the old treaties must be agreed to. Only then would they discuss indemnities. In short, if France were to indemnify, it should be for violations of existing treaties, "not as a preliminary to a new one." This view, of course, overlooked the fact that as far as the Americans were concerned there were no "existing treaties." Congress had abrogated them. As Ellsworth explained it, France by her conduct had compelled Congress to do away with the treaties. The treaties of 1778 were dead now, abrogated by "solemn public act" and beyond the power of the envoys to resurrect. They were

10. Entry of April 16, 1800, "Some Remarks"; for the French notes of April 9 and 13, see AAE EU, 51, folio 454–54v; for the American Ministers' answers, see *ASP FR*, II, 315.
11. Entry to April 18, 1800, "Some Remarks."

still relevant, however, as a basis for claims arising from infractions of those treaties prior to the date of abrogation. With this rebuttal the Americans now presented thirty more treaty articles.[12]

Whether or not France should abide by the death sentence which Congress had passed on the treaties of 1778 was a question which required the French ministers to seek fresh instructions. Unfortunately, Talleyrand was ill, and by the time he had recovered Bonaparte was a week on his way to Italy.[13] Murray, too, was sick (consumptive, he thought), and though more hopeful for this mission than were his colleagues, he worried about the political consequences of failure. Unless they won an "apparent and striking" success, they and the whole Federalist party would be "damned" at the next election. Moreover, their chances of success depended, in part, on the visible support of John Adams' peace policy by his own party. He cautioned Secretary of War McHenry that "there could not be a more triumphant event for F[rance] than the abandonment of the P[resident] by the Fedl. party." [14]

During the enforced lull, which lasted from May 8 until July 15, 1800, Murray began to emerge as the chief spokesman for his delegation. Even his colleagues admitted that a lengthy conversation which Murray held with Pierre Roederer on May 23 proved to be "exceedingly important" because it warned of an approaching crisis. On discovering that Roederer was drafting the request for new instructions, Murray lectured him on why the old treaties could not be revived. The reason was simple: Jay's treaty now stood in the way. Certain privileges relating to privateers and prizes had accrued to Britain with the demise of the Franco-American commercial treaty. These privileges, though provided for by Jay's treaty, had been inoperable between 1794 and 1798. Britain could not claim them because nothing in Jay's treaty was allowed to "operate contrary to former and existing Public Treaties." With the abrogation of the French treaty, the British could now claim the full range of privateer and prize privileges which had lain latent in Jay's treaty. But, asked Roederer, could not France be accorded at least *equal* privileges? No, Murray replied, because Jay's treaty conferred them on Britain ex-

12. French Ministers to U.S. Ministers, May 6, 1800, and U.S. Ministers to French Ministers, May 8, 1800, *ASP FR*, II, 319–20, 321–24.

13. U.S. Ministers' "Journal," May 23, 1800, *ASP FR*, II, 325; see also Albert Du Casse, *Histoire des négociations diplomatiques relatives aux traités de Mortefontaine, de Lunéville et d'Amiens* (Paris: A. Du Casse, 1855), 273–74.

14. Paris, May 18, 1800, Steiner, *McHenry*, 493–95; See also WVM to JQA, Paris, letters of April 4 and May 11, 1800, *AHA Report of 1912*, 645–46.

clusively. In that case, Roederer said vehemently, the United States should not expect France to pay indemnities.

The Frenchman was not persuaded that the old French treaties were dead beyond recall, however. War, he insisted, was the only valid ground for a unilateral abrogation of treaties, and neither France nor the United States had declared war during their difficulties. If, in fact, a state of war had existed since 1798, France might accept the concomitant of treaty abrogation, but she would not then pay for wartime spoliations. "A nation can give up cities at a peace, but not pay money—never." [15]

To this outburst Murray replied heatedly that all Europe had its eyes fixed on the present negotiation, watching to see whether the new regime would do justice to the United States. "Hence we are tranquil as to the issue." Roederer refused to be bluffed and observed ominously that thirty French frigates would suffice to reduce American naval power. Murray rejoined laughingly that be that as it might, his own country was quite capable of destroying French colonial commerce. The Frenchman sobered at this, admitting that France was indeed exposed in the West Indies. As they parted, Murray drove home still another threat. Any renewal of hostilities, he warned, would result in an Anglo-American alliance which would be "decisive against the whole colonial system of Europe for ever." Both warnings found their way into the French ministers' report to Talleyrand.[16]

Murray's encounter with Roederer convinced the Americans that they should consider possible compromises. Perhaps France would settle for a promise of *future* equalization of port privileges. They agreed to propose that, once Jay's treaty had expired, France be accorded access to American ports on a most-favored-nation basis. Murray hurried this proposal to Roederer so that the latter might include it in his report. He was ushered into the Frenchman's study only to meet a swift rebuff. Roederer balked at the prospect of future most-favored-nation treatment. Why not equality now? Surely Congress could undo the consequences of having abrogated the French treaty. If the British treaty now had priority, certainly an act of Congress could restore to France at least an equality of privileges for her privateers.

The Frenchman recoiled in disbelief when Murray explained that regardless of what action Congress might take, the courts of his country would uphold the exclusivity of the anterior treaty, Jay's treaty. Roederer exclaimed: "Then the Judiciary are your masters—They set up to direct

15. Entries of May 23 and 24, 1800, "Some Remarks"; also U.S. Ministers' "Journal," *ASP FR,* II, 325.

16. See French Ministers to Talleyrand, May 26, 1800, AAE EU, 52, folios 47v–48; and Murray's entry of May 23, 1800, "Some Remarks."

the diplomatic interests of the U. S." Their conversation ended with the Frenchman still unconvinced. His subsequent report to Talleyrand plainly reflected Roederer's conviction that the United States could, if she wished, revive the port privileges. Throughout the interview Roederer had been markedly candid. He allowed Murray to read Talleyrand's original instructions to the French delegation. He even read aloud to Murray the report he was drafting to Talleyrand, speaking so rapidly, however, that Murray missed parts of it. What he did learn—and this was significant—was that the French ministers were strongly advising the Foreign Office not to try to resurrect the old treaties *in toto*. For example, the U.S. treaty pledge to guarantee France the possession of her West Indies came in for particular ridicule. Murray reminded Roederer, however, that France had not invoked the "guarantee" and urged him to "dismiss those passages." This Roederer did.[17]

Amid all the ramifications of multiple treaty abrogation, the American commissioners now knew that the French felt most keenly the loss of Articles 17 and 22 of the old commercial treaty. Article 17 had permitted French warships access to American ports in possession of any prizes they might have taken. By the same article, American ports had been closed to the prize-bearing warships of any power at war with France. Article 22 had made American ports off limits for either the fitting out of enemy ships for hostility against France or for the sale of French vessels taken prize by an enemy of France. Once exclusive to France, these privileges were now exclusive to England under Articles 24 and 25 of Jay's treaty. What made possible the proffer of *future* most-favored-nation treatment was the fact that Articles 24 and 25 would expire two years after the signing of an Anglo-French peace. The French, however, wanted equality *immediately*.

The French ministers, meanwhile, put the question to Talleyrand. Should they try to argue the old treaties back to life? They advised against it. Those treaties had proved their worthlessness to France, and had merely jeopardized the neutrality of the United States. What they proposed, therefore, was to abandon the old treaties, salvage the port privileges, and resist all claims for indemnification. Talleyrand was easily persuaded; he relayed all three proposals to the First Consul on June 3.[18]

A month passed before Bonaparte's presence could be brought to

17. Cf. Murray's entries of May 24 and 25, 1800, *ibid.;* and French Ministers to Talleyrand, May 26, 1800, AAE EU, 52, folios 36–49.

18. See French Ministers to Talleyrand, May 26, 1800, *ibid.;* Talleyrand's report to the First Consul: "Point de vue actuel de la négociation avec les Etats-Unis," June 3, 1800, *ibid.,* folio 63.

bear. During the hiatus, Murray and Charlotte gave themselves over to the simpler pleasures of Paris. They strolled the boulevards, stopped at cafés, and rhapsodized at the sights and sounds and even the air of that city. As usual, when good health returned to him, Murray took an avid interest in the smallest details of his surroundings. Out of curiosity, perhaps, or an American's admiration for feats of engineering, he paced off the Bridge of the Revolution and solemnly recorded in his diary that it was 180 yards long. Later, a visit to Versailles evoked his observation that in its stillness and splendor the palace of the Sun King was "a graveyard of the imagination." Also at Versailles the Murrays met an old Frenchman who claimed to have fought in the American War for Independence. Murray promptly pensioned him with a fifteen-sou piece and listened amiably while the soldier's ancient spouse "who seemed half drunk cursed the Revolution heartily." [19]

Bonaparte returned to his capital on July 3, 1800, having won a stunning victory against the Austrians at Marengo. His return was the signal for some preliminary sparring between the French and American delegations. Early July might be called the "option" period of the negotiation as Ellsworth and his colleagues, hoping to keep intact the American claims for indemnity, began to emit a series of conditional concessions. One "option" plan would hold France liable for indemnity if within seven years the United States chose to restore France's exclusive port privileges. Failing a restoration of privileges, France would be forever quit of any liability. A second plan would erase Article 11 of the old alliance treaty by which each party had guaranteed the other's New World possessions. Again, the United States would have seven years in which to commute this obligation to a payment of eight million dollars.

This sum would erase both the "guarantee" and the port privileges, but leave France still liable for indemnity claims.[20]

On July 11 a discussion of the "option" plans only produced more bickering over Jay's treaty. On July 15, however, Ellsworth laid down a virtual ultimatum. Certain that their instructions would stretch no further, the Americans had agreed that Ellsworth should present the *ne plus ultra* of optional solutions. The spoliation claims against France were to be ascertained but not paid until such time within seven years as the United States should choose to restore all the exclusive port privileges of Articles 17 and 22. To this proposition the French ministers

19. Photostat Diary, 28–30, 136–136v.
20. French Ministers to Talleyrand, Messidor, An 8 (June 20–July 19, 1800), AAE EU, 52, folios 117–18v.

retorted sharply that port privileges would never constitute a *quid pro quo* for indemnities. Moreover, France did not want exclusive port privileges at some future time; she wanted equality with Britain at once. Impossible! answered Ellsworth; Jay's treaty had superseded. Warning that this was the "ultimate proposition," Ellsworth urged the French to weigh it carefully and not to hasten with an answer. As the meeting broke up, Roederer whispered to Murray that Ellsworth's proposal had little chance of being accepted. Murray could only reply that he hoped it would, because the envoys had reached the limits of their instructions.[21]

Bonaparte himself cut short the talk of "options" when on July 20 he told Roederer to tell the Americans that he would not sign any treaty which recognized, however temporarily, Britain's superior rights in American ports.[22] Thereafter, it was William Vans Murray who did more than either of his colleagues to keep the negotiation alive and flexible. He conducted most of the envoys' research, opened several hopeful avenues of compromise, and kept in close touch with Roederer. Until the hope vanished, he worked to save the indemnities. When the question of indemnity claims passed beyond reach he redoubled his effort to conclude at least a peace settlement. This last was imperative, for only a genuine *détente,* honorable to his country, could save John Adams and the moderate Federalists in the forthcoming election.

Murray's first opportunity for positive action came on July 25, when he learned that Pichon had roused Ellsworth out of bed the night before to ask if the Americans would agree to revive Article 17 merely to the extent of according most-favored-nation treatment to French privateers and prizes. Ellsworth liked this proposal. Murray, however, at first saw no hope for it because "equality was on the same principle as revival," and revival was precluded by Jay's treaty. Then, struck forcibly by what appeared to be Pichon's implication that the U.S. indemnity claims might thus be saved, Murray executed an abrupt about-face. Parenthetically, Pichon's nocturnal visit wore the mark of a Talleyrandian duplicity. Twice Talleyrand had counseled Bonaparte to revive the old treaties, not *in toto* but with "interpretive stipulations" yielding France's exclusive rights under Article 17 in exchange for equal rights with England. When

21. U.S. Ministers' "Journal," July 15, 1800, *ASP FR,* II, 327–28; entry of July 15, 1800, "Some Remarks."
22. Entries of July 20 and 21, 1800, *ibid.;* for the exchange of notes which halted discussion of the options see U.S. Ministers to French Ministers, July 23, 1800, *ASP FR,* II, 328–29; French Ministers to U.S. Ministers, July 27, 1800, AAE, EU, 52, folios 182–84v.

Pichon brought this proposal to Ellsworth he must have hinted that by conceding equal port status the U.S. might keep her indemnity claims intact. Why otherwise would Ellsworth and Murray have welcomed it? Quite likely, however, Talleyrand's purpose was not to lay a basis for American spoliation claims, but rather to weaken the Americans' contention that no part of the old French treaties could be revived. If such was his intent, he succeeded. Murray began at once to build a legal case for restoring as much of the old treaties as would satisfy France that she was receiving a *quid pro quo* for indemnities. He also set about convincing his colleagues that such restoration, though counter to their instructions, was legally possible, politically safe, and perhaps rendered unavoidable by Bonaparte's victory at Marengo.[23]

Had the British treaty been signed after July 7, 1798, Murray argued, any return to the exclusive features of the French treaties would be impossible. But Jay's treaty dated from 1794, at a time when London had accepted the exclusiveness of the French-American engagements. Britain could not, therefore, claim treaty rights resulting from a Franco-American dispute if, subsequently, France and the United States chose to recall a status quo under which Britain had not possessed those rights. Moreover, it could be argued that the French treaties had not been voided by war, and only one party had repudiated them. Despite what he had earlier said to Roederer, Murray now contended to his colleagues that Congress must still have the power to reverse its act of abrogation. To deny the existence of such power was to place the Franco-American dispute beyond congressional remedy.[24]

Murray was roundly rebuffed when he repeated these arguments to his colleagues at the rue de Sèvres. Davie was particularly hostile. London, said Davie, would never acquiesce to a loss of port privileges. "The British will say, 'you can settle with F[rance], but your settlement cannot displace our vested rights.' " Again, Murray denied that this was so. Davie's argument would be valid only if Jay's treaty had been signed *after* the abrogation of the French treaties. But Jay's treaty dated from the time when the French treaties were still in force. Any revival of those treaties now would return Britain to the status of 1794. Moreover, Britain might consider herself the gainer inasmuch as France was only asking for most-favored-nation treatment, not a restoration of exclusive privileges. Still, Murray recognized the force of Davie's argument. It

23. See Murray's entries of July 25 and 27, 1800, "Some Remarks;" also Talleyrand's "Raport au Premier Consul," 6 Thermidor, An 8 (July 25, 1800), AAE EU, 52, folio 175v; French Ministers to U.S. Ministers, 8 Thermidor, An 8 (July 27, 1800), *ibid.*, folios 182v–183; and French Ministers to Talleyrand, same date, *ibid.*, folio 179–179v.

24. See especially entries of July 25, 27, and 28, 1800, "Some Remarks."

would sit badly with London to lose the recently acquired and exclusive port rights—unless, of course, it could be shown that Britain herself had revived old treaties to the detriment of parties to newer ones.

To that end, Murray began to search the annals of European treaty practice. He found a French precedent immediately. France, in 1783, had recalled the Treaty of Utrecht so far as to renew an exclusive right of British privateers to bring prizes into French ports, despite the obvious conflict between this Utrecht provision and Article 17 of the Franco-American treaty of 1778. Because a British precedent was harder to find, Murray turned to Roederer for help, explaining to the somewhat embarrassed Frenchman what he had already uncovered. Roederer proved to be less knowledgeable than Vattel and Mably, but by August 5 both men had found what they were looking for. Lord Malmesbury, during the abortive peace mission to France in 1797, had offered to renew the Anglo-French treaties of 1678, 1715, 1763, and 1783. This meant that London had been prepared as recently as 1797 to restore port privileges to France of the type which had accrued *exclusively* to the United States under Jay's treaty.[25]

Although as an example of British practice the Malmesbury proposal was flawed by its not having been followed by an actual treaty, both Ellsworth and Davie agreed that Murray had found a good talking point. Davie displayed some irritation at Murray for fraternizing with Roederer, to which Murray replied soothingly that he and the Frenchman had already been "on the same ground." Ellsworth was less critical. Murray later recorded that when he read to Ellsworth the relevant passage from the Malmesbury proposal the Chief Justice "was charmed—as it goes home to the point." [26]

By early August Murray was persuaded that he and his colleagues might still save the indemnities if they restored to France the substance of Article 17. Legally, restoration was possible. It could be justified to England from precedent. But most important, the growing likelihood that France would make peace with her European enemies seemed to weaken the Americans' bargaining position. As Murray put it: "There is such a thing as being left in the lurch at a Peace"; any delay at this point in the negotiations would weaken the envoys' ability to wring concessions from France later.[27]

---

25. Murray's dealings with Davie and Roederer have been pieced together from dated (July 28 through August 3, 1800) and undated entries, probably within the same time-span, in "Some Remarks." These pages also include copies of Murray's note of July 30 to Roederer, and the latter's reply of August 3.

26. *Ibid.*, entry of August 6, 1800.

27. *Ibid.*; also U.S. Ministers to Secretary of State, Paris, August 15, 1800, *ASP FR,* II, 332.

How badly mistaken the Americans were in assuming that they could get France to pay indemnity in return for a modification of Article 17 became painfully clear on August 11 when the French ministers announced that Bonaparte had laid down an ironclad, either-or proposition. Either France would indemnify, but only if the old treaties were completely restored, or France would refuse to indemnify if the Americans insisted on writing a new treaty. In the latter event, France would at least require an equality with England in the matter of port privileges.[28]

That Talleyrand, through Pichon, had deliberately deceived the Americans into believing that they could obtain indemnification short of full treaty renewal cannot be proved. Talleyrand unquestionably preferred a no-indemnity settlement, but he was willing to discuss alternatives that were considerably broader than those now set forth by the First Consul.[29] Had Pichon's overture been calculated to disrupt and weaken the American position, however, it could not have succeeded more fully. The envoys, having been seduced from their initial contention that the old treaties were dead beyond recall, and having gone so far as to admit the possibility of partial treaty restoration, now found themselves vulnerable to Bonaparte's alternatives.

Although the injection of these alternatives seemed to dictate an abrupt narrowing of the negotiations, the diplomatic dialogue in fact continued to proceed down the path it had taken on the night of Pichon's visit: that is, indemnities versus partial treaty restoration. This was largely because Ellsworth and Davie refused to accept the immutability of Bonaparte's all-or-nothing options. Thus Article 17, and to a lesser degree Article 11 (the guarantee), remained the focus of ministerial exchanges.

Murray had little patience with his colleagues' subsequent efforts to break down the First Consul's alternatives. Put to a choice between old treaties plus indemnities or a new treaty without indemnities, Murray saw positive merit in the latter. To call back the old treaties, he believed, would be destructive of good relations. And French promises of indemnity payments would not be worth "three shillings in the pound." [30] Better to make a new treaty, he argued, and forego those claims for

28. Talleyrand received Bonaparte's instruction on August 5 (AAE EU, 52, 207–208), conveyed it to the French negotiators the same day (ibid., folios 209–10v); and the Americans received it on August 11, 1800, (ibid., folios 231–33v).

29. See Talleyrand's "Raport au Premier Consul," undated but probably of late July; and another report to Bonaparte dated July 25, 1800, ibid., folios 169–70v, 171–77v.

30. Entry of August 13, 1800, "Some Remarks."

maritime damages which France in all likelihood would never honor. Murray's line of argument with his colleagues would have been unanswerable had he known what instructions Talleyrand had already given the French negotiators with respect to indemnities. The French ministers had been told on August 5 that if they must agree to indemnities, they should arrange to pay as little as possible and at the remotest possible date. Ways could be found later to avoid payment altogether.[31] As it was, Murray strove in vain to persuade Ellsworth and Davie to give up the indemnities. He noted unhappily in his "Remarks on the Negotiation" entry of August 12, that his colleagues were "firm agt. abandoning compensation."

Ellsworth led off the meeting next day with a query. Did the French government intend that old treaties be recalled *"in totidem verbis,"* or would it entertain modifications? The French ministers replied that the treaties "must be renew'd in their integrity as if never interrupted." Any modifications would constitute a new treaty and come under the second, no-indemnity alternative. Once the old treaties were explicitly and totally recalled, however, France might agree to make such changes as would not diminish her exclusive port privileges.[32]

Though the choice was plain, Ellsworth and Davie refused to come to grips with it. A disheartened Murray analyzed his delegation's predicament. They would have to decide what part of their instructions to violate. The *sine qua non* of indemnities? The caveat against reviving the alliance? Or a revival of Article 17 without saving Britain's rights under Jay's treaty? His own view was unchanged. It was "better to relinquish money than to replace painful treaties." This truth was so evident to him that he again took it to Ellsworth and Davie, only to meet with another rebuff. Murray's temper flared. If his colleagues would not listen to reason, they should at least keep the State Department informed of the difficulties that had arisen. Specifically, a letter then being drafted to Pickering should include his own opinion that one or the other of the French alternatives be accepted. To Murray's chagrin, even on this point his colleagues "dissented absolutely." Next day he recorded cryptically in his diary: "we agreed to the letter to govt. & signed it." Angry and baffled by his colleagues' stubborn inflexibility, Murray nonetheless gave them credit where it was due. To John Quincy Adams he observed that whatever the truth of earlier reports that Ellsworth had been cool to the mission, the Chief Justice was now "heart and soul occupy'd to make

31. Talleyrand to French Ministers, 17 Thermidor, An 8 (August 5, 1800), AAE EU, 52, folio 210–210v.
32. Entries of August 13 and 14, 1800, "Some Remarks."

it succeed. So is D[avie]. So am I." [33] Thus, though the embassy was jarred by personal animosities and now rent by a severe difference of opinion, it retained that essential unity without which Murray knew it could not succeed. Murray had no wish to play the fatefully disruptive role of an Elbridge Gerry.

On August 15 the envoys began to press what Murray called "Mr. Ellsworth's propositions," a series of proposals which resisted Bonaparte's alternatives with schemes for saving the indemnities while writing off the worst features of the old treaties. Whether or not the French would accept these proposals, Murray ventured to the younger Adams that at least they would "bring things to a speedy conclusion." [34]

Despite Murray's doubts as to its acceptability, Ellsworth's proposal of August 15 devised an ingenious formula for saving the indemnities without quite meeting the French requirement that the old treaties be restored. It proposed a new treaty, but incorporated all of the former treaty provisions except the two which had caused the most difficulty. These two would be disposed of by cash payment. Specifically, the United States would offer to pay one million dollars and thereby reduce France's exclusive port privileges under Article 17 to the status of most-favored-nation. Another million dollars would be paid by the United States to erase forever that obligation embodied in Article 11 of the alliance treaty, wherein each party had guaranteed "forever" the other's possessions in the New World. In both cases the United States was to have seven years in which to comply. Significantly, however, the U.S. claims for maritime spoliation would be kept separate and intact.

Murray instantly saw a major complication. Until such time as the United States actually paid France for accepting a reduced status under Article 17, the French would insist on full and exclusive privateer-and-prize privileges in American ports. To avoid the awkwardness that such a claim would pose to Anglo-American relations, Murray suggested to his colleagues that a first installment of $100,000 be offered in order to effect an immediate reduction of Article 17. Ellsworth and Davie dismissed this suggestion, although they had to agree with Murray that London would certainly object to any arrangement which would allow France to assert exclusive rights in American ports during the seven-year waiting period. Their final draft, therefore, simply requested France not to ask for more than most-favored-nation status until the seven-year period had elapsed. Murray doubted that this would be accepted. He warned his colleagues that France would never consent to wait seven

33. Paris, August 20, 1800, *AHA Report of 1912*, 652.
34. *Ibid.*, 652; see also entry of August 15, 1800, "Some Remarks."

years before demanding the privileged status of Article 17—or its monetary equivalent.[35]

The French reply of August 25, while it did not reject the Ellsworth plan flatly, introduced a new element which defeated the Americans' purpose. The French replied that they might accept seven years of most-favored-nation port status, but, if by the end of that time the United States had not offered—*or France had not accepted*—the full restoration of Article 17, France would be relieved of all obligation to pay indemnities. Murray doubtless spoke his colleagues' chagrin when he wrote: "They absurdly supposed that we cd. accept 7 yrs suspension of their exclusive right as an indemnity." [36]

This fruitless exchange might have brought the negotiations to a standstill had not Murray received intimations from Roederer, during a dinner meeting on August 24, that the Alsatian had been busying himself with compromise proposals which might fit within the Ellsworth framework. Next day Murray and Davie, armed with a variant of the Ellsworth plan, conferred with Roederer in his study. Would France, they queried, agree to expunge Articles 17 and 22 from the old commercial treaty as well as Article 11 of the alliance if the United States would pay its own citizens' claims up to $1,600,000? France, of course, would remain liable for claims over and above this amount. Roederer's response indicated that this was not what he had had in mind. Like his colleagues, Roederer intended to resist the demand for indemnities. Where he differed from the others was in his willingness to write off not only Article 17 but the other two controversial articles as well. This became clear when Murray and Roederer met alone on September 5. The United States, said Roederer, could rid herself of her obligations under all three disputed articles, but only if she agreed to indemnify her own citizens for *all* the maritime spoliations committed by France.

Murray reacted sharply. His countrymen would regard it as a "slap in the face" to be asked to assume the full amount of French damages. Then, with more guile than was his wont, Murray contended that the U.S. payment of $1,600,000 might conceivably cover France's liability He could scarcely have made a convincing case on this point, inasmuch as he privately reckoned that France had done nearly forty million dollars' worth of damage to American shipping. When the two men parted, Louis Pichon, the sole witness to this meeting, observed with

35. See entries of August 15, 16, 18, and 20, 1800, *ibid.;* also U.S. Ministers to French Ministers, August 20, 1800, *ASP FR,* II, 333–34.
36. Cf. French note of August 25, 1800, AAE EU, 52, folio 258; entry of August 25, 1800, "Some Remarks."

misplaced optimism that Murray seemed inclined to accept Roederer's proposal. Next day, however, a note from the American commission termed it "altogether inadmissible." [37]

The final version of Ellsworth's payoff plan, broached to the French on September 6, proposed to revive the old treaties but commute the "guarantee" to a money payment and require each party to indemnify the other's claimants—with this condition: that the United States might later opt for a complete release from the old treaties by agreeing to drop all claims for indemnification. Although this last condition closely approximated Roederer's proposal, it differed significantly in its insistence that the decision to forfeit the claims must belong to the United States alone. This the French could not accept. When the French delegation replied that France must have an equal right of choice, the negotiation reached its final deadlock. The Americans observed unhappily that to give France this choice would be "to abandon absolutely the indemnities." [38]

Tempers ran short at a climactic meeting on September 12. After wrangling with the Americans over the question of whether both parties or only one should be permitted to wipe out the indemnities, the French fell back on their immutable alternatives of August 11. As he watched the Americans leave the room for consultation, Louis Pichon thought they wore "an air of satisfaction and almost triumph." He overheard Murray remark that "all is finished at present." When the envoys returned they were met with Joseph Bonaparte's angry accusation that they had tried to modify the old treaties while still claiming indemnities. He would resign from the commission, said Bonaparte, rather than put his signature to a treaty which accorded both alterations and indemnities. At some point in this meeting, and perhaps explaining the Americans' "air of satisfaction," the French ministers blurted out that their purpose throughout had been "to avoid, by every means, any engagement to pay indemnities." Such an explanation was "quite unnecessary," the Americans replied smugly. As the delegations ended their

37. The substance of these conferences has been reconstructed from the U.S. Ministers' "Journal," August 26, 1800, *ASP FR,* II, 335–36; entry of August 26 in "Some Remarks;" Murray and Davie to Roederer, August 26, and U.S. Ministers to French Ministers, August 29, AAE EU, 52, folios 262–262v, 265–265v, respectively; French Ministers to Talleyrand, "Conférence du 17 fructidor, An 8" (September 4, 1800), *ibid.,* folios 268–71v; and U.S. Ministers to French Ministers, September 6, 1800, *ASP FR,* II, 336–37. For Murray's earlier estimate of French damages see his letter to JQA, The Hague, April 26, 1799, *AHA Report of 1912,* 545.

38. U.S. Ministers to French Ministers, September 6, *ASP FR,* II, 336–37.

session, the French promised to make a written reply to the American note of September 6. There was no indication that it would be anything but negative.[39]

The negotiation seemed to have run its course. For more than four months the French position had gradually hardened, and was now at the point where the Americans could no longer remain deaf to the voice from Paris which said: You may have a new treaty if you will forsake the hope of being indemnified for maritime losses. But, if you will take back the alliance and commercial treaties of 1778, we will indemnify you. To this last, Murray could only have added the word "maybe."

39. French Ministers to Talleyrand, "Conférence du 25 fructidor An 8 (September 12, 1800) et jours suivans jusqu'au 4 vendémiaire An 9 (September 26, 1800)," AAE EU, 52, folios 289–307v; also U.S. Ministers' "Journal," September 12, 1800, *ASP FR*, II, 337.

15

The Franco-American Convention of 1800

IT WAS THE Americans who broke the diplomatic logjam when on September 13, 1800, they called on their French counterparts to sign a temporary convention. Postponement was the key. By making a convention, the envoys arranged to put off the resolution of both the treaties and indemnities questions until such time as they might be settled "with fewer embarrassments." Until then they made good their insistence that the old treaties would "have no operation." Failing of their major endeavor, the Americans aimed now simply to end the hostilities, secure the return of captured vessels not yet condemned, and prevent future seizures by reaching agreement with France as to future maritime practices.[1]

That the long months of negotiation ended with a convention instead of a rupture was largely the accomplishment of three men: Talleyrand, Murray, and Ellsworth. From Talleyrand came the will to persevere lest all hope of Franco-American reconciliation be dashed by France's recovery of Louisiana. The Frenchman knew that no accommodation with the United States would long survive the news that "Spain is to restore New Orleans to us." Whatever was to be salvaged for France in her relations with the United States must be put on paper before the news broke.[2] From Murray came the relentless argument that an end to hostilities and a release from the old treaties were national advantages of far greater worth than French promises of indemnity. In the end, his colleagues tacitly accepted the hardheaded wisdom of Murray's contention. Oliver Ellsworth's contribution was, simply, that to this day

1. U.S. Ministers to French Ministers, September 13, 1800, *ASP FR,* II, 339.
2. See Talleyrand's "Raport au Premier Consul," undated and not sent, probably written in late July and certainly illustrative of Talleyrand's concern, AAE EU, 52, folios 169–70v.

Americans may rest assured that no alternative was left untried before one of their greatest legal minds concluded that the United States had to be extricated "from a contest which it might be as difficult to relinquish with honour, as to pursue with the prospect of advantage." [3]

Few of the twenty-seven articles contained in the finished convention caused any serious controversy during the drafting sessions. The decision to defer to the future the two major items of difference made these sessions largely a process of adapting the American proposal of May 8, 1800, to the minor alterations which Talleyrand had suggested to the First Consul in August. Old specters, however, were not entirely laid. The French found it necessary to repulse a last-ditch effort by Ellsworth to get a more definitive commitment as to the future of indemnities, and the Americans suspected the French of trying to resuscitate the old commercial treaty in the latter's suggestion that Article 2 of that treaty be made the basis for restoring vessels not yet condemned. On this last point, the envoys insisted that vessels be restored under procedures delineated by the new convention. The only serious crisis developed on September 26, when the French grandly announced their hope to convert the draft convention into a full-fledged treaty of amity and commerce. Only by threatening immediate rupture did the Americans persuade their opposites that they were determined to make nothing more pretentious than a convention.[4]

For diplomats, who sometimes brood over the reactive potential of their own triumphs, no victory is so satisfying as that which can also be claimed by the other side. Such was the easy decision to reaffirm that principle of neutral rights known as "free ships, free goods," by which the neutral flag of the merchantman confers immunity from seizure on its cargo. By their instructions, the envoys could have omitted this principle because it had also been omitted from Jay's treaty. To have left it out of the convention, however, would have conceded to France a tacit right to seize British-owned goods from American bottoms. The French, with a show of magnanimity unwarranted by their motive, nonetheless insisted on renewing this tenet of neutral privilege. Their motive, which was not apparent to the Americans, was to raise France's

3. Ellsworth to Pickering, quoted in Pickering's letter to Oliver Wolcott, Philadelphia, January 3, 1801, Gibbs, *Wolcott*, II, 462. This phrase first appeared in the envoys' dispatch to Secretary of State John Marshall, Paris, October 4, 1800, *ASP FR*, II, 343.
4. See French Ministers to Talleyrand, reports entitled: "Conférence du 2e jour Complémentaire" (September 19); "Conférence du 3e jour Complémentaire" (September 20); and "Conférence du 4e Vendémiaire (September 26) in AAE EU, 52, folios 293, 295v–298, and 301–307v, respectively.

standing as a champion of neutral rights in the eyes of the neutral nations of northern Europe. As Talleyrand had impressed on Bonaparte, it would be impolitic for France to thrust aside a liberal reading of neutral rights at a time when the northern powers were organizing to resist the illiberal practices of Great Britain.[5] Each side, then, was gratified: the Americans, because they had won a point they had been willing to yield; the French, because they had won the same point under the guise of making a concession. Murray was pleased but not altogether convinced by the ease with which the French had been persuaded. He wrote John Quincy Adams that as an earnest of France's future behavior the French promise to observe "free ships" was probably not worth a thousand guineas. He admitted to McHenry, however, that immediate application of the principle would probably expedite the release of American vessels.[6]

Minor controversies were easily disposed of. The French made only minimal protest when the Americans insisted that the *rôles d'équipages* (crew rosters) no longer be required among the ship's papers of American vessels on pain of confiscation. For their part, the Americans put up only token resistance to the return of captured naval vessels, notably the *Insurgente,* taken in battle by Commodore Truxtun in 1799. Nor was either delegation disposed to object to the mutual recovery of public and private debts—so long as they were not classified as indemnities.[7]

During the last four days of September the peacemakers haggled briefly over what to name the document and what language to designate as the original. Thanks to Bonaparte's intercession, it was declared to be a "convention" and signed in both languages. Since this met the Americans' specifications, the envoys were pleased to gratify the First Consul's wish that the convention state that it was made in his own name and that of President Adams, rather than in the names of their respective governments. Dated September 30, 1800, but signed at two o'clock in the morning of October 1, the convention received Bonaparte's formal ratification the following day during a ceremonial fête given by Joseph Bonaparte at "Mortefontaine," the latter's country estate outside Paris.[8]

5. Talleyrand to the First Consul, 22 Thermidor, An 8 (August 10, 1800), *ibid.,* folios 227–227v.

6. To JQA, The Hague, December 22, 1800, *AHA Report of 1912,* 666; to McHenry, Paris, October 3, 1800, Steiner, *McHenry,* 495–96.

7. U.S. Ministers' "Journal," September 22, 1800, *ASP FR,* II, 340; also the French Ministers' "Conférence" reports of September 20 and 24, AAE EU, 52, folios 295v–298, 301–307v.

8. For more detail on these last-minute changes see the French Ministers' "Conférence" reports of "4e Vendémiaire" (September 26) and "4e Vendémiaire

Incisively, with sharp, deft strokes of his pen, Murray spread the festive panorama of Mortefontaine across the pages of his diary.[9] His quick, discerning eye perceived the pathos as well as the grandeur of France's new order. His host, the fierce Joseph Bonaparte who had recently vowed to rupture the negotiation rather than put up with Ellsworth's further equivocations, now subsided before Murray's eyes into an indolently graceful, mild-mannered man whose surprising "flow of literary knowledge comes from him like an insensible perspiration"— and beside him his wife, Madame Bonaparte, who seemed "a small delicate woman—a little jealous."

Later, Murray found Pichon standing alone and dejected in a room crowded with many of the nearly two hundred diplomats and high government officials who had made Mortefontaine their place of business mixed with relaxation for the weekend. Pichon explained miserably that he lacked the social connections that might have made this gathering, for him, an opportunity to advance his career. Murray, whose sympathies were instantly touched, did what he could to introduce Pichon to the "right people." But even the "right people" looked somehow ill at ease in their own setting—the aging Josephine, for example, whom Murray saw sitting in a corner suffering visibly, he thought, amidst the youthful tribe of Bonaparte.

In late afternoon the clatter of an armed and mounted escort announced the arrival of the First Consul. Five minutes later Murray found himself alone in the garden with the Man of Brumaire. Here they walked and talked for half an hour, Murray trying to keep the conversation general but yielding finally to the temptation, offered by their solitude, to urge on the master of France that he make peace with England. As long as the two great powers remained at war, he pointed out, the virtually uncontrollable activities of French privateers would continue to abrade Franco-American relations. Only a peace between France and England could assure that the newly made convention would succeed in its purpose. Whatever Bonaparte may have responded, Murray was more impressed by what the man was than by what he said. The First Consul, he wrote, was

> grave, rather thoughtful, occasionally severe—not inflated nor egoistic—very exact in all his motions wh. show at once an im-

et jours suivans" (September 26 and days following), *ibid.*, folios 316–19, 320–320v; also WVM to JQA, Paris, October 5, 1800, *AHA Report of 1912*, 654–55; and Roederer to WVM, September 25, 1800, Misc. Letters, WVM MSS, LC.

9. The following account is drawn from a twenty-four-page entry in a small green diary which Murray entitled "Fete given by Mr. Joseph Bonaparte at his Chateau of Morfontaine [*sic*] on Friday the 3rd Oct. 1800," WVM MSS, LC.

patient heart & a methodical head—not the exactness of a special
pleader—but of a most skilful self possest Fencing master. . . .
he speaks with a frankness so much above fear that you think he
has no reserve—He is a pleasing man with the Soldier drawing
into the politician—He could never have been a trifler in his life."

Next day, returning from a hunt (he had shot a doe), Bonaparte caught
Murray by surprise with his questioning of the American reaction to 18
Brumaire. What did Americans think of the new regime? Murray's reply was as candid as he could make it. "The friends of order & rational
liberty," he said, speaking of the Federalists, "rejoiced at it as bringing
France back to reason." Those of his countrymen who were attached
to the ideal of stable and orderly government would welcome Bonaparte
as the pacifier of political extremism. Among American Republicans,
however, Murray admitted that the highly centralized nature of the new
French regime would not sit well. As for himself, he told Bonaparte, he
believed that France "could not do with govt. less strong."

Some of Murray's vignettes were sketched straight-faced, others
tinged with amusement. Charlotte, he reported, on arriving at Mortefontaine "after a ride of 22 miles & a dish of tea," had found that she
required the escort services of two ambassadors and their wives to
reach the nearest water closet. Murray described delightedly the elaborate protocol which attended this mission of urgency. A short while
later another crisis occurred when Ellsworth's son was seized by two
dragoons who mistook him for an intruder. Murray effected a rescue,
however, and sent the younger Ellsworth upstairs to join his father. The
Chief Justice, unhappily, spent most of his time at Mortefontaine in bed,
suffering what Murray diagnosed as an attack of kidney stones.

Throughout the fête the entertainment was lavish. A "superb" state
dinner was followed by a fireworks display that was somewhat dampened
by an evening rain. There was a prophetic note in Murray's observation
that because of the wet "the emblems of amity between U. S. & F." did
not go off. But the evening banquet remained the most memorable high-
light to Murray, replete with toasts to Franco-American amity, drunk by
150 French notables while cannon boomed a salute to the new era.
Later that evening the guests repaired to a small theater to watch a
comedy and to hear songs specially composed to commemorate the
occasion. Not until three o'clock in the morning did the festivities cease.

Next day, while Ellsworth and Davie set off for Le Havre to take
passage home, the Murrays returned to Paris in their coach. Lafayette
rode with them. The marquis alternately slept and talked politics during

the ride, convincing Murray that estimable though it was, the general's revolutionary idealism was somewhat out of date. He recalled that at Mortefontaine Bonaparte had been "very civil to him [Lafayette], notwithstanding he would talk about liberty." [10]

The Murrays had planned to return to The Hague within the week. Their departure from Paris was delayed, however, when Charlotte contracted chills and fever after a day's excursion to Ermenonville, where they had visited the grave of Rousseau. Not until October 17 did they leave Paris, even though Charlotte was not fully recovered. As they passed through the countryside between Valenciennes and Brussels, Murray was struck with nostalgia and a longing for home. This is "a low country like Dorset," he wrote.[11]

Murray now foresaw the approaching end to his mission at The Hague. His presence there, now that the quarrel with France was healed, no longer served its earlier purpose. Even if John Adams were reelected, Murray had no wish to prolong his mission. Moreover, his health was poor and his vitality low. Once back at The Hague he wrote John Quincy: "I neither read nor write, for as yet my books are unpacked, and I do not know but it is best to let them sleep as undisturbed as I do." What he could not foresee was that his mettle as a diplomat would be tested by that most delicate phase of the negotiation, the exchange of ratifications. Until May 20, 1801, when he received orders to proceed once more to Paris, he assumed that whoever Jefferson appointed minister to France would transact the final business.

Though he threatened to sleep, the politician in Murray remained alert. The months following the signing of the convention posed several questions, the answers to which, he knew, must have a political reading. Would France observe the convention in good faith and thereby add to Adams' chances for reelection? What if London, by protesting the new treaty, gave Adams' enemies an argument against his diplomacy? And finally, would the Senate itself, still Federalist but split, give the necessary two-thirds approval? Murray wrestled uneasily with possible answers. He sensed, however, that no matter how fully the success of the convention might vindicate Adams it had come too late in the political season to help in his reelection. And this he deeply regretted. He explained to the President's son that at Paris the envoys had been balked, time and again, in their efforts to speed the negotiation. "All was done—

10. To JQA, Paris, October 5, 1800, *AHA Report of 1912*, 654–55.
11. WVM to JQA, Paris, October 10, 1800, *ibid.*, 657.

all—that could hasten it; in vain." Now, only the "good sense" of his countrymen could still save the election for Adams.[12]

As weeks passed, Murray and the younger Adams agreed with philosophical resignation that, whatever the outcome of the election, the President had won a victory for the national interest that would be remembered long after his detractors were forgotten. Gradually both men concluded that Adams would be brought down by the irrational enmity of the Hamiltonians, regardless of the success of the convention.[13]

The convention, meanwhile, *did* succeed. Even before the signing, Talleyrand promptly responded to the envoys' request that prize cases be suspended forthwith. The Foreign Minister immediately notified the French Council of Prizes that the principles of "free ships" was now in force, and that American vessels were no longer subject to condemnation for lack of *rôles d'équipages*. Talleyrand also wasted no time in alerting the Ministry of Marine to the likelihood that the United States would demand indemnification for any American vessels illegally seized between the time of signature and the exchange of ratifications, a warning that was quickly heeded. Within a week the Minister of Marine had circularized this warning to the six naval districts of the metropolis, as well as to the appropriate colonial officials.[14]

Back at The Hague, Murray was inclined to be doubtful. When the first American vessel was released, he noted that the French "always begin well." By December, however, even Murray was impressed when the Prize Council released eleven more ships. When news arrived that the Senate had acted favorably on the convention, still more vessels were returned to their owners. That France intended to carry out the spirit as well as the letter of the convention was further confirmed by Major Mountflorence, now American consul in Paris, who reported intermittently to Murray throughout the early months of 1801.[15] Perhaps more than anything else, Louis Pichon's appointment as chargé d'affaires in Washington attested most clearly to France's wish to couple the

12. The Hague, November 7, 1800, *ibid.*, 660–61.

13. See Murray's letters to Adams of December 22 and 30, 1800, *ibid.*, 667, 670; and JQA to WVM, letters of October 30, December 16, 1800, and January 10, 1801, Adams MSS, MR 134.

14. See Talleyrand to the Government Commissioner at the Council of Prizes, AAE EU, 52, folios 328–328v, 368–70v; also Talleyrand to Minister of Marine Pierre-Alexandre Forfait, Paris, 16 Vendémiaire, An 9 (October 8, 1800), and 18 Vendémiaire, An 9 (October 10), *ibid.*, folios 371–74v, 383–84v; and Forfait to Talleyrand, 21 Vendémiaire, An 9 (October 13), *ibid.*, folio 386–386v.

15. To JQA, The Hague, November 7, 1800, *AHA Report of 1912*, 661; WVM to Marshall, No. 121, The Hague, December 28, 1800, and a private letter to Marshall, dated January 30, 1801, in Netherlands Despatches, I.

convention with a genuine détente. Pichon was Talleyrand's personal choice for the interim post. Murray, who liked Pichon, would have agreed with Talleyrand's recommendation to Bonaparte, in which Pichon was described as a man of "discernment and conciliatory nature." He would have applauded even more the content of Pichon's instructions, for not only was Pichon to bend every effort to suppress illicit privateering in the French West Indies, but he was also strictly enjoined to keep himself out of American politics. Pichon followed these instructions to the letter.[16]

The road to rapprochement was not entirely without potholes, however. Murray encountered two minor difficulties with the convention itself, and worried at greater length about the effect of French sponsorship of a new "armed neutrality."

As to the convention, Murray chafed irritably when the French Foreign Office allowed its text to be published in the *Moniteur* only two days after his colleagues had left France. Publication violated an earlier agreement that only Article 4, which stipulated the return of vessels not yet condemned, be made public. The envoys had insisted on secrecy lest the convention "become the subject of popular discussion even before the Govt. has it officially." [17] Anticipating a protest from Murray, Talleyrand authorized the French minister at The Hague to convey an apologetic explanation. France had published the full text of the convention, Murray was told, in order to quash rumors that it was not being executed. Murray also discovered the real reason: France wanted her championing of maritime neutral rights to be known among the northern powers of Europe. As Murray and his colleagues had predicted, however, the convention became a matter of public knowledge when copies of it arrived in Baltimore more than a month before Davie was able to reach Washington with the official text.[18]

Although he deprecated this premature disclosure of the treaty, Murray was far more alarmed by the uncertainty which suddenly appeared

16. See Talleyrand's "Report au Premier Consul," 29 Vendémiaire, An 9, (October 21, 1800), AAE EU, 52, folio 390–390v; and Talleyrand's instructions to Pichon, Paris, 11 Brumaire, An 9 (November 2), followed by supplementary instructions simply dated Brumaire, *ibid.*, folios 403–403v, 417–18v.

17. WVM to Jean Luzac, editor of the *Leyden Gazette*, The Hague, October 28, 1800, Misc. Letters, WVM MSS, LC.

18. Talleyrand to Sémonville, Paris, 13 Brumaire, An 9 (November 4, 1800), AAE EU 52, 410–11; see also Murray's entry of March 15, 1801, Photostat Diary, 174v.

to exist in Article 6. Here, in familiar shape, was the ghost of Article 17 of the old commercial treaty which, when alive, accorded exclusive U.S. port privileges to French privateers. As embalmed in Article 6, those privileges had been reduced to those of the most-favored-nation. Whether or not the ghost walked depended on whether France became the immediate possessor of this equal status, or would have to await the expiration of Jay's treaty.

Two weeks after the signing, Murray learned from Pichon that France intended to enter an immediate claim. Murray recorded that at that time he had "made no reply—as we had agreed not to give, individually, any construction—." Later, when he heard that the Senate was questioning this article, he recalled that the envoys had seen no violence to Jay's treaty in reviving a prior obligation to France. Morever, without this concession contained in Article 6 there would have been no convention. Still, the question remained: did France benefit immediately or must she wait? Because neither the Senate nor the administration was able to answer this question, Murray was vastly relieved to learn in early October, 1801, that Britain and France had made peace. Two years later, Britain's exclusive port rights under Jay's treaty would automatically expire, leaving France with equal status in U.S. ports should the Anglo-French duel be renewed. The Peace of Amiens provided the solution to Article 6. "Ah," wrote Murray when he heard the good news, "it settles all our disputes [including] the questions which wd. have arisen on the operation of the 6 article of our convention." [19]

Though nagged by treaty matters, Murray showed much greater concern for the implications of that short-lived coalition of northern European powers known as the Armed Neutrality of 1800. Diplomatically, the conjuncture was "Franco-Russe"—born of Bonaparte's hope to win maritime allies and of Czar Paul's impatience with his erstwhile allies, Britain and Austria. By late 1800 the Czar appeared ready to lead Russia, Prussia, Sweden, and Denmark into a coalition which, though it would be technically neutral, would support France by its armed resistance to British maritime practice. Murray was fascinated by what the Armed Neutrality portended. He doubted, in the first instance, that the smaller neutrals could stop their own internecine bickering long enough to cooperate against England. Further, he doubted France's wisdom in seeking to extend the war into an element where British naval power would have telling effect. To be sure, if the armed neutrals succeeded, Britain would be cut off from her Baltic sources of naval

19. Undated entry of early October, 1801, Photostat Diary, 206v; also WVM to JQA, The Hague, February 9, 1801, *AHA Report of 1912*, 681–82.

supplies. To American suppliers as well as American carriers, to whom Britain must turn, this eventuality promised fat profits. "Should this miserable neutrality last three years," Murray predicted, "we may be great gainers . . . ," unless, of course, France tried to force the United States to cooperate with the armed neutrals to the extent of foregoing that profitable trade.[20]

That France earnestly desired American adherence to the Armed Neutrality Murray never for a moment doubted. He guessed correctly that Pichon bore instructions to persuade Jefferson of its usefulness. Morever, his soundings of political talk at The Hague fully convinced him that France would spare no effort to secure American participation. Few persons approached Murray directly on the subject because he made it known that he opposed it. On one occasion, however, the French minister at The Hague, a man named Sémonville, regaled him with a number of reasons ("facetious," Murray called them) why the United States should cooperate. Sémonville listed such advantages to the United States as "glory in obtaining Liberty of the Seas—that money is the root of evil & by making too much we shd. lose our virtues—besides our population wd. be thinned . . . an advantage to those who survived." [21]

Despite such nonsense, Murray was relieved when the Armed Neutrality fulfilled his predictions of internal weakness, then collapsed altogether with the death of the Czar. Having been chastened by Nelson's destruction of the Danish fleet at Copenhagen, the league of armed neutrals melted away entirely when the new Czar, Alexander I, found Britain receptive to a rapprochement. Thus, by May of 1801, the few clouds which had darkened the prospect of Franco-American reconciliation were blown away, leaving only the problem of Louisiana (which did not involve Murray) and the delicate business of exchanging ratifications (which did).[22]

Senatorial insistence on modifying the terms of the convention was bound to complicate the later exchange of ratifications. It was possible, even, that the Senate might defeat the treaty, so formidable were the

20. WVM to JQA, The Hague, January 20, 1801, *ibid.*, 675.
21. Entry of February 11, 1801, Photostat Diary, 165v; see also WVM to JQA, February 3, 1801, *AHA Report of 1912*, 680.
22. For Murray's running disparagement of the armed neutrality see especially his dispatches to Secretary of State Marshall, No. 118 (November 1) and No. 120 (December 4, 1800); No. 122 (January 4, 1801), No. 126 (January 30), No. 127 (February 7), No. 130 (April 10), and No. 132 (May 7), Netherlands Despatches, I.

forces ranged against it. Certainly the voices of party leadership on both sides spoke with strong reservation. Thomas Jefferson called it "a bungling negotiation," and foretold that, unmodified, the convention with France might compromise good relations with Britain. Madison, too, found it "remarkable" that Ellsworth and his colleagues had revived Article 17 in such a way as to deprive Britain of the exclusive port rights which had accrued to her by Jay's treaty.[23]

Republican misgivings were more than drowned out by the strident chorus of objections which arose from the ranks of the High Federalists. Timothy Pickering, who laid the treaty's defects to Davie and Murray, was plainly astonished to learn that Ellsworth himself had endorsed the whole. Pickering gladly accepted Wolcott's explanation— that Ellsworth must have been "enfeebled by sickness"—and proceeded to denounce the treaty in four particulars and damn it in entirety as being worse than no treaty at all.[24] Similar utterances, ranging from amazement to dire warnings of British hostility, came from others in the High Federalist hierarchy. Almost alone, Alexander Hamilton counseled restraint. Amid the High Federalist outcries came Hamilton's cool warning that unless the convention were ratified the Federalist party would be "utterly ruined." "Moreover," he added, "it is better to close the thing where it is, than leave it to a Jacobin administration to do much worse." Nor was Hamilton willing to argue the possibility of British objection. Britain, he wrote, has "no good cause to complain." The United States, he felt, was well within its rights to rescind its earlier act of treaty annullment "even to the restoration of the *status quo*." Murray had made the same argument in Paris.[25]

As it turned out, London had no objection. Rufus King reported— and John Adams forwarded the report to the Senate on January 21, 1801—that Lord Grenville "saw nothing in the convention inconsistent with the treaty between them and us, or which afforded them any ground of complaint." [26] Knowing full well that Federalist opponents of the convention would snatch at any word of demurrer from London, Murray was elated when he heard the news. British acquiescence, he wrote, was

23. Jefferson to Madison, Washington, December 19, 1800, Ford, Jefferson's *Writings*, IX, 159; Madison to Jefferson, January 10, 1801, Hunt, Madison's *Writings*, VI, 413.

24. To Wolcott, Philadelphia, January 3, 1801, Gibbs, *Wolcott*, II, 462–63.

25. Cf. Hamilton to Sedgwick, New York, December 22, 1800, and Hamilton to Gouverneur Morris, New York, December 24, 1800, in Hamilton, *Works*, VI, 495, 496; and Murray's entry of July 27, 1800, "Some Remarks."

26. King to Secretary of State, London, October 31, 1800, *ASP FR*, II, 343–44; JA to the Senate, January 21, 1801, Richardson, *Messages*, I, 314.

"a triumph the completest over the 'mob of gentlemen' who have chirped so much against it, and filled their eyes with prophetic tears about certain consequences, etc., etc!" [27]

Finding the "British" argument blunted, the High Federalists turned their attack on specific clauses of the treaty which, in their eyes, made it unsuitable to the future of Franco-American relations. Under the onslaught, the convention went down to defeat on the Senate floor on January 23, 1801, only to be revived by its friends and passed in modified form on February 3.

When the news reached him in late January, Murray was not surprised to learn that John Adams had been defeated. The Federalist Party's deep schism, widened during the campaign by Hamilton's published attack on the President, combined with what he knew of his party's "gentlemen" politicians and their reluctance to soil their hands on the hustings—all prepared him for news of a Republican victory. Not expected, however, was the tie vote in the electoral college that resulted when each Jefferson elector also cast his second ballot for Aaron Burr. Although the Republicans had plainly intended to elect Jefferson to the presidency, the constitutional inability of the electors to differentiate between the offices of President and Vice President in casting their ballots had given Aaron Burr an equal claim to the highest office, and thus thrust the final decision into the House of Representatives. Of the two, Murray hoped that the House would elect Jefferson, a preference he did not explain except to note that "some of the first rate" Federalists in his own state of Maryland also preferred the Virginian.[28]

No matter whether Jefferson or Burr came from the House with the presidency, Murray could be sure that his days as a diplomat were numbered. Had Adams been reelected, Murray knew that he might have been appointed to Paris. Failing that, he would have agreed to stay at The Hague had Adams asked him to do so. The prospect of retirement —which had seemed so welcome to Murray after the months of arduous negotiation in Paris—had given way, perhaps inevitably, to ambition's hope for preferment. With the Republican victory, however, Murray saw no future for himself in the diplomatic service. He and William L. Smith at Lisbon were certain to be retired by the new administration. In their House days, he and Smith had been too articulate in their defense of Jay's treaty. Republican vengeance would be swift.

When he learned that James Madison had taken over the State Department, Murray became even more certain that partisan consider-

27. To JQA, The Hague, November 18, 1800, *AHA Report of 1912*, 662.
28. To Sylvanus Bourne, undated, Misc. Letters, WVM MSS, LC.

ations would dictate changes in the diplomatic corps. Still, of the party
Republicans he knew, Madison, he felt, was "the best of them all."
If good judgment had any claim on the new administration, men like
John Quincy Adams, Rufus King, and David Humphreys (at Madrid)
might still be kept at their posts. Even if the Republicans saw fit to
appoint one of their own to Berlin, Murray hoped that they would have
the good sense to keep his friend John Quincy Adams in the service,
either at Copenhagen or St. Petersburg.[29]

Whether Murray would have agreed to serve a Jefferson administration either at Paris or The Hague he himself did not record. The
possibility that Jefferson might appoint him was too remote. He could
only hope that whoever was named to Paris would also be charged
with exchanging the ratifications of the convention. In view of the
alterations which the Senate had effected in that document, he had no
wish to undertake such a mission.[30] In its final passage, the convention
had been modified by the Senate in two respects. Article 2, which lumped
old treaties and indemnities for future negotiation, had been expunged
altogether. What this deletion signified of the Senate's intentions re-
garding these two items was not clear of itself. Second, and less puzzl-
ing, was the protocol the Senate attached, limiting the duration of the
convention to a period of eight years. President Adams had reluctantly
acceded to these two alterations on February 18 and had ratified, leaving to his successor, however, the matter of securing France's consent.
Exactly one month later Jefferson's acting Secretary of State, Levi
Lincoln, addressed letters to Murray and Ellsworth instructing either or
both to proceed to Paris. Ellsworth had already left for home after
wintering in England. This letter meant, therefore, that Murray alone
would have the delicate task of persuading Bonaparte that the Senate's
alterations should not preclude an exchange of ratifications.[31]

29. WVM to JQA, The Hague, letters of April 25 and May 2, 1801, *AHA Report of 1912*, 694–95.
30. Entry of February 17, 1801, Photostat Diary, 168; also WVM to JQA, The
Hague, February 17, 1801, *AHA Report of 1912*, 683.
31. Murray's new instructions reached him on May 20. See entry of that date
in Murray's diary entitled "Another Mission to Paris," WVM MSS, LC, hereinafter referred to as "Another Mission."

16

The Final Mission to Paris

NEWS OF HIS last assignment reached Murray on May 15, 1801. It came from a Virginia congressman named John Dawson who, acting as courier for the State Department, arrived in Paris in early May. Dawson bore with him the official instrument of ratification which he was instructed to deliver to either Ellsworth or Murray. Finding neither man in the French capital and learning that Ellsworth had sailed, Dawson wrote Murray that he should come to Paris at once. Murray replied testily that he had no intention of going to Paris unless Dawson could produce official instructions. As Murray explained to John Quincy Adams, "I know the importance of finishing the business but . . . I cannot act so ridiculous a part as to run to Paris on the letter of a private man whom I do not know, that I know of, and who is but the mere bearer of the papers." He would go to Paris when ordered, but not before. Five days later, much to Murray's discomfiture, the order arrived from Acting Secretary of State Levi Lincoln.[1]

Murray's irritation with Congressman Dawson now turned to despair at what had emanated from the State Department. Lincoln's letter stated only what changes had been made in the treaty—not why they had been made, nor how they were to be construed, nor, except in the broadest sense, what room for maneuver Murray might allow himself in dealing with the French. Lincoln blandly supposed that France would not object to the Senate's modifications and that the exchange would be "a matter of course." He offered no explanation of the Senate's action in expunging Article 2 except to say that there had been "considerable diversity of sentiment on it." Should the French protest the suppression of that article, Lincoln proposed a solution that could result in endless circling. That is, Murray might agree to let the French restore Article 2,

1. Entry of May 15, 1801, Photostat Diary, 180; WVM to JQA, The Hague, May 16, 1801, *AHA Report of 1912*, 697.

but he must warn Paris that the Senate might subsequently "refuse a ratification in that form." On the eight-year limitation he was not to budge. The new administration, he was told, believed it unwise to make treaties of unlimited duration because "what is now advantageous, may soon become otherwise."

In his answering dispatch Murray remarked pointedly on the large number of unanswered questions. Was there any room for bargaining? Could he, for example, relinquish the eight-year limitation if the French agreed to the suppression of Article 2? Or could he make the restoration of Article 2 the price of French acquiescence in the limitation? And where, precisely, did the Senate's erasure of Article 2 leave the whole question of old treaties and indemnities? If Lincoln had sent further instructions to Paris, perhaps the answers to these questions were await- ing him there. He discovered that they were not.[2]

Because he left The Hague in such haste, Murray took the precaution of explaining the reason for his departure to the press. He had come to know the Dutch capital well enough to know how quickly rumors could multiply in the wake of any unexplained movement by a diplomatic person. On May 22 he drew a thousand florins on the Dutch bankers, packed Charlotte and her chambermaid, Mary, into a coach, and settled back to enjoy the scenery along the road to Paris, spending evenings recording each vignette in his diary. The first day out he got a painful bump on the head when, eager to see how his carriage was to be ferried across the Maase, he made the mistake of leaning out of the carriage window just as the vehicle jolted aboard the ferry boat. The blow was not disabling, just painful, and on the second day he wrote that "nothing could have diminished the pleasure of so sweet a ride but the idea of going on such a mission—ignorant as yet I am of my in- structions." [3]

The administration's failure to give him adequate instructions cost Murray two months of agonizing negotiation. It also cost American ship- owners that much more delay in recovering vessels on which legal proceedings were halted when word arrived in France that ratification had been made conditional. Had Murray known with certainty that the Senate meant to forego forever the indemnity claims against France

2. Acting Secretary of State Levi Lincoln to Ellsworth and Murray, Wash- ington, March [18], 1801, Despatches to Consuls, I, NA; and WVM to Lincoln, No. 134, The Hague, May 20, 1801, Netherlands Despatches, I. See also entry of May 20, 1801, Photostat Diary, 182–182v.
3. Entries of May 22 and 24, 1801, "Another Mission;" also WVM to Sylvanus Bourne, The Hague, May 22, 1801, Misc. Letters, WVM MSS, LC.

by its excision of Article 2, he might have completed the exchange within a week and a half of his arrival. (Exactly what effect the Senate intended is difficult to ascertain, although Hamilton's view that the spoliation claims had been "virtually relinquished" was probably representative.) [4] Unsure on this point, Murray spent weeks parrying French demands that he stipulate that relinquishment. Because his instructions were unclear, he finally agreed to a form of French ratification so unusual as to move President Jefferson to resubmit the convention to the Senate. Not until the Senate's further action of December 19, 1801, was the convention considered to be "fully ratified." [5]

Murray reached Paris on May 28 and lost no time in making his approaches to the Foreign Office. He spoke with Talleyrand on June 1 and learned that Bonaparte, Fleurieu, and Roederer would confer with him at the earliest possible moment. The American sensed an impasse, however. He found the Foreign Minister evasive, unwilling to commit himself to the expectation of "no difficulty." When they discussed the Senate's alterations, Talleyrand merely repeated that the French ministers would meet him in the near future. Suspecting that the French were in a mood for bargaining, Murray consoled himself with the thought that at least the Armed Neutrality was dead and there would be no pressure on him from that direction. On June 6 Murray was troubled when, on presenting his credentials, he found that the First Consul "did not appear much pleased with the provisional Ratification," though he was reassured that Bonaparte did not foresee any "insurmountable difficulties."

Two days later Murray conferred with the French commissioners. When he explained the Senate's action, they all agreed that the Frenchmen's "powers" would have to be broadened to permit them to treat with Murray in this unforeseen circumstance. Although this meeting lacked substance, something Roederer said after dinner confirmed Murray's suspicion that France would "insist on a formal abandonment" of the indemnity claims.[6] Still, Murray remained optimistic. He wrote John Quincy Adams the next day that his mission had thus far met with "no palpable obstacle except in the *delays*." [7]

Between June 13 and 19 the battle lines were drawn athwart the

4. Hamilton to Gouverneur Morris, New York, January 10, 1801, Hamilton, *Works*, VI, 515.

5. Jefferson to the U.S. Senate, December 11, 1801, Richardson, *Messages*, I, 332; U.S. Senate, *Executive Journal*, I, 398.

6. WVM to Talleyrand, letters of May 29 and June 1, 1801, AAE EU, 53, folios 129, 130, 132–132v. See also Murray's dispatches to Levi Lincoln, No. 1 of June 1 and No. 2 of June 9, 1801, Despatches from Paris, NA, the latter enclosing French Ministers to WVM, 18 Prairial, An 9 (June 7, 1801).

7. Paris, June 10, 1801, *AHA Report of 1912*, 698; also WVM to Henry Maynadier, Paris, June 13, 1801, WVM MSS, Maryland Historical Society.

meaning of the Senate's suppression of Article 2. Murray was closely pressed to explain the Senate's motives. Should France accept the removal of Article 2, would not the old treaties be dead beyond recall but the indemnity claims against France still be valid? The French obviously thought so. Roederer cited the maxim that treaties neither renewed nor recalled by subsequent treaty were understood to be abrogated. The only place in the convention where the old treaties were mentioned was in Article 2. Expunge that article, Roederer contended, and France would lose forever the benefits of the old treaties. Only if France were assured that Americans would *also* give up their claims for indemnity could she agree to forego the treaties. Could Murray give that assurance? [8]

In his diary Murray wrote: "This is tough for me—as I was for that article—& my instructions are silent upon the motives for its suppression! But I must make the best of it." By June 19 Murray was ready to confess to the French ministers that his government had not informed him as to the Senate's motives, but he supposed that Article 2 had been struck out lest it cause further difficulty between the two governments. He could only conclude that the removal of Article 2 had left matters just as they would have been had that article not been included in the convention in the first place. Indemnities were not claimable, as the convention now stood, but the United States might press them later. Old treaties were also dead, but they too might be subject to later revival. To Roederer's fretful assertion that old treaties became defunct unless they were explicitly recalled, Murray noted that several of the Utrecht treaties not renewed during the European settlement of 1763 had nonetheless been reinstated in 1783.[9]

The French ministers were not so easily persuaded. They reported to Talleyrand that while the eight-year limitation could be agreed to, the removal of Article 2 appeared to be a calculated scheme to keep the indemnity claims alive while killing off the old treaties. Further, with the disappearance of Article 2 the controlling principle for the future would be contained in Article 6 which prescribed most-favored-nation treatment. Moreover, Article 6 seemed to be "a positive recognition of the destruction of the old treaties" now that the second article had been removed. The French commissioners therefore advised the First Consul that should he decide to ratify, he do it conditionally. Bonaparte was

8. WVM to Madison, No. 3, Paris, June 23, 1801, Despatches from Paris, NA; also entry of June 17, 1801, "Commonplace" of 1800–1801.

9. Entries of June 17 and July 3, 1801, *ibid.;* also WVM to French Ministers, June 19, 1801, AAE EU, 53, folios 161–62 (original draft in WVM MSS, LC); and WVM to Madison, No. 3, June 23, 1801, Despatches from Paris, NA.

urged to stipulate that the suppression of Article 2 "signifies a renunciation by the United States of all indemnity, as well as a renunciation by France of old treaties." [10]

It remained now for the French to discover whether Murray had sufficient authority to consent to a conditional exchange. To that end the American was summoned into the presence of the First Consul. Bonaparte put the question bluntly: "Monsieur, avez-vous le pouvoir de discuter et signer?" Murray replied that he did, "conformement à mes instructions." Those instructions, he added gave him full power to execute all the business connected with the exchange of ratifications. Satisfied, Bonaparte turned to Talleyrand and told him to proceed with the negotiation. Murray was somewhat puzzled at being catechized in this manner and decided to make his own investigation of Bonaparte's "ratifying powers." To satisfy himself that Bonaparte's signature did not require legislative sanction, Murray drove directly from his audience with the First Consul to the Hôtel Chatillon to get the opinion of Count Cobenzl, the Austrian ambassador. Murray's doubts were set at rest when Cobenzl obligingly showed him a copy of the Lunéville treaty and assured him that Austria considered Bonaparte's sole signature perfectly binding on any diplomatic instrument.[11]

An uneasy quiet prevailed at a meeting on June 23. The French ministers were still waiting for fresh instructions, and both sides found themselves going over old ground. Although the delays began to tell on Murray, he refused to attribute them to "any fixed Intention" to defeat the exchange altogether. It was disturbing to know that James Mountflorence had picked up a rumor that France intended to reject the amended convention flatly.[12] Nor was Murray pleased with the conduct of John Dawson, the courier-congressman, who was hounding him to be quicker with the exchange of ratifications. Not only had Dawson offended him with his peremptory summons to Paris, but Murray had arrived in the French capital to find Dawson being described in the press as the new American minister. It appeared to Murray that Dawson rather enjoyed the illusion. He pointed out to the Virginian that twice in his presence the latter's French servant had addressed his employer as "monsieur le ministre." He swallowed hard at Dawson's efforts to pass off the deceit, in fact to deny it, on the plea that he was ignorant of the French language.

10. French Ministers to Talleyrand, 30 Prairial, An 9 (June 19, 1801), AAE EU, 53, folios 157–60v.
11. Entry of June 21, 1801, "Commonplace" of 1800–1801.
12. Entries of June 22 and 23, 1801, *ibid.*

While it bothered Murray that Dawson should pose as an accredited diplomat, it disturbed him even more that in such a false context the congressman should be consorting openly with such expatriate American Republicans as Thomas Paine and Joel Barlow. But most annoying of all was Dawson's nagging at him to be done with the exchange so that he, Dawson, could return to Washington with the instrument of ratification. Behind such importunings lay the unspoken accusation that Murray was deliberately delaying the exchange. Undoubtedly, the American community in Paris was beginning to wonder why Murray had not brought matters to a speedy conclusion.[13]

On June 25 the diplomatic battle began at close quarters. Murray discovered that afternoon why his "powers" had been so carefully scrutinized: the French were planning to offer a conditional ratification. As evening approached, the French ministers made it plain that they would not accede to the suppression of Article 2 unless Murray would sign a protocol abandoning both indemnities and old treaties. Ironically, this was the solution Murray had urged on Ellsworth and Davie nearly a year before. His arguments had been resisted then. Now he was alone, his retirement certain, his disgrace probable no matter what the outcome. It was possible to wipe the slate clean, to set at rest forever the nettlesome old French alliance at the mere cost of giving up his country's claims for indemnity, claims which he doubted could ever be collected. But what was now within his reach was not within his power. With scarcely a backward glance Murray turned, instead, to the unlikely arsenal of his instructions and drew forth Levi Lincoln's alternative: the reinstatement of Article 2. He warned the French ministers, however, that if Article 2 were restored, the convention would once more be thrown into the United States Senate where its chances of passage would be slim. Either France must ratify "purement et simplement," he told them, or face the likelihood that the Senate would reject the convention in its entirety.[14]

When the French commissioners shied at this offer, Murray guessed the reason. The Senate's removal of Article 2 was not without potential

13. See Murray's letters to Sylvanus Bourne (June 13, 1801), Jean Luzac (July 3), and Rufus King (July 5), all in WVM MSS, LC. See also Joshua Barney to General Samuel Smith, Paris, July 11, 1801, Jefferson MSS, LC, as cited by DeConde in "The Role of William Vans Murray," *loc. cit.* 194.

14. Entries of June 25 and 27, 1801, "Commonplace" of 1800–1801; also WVM to Madison, No. 5, Paris, June 26, 1801, and No. 6 of July 1, 1801 (enclosing WVM to French Ministers, June 27), Despatches from Paris, NA.

advantage to France. If the Senate's excision were carefully construed, France might spare herself a liability for maritime claims for all time. The French had no wish to reinstate Article 2 as long as they stood a chance of persuading Murray to sign away the indemnities once and for all. To that end Roederer put Murray to a choice of procedures on July 1. Either he might sign a *procès verbal* agreeing that within a year the two governments would exchange a treaty article declaring that the "respective pretentions which were the object of the Second Article shall never be reproduced," or Murray might sign an instrument of exchange in which this French construction was set forth. Either way, Murray's signature was called for—and to Murray this was the rub. He now recognized, however, that *form* was the all-important consideration. He could not put his signature to either a *procès verbal* or a conditional ratification. He could sign only a simple ratification, with or without Article 2. When he rejected Roederer's alternatives, Murray made it very clear that it was not the purpose of the French proposals that stood in his way; it was only the form they took which left him powerless.[15]

Ultimately, it was Murray himself who solved the dilemma and hit on the solution which broke the deadlock. After dinner with Roederer on July 5 he proposed to the Frenchman that he should "enter your article as you propose in the process verbal of Exchange, sign it & I can certify that fact—viz that you did exchange & that you signed that reserve." In sum, Murray agreed to bear witness to whatever the French might stipulate, without himself agreeing to the stipulation.[16]

There now followed some desultory skirmishing, and more delay. Bonaparte succumbed to a brief illness, and Talleyrand himself went off to take the waters. By July 25, however, Murray was nearly certain that his solution would be accepted, and was pleased when he weighed what might have been the alternative. Had he signed a conditional ratification, the convention would have had to have been resubmitted to the Senate. But a simple ratification accompanied by an interpretive statement would, he believed, finish the business once and for all.[17]

Murray's hopes were not disappointed. On July 23 he was notified that Bonaparte had agreed to his procedure. Accordingly, on July 31 Murray

15. French Ministers, to WVM, 14 Messidor, An 9 (July 3, 1801), AAE EU, 53, folio 166; entry of July 3, 1801, "Commonplace" of 1800–1801; and WVM to Madison, No. 7, Paris, July 2, 1801, Despatches from Paris, NA.

16. WVM to French Ministers, July 5, 1801, enclosed in WVM to Madison, No. 8, Paris, July 9, 1801, *ibid.*

17. See WVM to Madison, No. 9 of July 15, and No. 13 of August 3, 1801, *ibid.;* also WVM to JQA, Paris, July 15, 1801, *AHA Report of 1912,* 701.

and the French ministers signed an instrument in which there was no reference to qualification or condition. Then, in Murray's presence, the French commissioners signed a separate declaratory statement—written only in French and signed by them alone—stipulating that the First Consul consented to the amended convention "with the addition, however, that the Convention shall be in force during the space of eight years and with the suppression of Article 2; understood that by that suppression the two states renounce the respective pretensions which are the object of said article." [18]

Now that it was done, Murray suffered few of the misgivings which characteristically beset him in the aftermath of decision-making. He had "hazarded a little" in submitting to the French declaration, he told John Quincy Adams, but the business was now complete, and both could rejoice that the former President's policy of reconciliation with France had finally been vindicated.[19] To James Madison he wrote without apology that he had pursued what he believed would have been Jefferson's instructions. Under the circumstances, "nothing better can be gained"— a plain aspersion on the administration's failure to instruct him fully. If his letter to Madison was cool, it was also because, five days before the exchange, Murray had received notice that he was being recalled from his post at The Hague. "It was a gauche thing," he wrote privately, "to recall me before an end to this negotiation." He had fully intended to resign at the end of the Paris mission, postponing the act only for the most obvious of political reasons: ". . . had this affair failed, they wd. have said I intentionally spoiled it! from ill humor to Mr. Jefferson!" Now, he added, "Govt. has saved me this delicacy!"

Stung by the humiliation of not being allowed to resign in due course, Murray next discovered "to my great surprise [he told Madison] that the French Government knew of my recall long before I did." Dawson, he suspected, was the informant. But when he pressed the Foreign Office as to their source of information he was told merely that they had "heard it" some two months before. Murray could scarcely comprehend the folly of an administration that could undercut its own minister "at a moment when he needs the certainty in the eyes of a foreign govt. that he had the confidence of his own govt.—! —This is a precious policy— and a strange fact!" he wrote in his "Commonplace" on August 6.[20]

18. WVM to Madison, No. 12, Paris, July 31, 1801, Despatches from Paris, NA; French Ministers to Talleyrand, 12 Thermidor, An 9 (July 31, 1801), AAE EU, 53, folio 198–198v.

19. Paris, August 8, 1801, *AHA Report of 1912*, 702.

20. For Murray's recall see Madison to WVM, Washington, D.C., June 1, 1801, Despatches to Consuls, I, NA; and Murray's response in his No. 11, Paris,

His sense of outrage made it easy for Murray to accept the fact of his recall. But even before the fact, he had decided that he did not care to serve Jefferson at The Hague. Moreover, he had personal affairs to attend to, not the least of which was the prospect of having to build a new house in Cambridge to replace the house his father had left him, which had been destroyed by fire that spring. What nettled him most, perhaps, was Jefferson's decision to close down the Hague and Lisbon legations altogether. As Dawson explained, the new President hoped to make economies—an explanation that sat so ill with Murray that he wrote to the administration urging it to reconsider.

The economy argument, he told Madison, broke down when measured in terms of diplomatic services rendered to American merchants. An American minister at The Hague, for example, "saves twice his salary to those concerned in trade." Moreover, the Dutch would be sorely offended to have the American legation closed. His chief objection, however, bore on the issue of national self-respect. American diplomats, he wrote, "add a lustre to our nation. They are the respected Seedsmen of opinions of slow but useful growth. They are besides, an important idea for us, a clear demonstration of an independence & free will." [21]

While Congressman Dawson rode off to Dieppe with the ratification documents, Murray spent his last days in Paris pressing the Foreign Office to get the Council of Prizes to resume the freeing of American vessels. In this Murray turned to Pierre Roederer, whom he had come to trust and respect. Roederer, however, did not see how the prize proceedings could be resumed until the Senate had acted with finality on the convention. Murray countered that even if the convention failed of final approval (though he did not believe it would) the United States was nonetheless presently executing its terms; therefore France was "bound to do so." Roederer was sufficiently impressed by this argument to promise Murray that he would take up the matter with Talleyrand. Having made this indirect approach, Murray then sought out Talleyrand personally and pressed the point again. The Foreign Minister seemed eager to oblige. What jostled Talleyrand into action was the possibility

---

July 27, 1801, Despatches from Paris, NA. Except for his August 8 letter to JQA (*AHA Report of 1912,* 702), Murray confined most of his bitterness to the pages of his "Commonplace" of 1800–1801; see, for example, entry of July 30, 1801.

21. WVM to JQA, Paris, Letters of June 10 and July 15, 1801, *AHA Report of 1912,* 699, 701; WVM to Madison, No. 11, Paris, July 27, 1801, Despatches from Paris, NA. See also entry of July 27, 1801, "Commonplace" of 1800–1801; and Murray's draft essay entitled "Foreign Relations U.S.," Photostat Diary, 188v, WVM MSS, LC.

that any delay in freeing American vessels might bring renewed claims for indemnification. He wrote at once to the Council of Prizes. By early September, Murray could report that Talleyrand was as good as his word: American vessels were once more being released by the prize authorities.[22]

Murray's mission ended amid a scattering of official reactions. Talleyrand wrote Pichon that Murray's reading of what the Senate had intended to accomplish by the removal of Article 2 was "full of wisdom," although the Senate's ratification itself he termed "inevitably unusual, irregular and incomplete." Only France's desire for harmony, he told Pichon, had kept the government from refusing to complete the negotiation.[23] On the other side of the Atlantic, Madison and Jefferson— though they fully understood the difficulty Murray had felt in his lack of instructions—could not understand why he had hesitated to erase the indemnity claims. Madison so completely accepted this meaning of the Senate's expungement of Article 2 that he suspected France of holding Murray up for altogether new treaty terms that would more nearly match her improved posture in Europe since the original signing. Other than this, Madison was becoming far more preoccupied with the Louisiana question. Whatever the reasons for Murray's delay, Madison was now singlemindedly intent on urging Robert Livingston to hasten to Paris—not only to assure the French that the convention was being executed, but also, and more importantly, to dissuade France from accepting the retrocession of Louisiana from Spain.[24]

Jefferson, too, was mystified that Murray should balk at "nothing more than a [French] desire to obtain an express renunciation of the demand of indemnities." If this were the only obstacle, the President expected that Murray would surely complete the exchange. By mid-September, however, Jefferson was citing Murray's slowness as a good reason for speeding Livingston to France. More overtly slighting was Jefferson's observation that "the state of the treaty there calls for the presence of a person of talents and confidence; we would rather trust him [Livingston]

22. Entry of August 9, 1801, "Commonplace" of 1800–1801; also Talleyrand to Collet-Descoutils, member of the Council of Prizes, Paris, 29 Thermidor (August 17, 1801), copy enclosed in Consular Despatches from Paris, I, NA; and WVM to Madison, No. 14 (Part 2), Paris, August 11, 1801, *ibid.;* and same to same, No. 135, The Hague, September 2, 1801, Netherlands Despatches, I.

23. No. 4, Paris, 16 Thermidor, An 9 (August 4, 1801), AAE EU, 53, folios 211–12v.

24. Madison to Robert R Livingston, letters to September 4 (Monticello) and September 28 (Washington), 1801, Despatches to Consuls, I, NA.

than Murray in shaping any new modification." This reference to "modification" alluded to Jefferson's plan, if the convention failed, to have Livingston offer a single treaty article stipulating the return of prizes and thereafter leaving Franco-American maritime relations to trust, goodwill, and a promise of future most-favored-nation treatment.[25]

Ultimately, when Murray's talents proved equal to the task, Jefferson made no comment, either in his private correspondence or in his first annual message to Congress. What John Adams had begun William Vans Murray had completed and, although the Republicans were the political beneficiaries of the *détente* with France, their only show of approval was their overwhelming vote on the convention when it reached the Senate again in December of 1801. Although Murray had hoped that no further Senate action would be required, he had also foreseen that Jefferson might request it. In this he was correct, and in the Senate's ready acceptance of his handiwork lay Murray's ultimate vindication.

As to the worth of the convention itself, any historical appraisal must necessarily be inconclusive in some particulars. The treaty ended a phase of open hostilities with France and thereby served an important national interest. The year 1803, however, brought a renewal of war in Europe and a return to French transgressions against the neutral maritime principle of "free ships, free goods." In this sequel, Murray's impatient prediction was fulfilled: that no mere treaty could protect American shipping from indiscriminate seizures by warring powers. Too, whatever climate of Franco-American good will the convention might have engendered was almost immediately clouded by the Louisiana question. To say that the treaty cleared the air or contributed importantly to the U.S. purchase of Louisiana would be to scant the much more relevant causative factors in that transaction. Perhaps the most that could be said of the convention in this context is that it had a pacifying effect on Franco-American relations without which Louisiana diplomacy would have been complicated by unsettled maritime questions.

On the domestic political scene, the convention was the symbol rather than the cause of the Federalist party's demise. The party's long decline can be partly explained by the High Federalist quarrel with John Adams over the expediency of making peace with France. Disintegration was foreshadowed when Murray first began to listen to Louis Pichon at The Hague in the summer of 1798. It became more probable when Adams,

25. Jefferson to Madison, Monticello, September 12, 1801, and Jefferson to Gallatin, Monticello, September 18, 1801, Jefferson's *Writings,* IX, 303 and 305, respectively.

setting aside the counsel of his cabinet, decided for peace. But it became certain only when the High Federalists revealed the narrow and inflexible purposes of a small-based mercantilist program and marched, ranks asunder, into the catastrophic election of 1800. For individual Federalists, marooned by the shipwreck, the day would come when they could sign on with the Jeffersonians and find comfortable berths in a party made broad-beamed by the stresses of national responsibility. John Quincy Adams would make that transition, and Murray might have done so had he lived. For the near future, however, Murray no longer saw himself playing either a diplomatic or a political role. What remained of his life was brief. What remained of his public career was to be even briefer.

The Murrays left Paris August 12, delayed at the last moment by Lafayette's appearance for a last, long round of philosophizing on what Murray called the marquis' "PRINCIPLES." Finally they boarded the carriage and began the trip back to The Hague. Charlotte had an upset stomach which was not improved by their first meal on the road, taken at a post-house in Cambray where the fish was rotten and the veal "villain." But at least the innkeeper was apologetic. Not so the stableman, who offered no apologies for keeping the travelers' horses in an abandoned church. Murray became so incensed at the sacrilege that he asked the man if he were "the priest," and felt no regret when the peasant stamped away angrily without answering. Next day, with Charlotte feeling somewhat better, the party took to the road again; and a week later they arrived at The Hague.[26]

Less than a month after their return to the Dutch capital the Murrays embarked for home, their stolid Dutch friends surprising them with tearful goodbyes as they boarded ship. As was the official custom, the Batavian Directory tendered Murray a parting gift—in Murray's case a gift of fine linen which he estimated was worth about 1,500 guilders. Sadly, Murray refused, knowing that he could not accept any sort of gratuity without the congressional permission which he refused to apply for. Later he inquired of Madison whether the President might make a distinction between customary and extraordinary gifts, this being a customary one. Whatever the answer, he made it clear that he wanted no "legislative notice" taken of his inquiry. Madison answered from

26. See entries of August 12 and 14, 1801, "Commonplace" of 1800–1801; and WVM to Madison, No. 135, The Hague, September 2, 1801, Netherlands Despatches, I.

precedent: no distinction could be made. Unless Murray were to ask the consent of Congress, "the compliment is understood to have been declined." [27]

On an evening breeze, the vessel which was to carry them home slipped out of the harbor at Helvoet Sluys. The date was September 16, 1801. More than four years had passed since the mission had begun. Now, standing on deck in the gathering dusk, Murray took one last look at the fast-receding town of Helvoet "whose little spire & low shore," he wrote, "I view'd in twilight with emotion." [28] A few days later, during a layover in Falmouth, they encountered another homeward-bound diplomat, William L. Smith, whom the new administration had recalled from Lisbon. It was a consolation, he wrote Adams, to meet "a brother in disgrace." [29]

The same head winds that had forced their vessel into Falmouth continued during the Atlantic crossing. It was a slow passage—eleven weeks in all—made anxious for Murray by the low state of Charlotte's health. He sometimes read to her from his diaries to pass the time, and spent other moments wondering about his own future. Ahead lay the tasks of rebuilding both a house and a law practice. Too, he had yet to collect part of his official salary, the amount of which was uncertain. Yet, for all these worries, his spirits rose as the voyage drew to an end. At four o'clock on the morning of November 27 Murray came on deck as their ship sailed past Cape Henry. Overhead, he wrote, was "a fine serene sky—bright sun—an American sky!" Then he recalled another homecoming, his return from London as a young man, and wrote proudly, "When I came in here 14 yrs. since there was no lighthouse—so rapidly speeds our country." [30]

When his ship docked at Alexandria on December 2, Murray evoked little curiosity from official Washington. When no one came to question him, he wrote Adams with some irony that, since he had little to report, he was content to keep what little he had to himself. Then bitterly: "This it is to be disgraced, and is among the means by which it is clearly demonstrated that a minister is a useless thing in my poor little Holland." Murray was not completely neglected, however. Although the administration did not seek his counsel on official matters it did treat him cordially. He dined with Madison one day, and found the new Secretary

27. WVM to Madison, Georgetown, Md., January 3, 1802, *ibid.;* Madison to WVM, Washington, January 7, 1802, Despatches to Consuls, I, NA.
28. Entry of November 10, 1801, Photostat Diary.
29. Cambridge, Md., April 3, 1802, *AHA Report of 1912,* 702.
30. Entry of November 27, 1801, Photostat Diary.

of State "more cordial than any one else." Jefferson also had him to dinner, but Murray left no account of it. Most important, he had no difficulty in collecting his salary for the earlier Paris mission. His old House rival, Albert Gallatin, now in the Treasury Department, paid him off on a scale equal to that of Ellsworth and Davie, thus satisfying an equity on which he had had some doubts earlier.[31]

Back on the Eastern Shore, Murray set about picking up the pieces of a private existence. His diary now began to record the details of a reviving law practice, its entries having to do mostly with land surveys and patenting. His less frequent letters to John Quincy Adams spoke of books still unpacked while work went forward on building a new house from the bricks of the old one. Here, too, on the banks of the Choptank, there were crops to be planted and landscaping to be supervised. His neighbors, he was sure, were laughing at him for planting forest trees along with the fruit-bearing varieties. But on the whole, life was emptier now. Instead of the excitement of people, places, and events, Murray filled his leisure hours peering through a new telescope by night and a solar microscope by day.[32]

One thing was certain: Murray had no intention of returning to politics. Not only could he not indulge the expense of campaigning, but also he felt that the field had become weed-choked. It repelled him. His district, he wrote Adams, was still Federalist among the gentry and generally so among the people, but from the ten or so Republicans who had infested it in 1797 there were now about a hundred. This decision not to return to public life cost him a price which, had he lived, he might not have been willing to continue to pay. Even as the isolation of life in Cambridge settled around him, there reappeared that deep pessimism which had so often before sent him back to the political fray. In his next-to-last letter to John Quincy Adams he spoke worriedly of the rumors of New England separatism. Nor was he consoled that only by war, never by mere political act, could the Union be dissolved. If it came to civil war, he wrote: "Dear me! we should have Great Britain and France by the hand in the struggle, and be fighting their European jealousies in the United States." Those who advocated disunion could have but one object, though to Murray it seemed far-fetched, which was "that by a dissolution we might have a civil war; and after, come together on the old ground of a STRONG GOVERNMENT, which I think we want. I know no nation that wants one more for the preservation of its

31. WVM to JQA, Cambridge, April 3, 1802, *AHA Report of 1912,* 703–704.
32. See WVM to JQA, Cambridge, August 10, 1802, *ibid.,* 706–708, and scattered entries following page 211 in the Photostat Diary.

liberties, and I never heard of one which had so few materials to make one!" From this prophetic note Murray went on to discourse on the uncertainties facing his countrymen in the future.

> The strange thing is that in America you can not tread in the past, nor can you . . . realize that *beau idéal,* of which the perfectionists have so much talked, here and in Europe of late. We are vibrating between both; our theories with the last, our manners with the first. How can a money loving people who have no prejudices but for income, get back into the track which the past indicates . . . or into the new doctrines which presuppose men to be angels? . . . As the patient can not die of the complaint, nature must be left to herself. What the cure will be God knows.[33]

Murray died on December 11, 1803, whether in Cambridge or while visiting in Philadelphia is not known. Neither the cause of his death nor his place of burial is known, although in the early 1950s workmen excavating the site of a new high school near the former Murray estate uncovered bones which may or may not be his. His passing went almost unnoticed except by John Quincy Adams, who published a lengthy tribute to his friend in the *Boston Portfolio,* January 7, 1804. Adams' most touching farewell, however, was scribbled at the bottom of Murray's last letter to him.

"In my memory and hopes his existence will cease but with my own."

33. Cambridge, Md., April 3, 1802, *AHA Report of 1912,* 704.

17

An Appraisal

SINCE MURRAY'S day, the American diplomatic establishment has grown from a nucleus of one Secretary of State, two clerks, and six ministers-resident to a staff of approximately 3,100 foreign service officers. Although this growth seems fully warranted by the complexity and variety of overseas problems which face the United States today, perhaps an even more fundamental change has occurred in the perceived role of the chief of mission. Few would deny, for example, that today's instant communication between the State Department and its embassies has drastically reduced the number and types of initiatives once expected of the ambassador. Today, when opportunity knocks or crisis explodes, the sound is heard immediately in Washington by those who have the responsibility for formulating an official response. The ambassador becomes the instrument of that response; he runs little risk of over-stepping his authority.

Such, obviously, was not the experience of the eighteenth-century American diplomat. His instructions were general, often irritatingly vague, and designed at most to cover only a few foreseeable contingencies. Faced with crisis or with an opportunity to secure advantage for the United States, he was expected to take the initiatives which the moment presented—to seize them, hold them, and pursue them with advantage until explicit instructions arrived from Philadelphia. Working in this milieu of great distances and long pauses, the diplomats of the Federalist era proved to be rather cautious men. As a group they were more than ordinarily sensitized by their political backgrounds to an awareness that precipitate action might have undesirable domestic consequences. They tended to move slowly, wait patiently, and to consult with one another before taking action. In a sense, they constituted an overseas cabinet whose members regularly sought one another's counsel but who, as individuals, knew that they alone would answer for any initiatives which good policy dictated they should take. The slowness of communication imposed on them responsibilities for independent action which today's diplomat would find hard to imagine.

Although Federalist emissaries enjoyed more latitude in performing their official duties than do their modern counterparts, they also suffered a greater likelihood of being superseded. In an effort to overcome the communications "lag," early administrations often sent special emissaries to deal with specific crises. Thus William Short, who laid the groundwork for the treaty with Spain, was joined by Thomas Pinckney—who concluded the negotiation and won the credit—just as John Jay had earlier superseded Pinckney in the treaty-making which had transpired at London. So, too, did Murray feel himself uncomfortably overshadowed when Oliver Ellsworth and William R. Davie were named first and second in the commission which subsequently negotiated the Franco-American convention of 1800. In Murray's case, it was partisan politics which required the additional appointees. Because Murray had offended war-hawk Federalists by appearing to be too receptive to French peace overtures, he was teamed with men who could be more confidently counted upon not to let France off easily. That he was not superseded altogether signified the trust in which he was held by John Adams.

Despite the uncertainties of their profession, Federalist diplomats never labored under any doubt as to the cardinal principle of American foreign policy. Amid the multitude of mere diplomatic objectives—such as opening the Mississippi, settling the Florida boundary, recovering the Northwest posts, or getting indemnities for maritime spoliations—they knew that Washington and Adams had no more important or sustained policy purpose than to keep the United States out of war. Parenthetically, one should make the distinction here between neutrality and noninvolvement. Neutrality was a condition of nonbelligerence partly defined by the rights which a nonbelligerent government must insist upon, and otherwise sustained by the duties which it must observe. By so insisting and so observing, neutral nations ostensibly immunized themselves from military involvement. This immunity was not certifiable, however, because the rights and duties themselves were not clearly agreed upon. Nor, in fact, were they all-important, because the end transcended the means; and the end was to prevent the United States from slipping into war on either the side of Britain or France. This is not to imply that Federalist statesmen were heedless of the protocols of neutrality. But their chief and overriding aim was to keep the United States at peace.

Thus, the Federalists who truly believed that Jay's treaty had averted a disastrous war with Britain could overlook the violence which that treaty had done to the Franco-American concept of what constituted this country's legitimate rights as a neutral. But France could not overlook it; nor could her partisans in the United States. The treaty which ostensibly averted war with Britain set the stage for a warlike crisis with France. How many early American statesmen recognized the primacy of peace to the nation-building process cannot be determined with any degree of accuracy. Until the crisis with France, however, one might search in vain to discover a prominent figure who actively advocated war with any country. There was talk of war, to be sure, during the crisis which Jay's treaty brought to a close, and some speculation, too, on the likelihood of hostilities with Spain until Pinckney's treaty settled the southwestern river and boundary disputes with Madrid. But it was only with the French crisis known as the Quasi-War that such positing passed beyond mere talk and speculation to engage the endorsement of an organized political following—in this case, the High Federalist war hawks.

Seldom in American history has foreign policy so deeply divided the people of this country as it did the late 1790s. Because the lines of division were partisan they were the more disruptive. To put it simply: Republicans were pro-French, Federalists were pro-British. How profoundly this alignment split the body politic can be illustrated by hypothesizing a modern parallel. Suppose, for example, that today's Republican party gave its support to NATO while the Democrats sided with the Warsaw Pact nations. One can well imagine the cries of outrage and the charges of treason that would be heard. And yet this parallel, however superficial, speaks to the highly emotional temper with which eighteenth-century Americans, neglecting what Murray called the "middle ground," became in fact apologists for one or the other of Europe's two battling giants.

Although as a Federalist he saw greater national advantage in his country's alignment with London than with Paris, William Vans Murray was nonetheless schooled in the Washington-Adams dictum that national survival depended on avoiding a major war. To Murray, peace was a substantial blessing, as nourishing to the young nation as the bread which men live by. But as a discerning nationalist Murray knew that nations cannot live by peace alone, especially if the approaches to peace are accompanied by national humiliation. Even powerful nations cannot afford to make peace settlements which are visibly dishonorable. For small nations the results may be fatal. This explains why Murray rejoiced at the disclosures of the XYZ dispatches: his country was not going to allow France to hide the fact that she had attempted to wheedle money out of the United States as the price for a treaty of accommodation. It explains, too, why Murray was elated by the warlike responses to XYZ that issued from Congress, and why his own responses differed little from those of the most ardent war hawk.

Murray contributed most notably to the drift toward peace when, in the first instance, he risked the disfavor of his Federalist compatriots by listening to the conciliatory overtures which Louis Pichon brought to The Hague from Talleyrand in the summer of 1798. Murray not only listened, but he also weighed carefully what Pichon told him against John Adams' stated requirement that if France wanted to end the quasi-war she must guarantee a respectful reception to any American mission that might be sent to Paris. In short, there must be no repetition of the shabby treatment accorded to Pinckney, Marshall, and Gerry. It was to Murray's credit that he succeeded in extracting from the French Foreign Minister assurances of diplomatic reception couched in language that admitted of no equivocation and that responded to Adams' requirement in every particular. Moreover, Murray made it clear to Paris that the assurances which he relayed to Philadelphia would in no way obligate the President to respond to them if he chose not to do so. As it turned out, Murray's diplomacy gave John Adams the soundest possible documentary basis from which to accept the French overture. Of itself, the decision to renew negotiations with France rested squarely on the President, but it was a decision made more fully acceptable because, as Adams himself remarked, "the diplomatic organs were all perfect and complete." For that perfection and completeness Adams could thank William Vans Murray.

The importance of Murray's accomplishment can best be understood, perhaps, in the context of the loud and clamorous opposition it evoked. For a time it seemed as though the party's war hawks might seriously impair the Chief Executive's authority for the conduct of foreign affairs. Had the French promises of good behavior been any less explicit than Murray had succeeded in making them, that authority might have been even more severely challenged. As it was, Murray put in Adams' hands the one document that gave official evidence that if another mission were sent to Paris it would be received with respect. With that assurance Adams could now move surely, despite opposition, toward the peace settlement which he knew must be effected sooner or later.

Once the negotiation began there seemed little likelihood that it would abort. From the time Ellsworth and Davie sailed from Newport in November of 1799 until the signing of the convention the following

September, nothing occurred in either France or America to reverse the progress toward reconciliation. Quite the contrary; while Ellsworth and Davie were still at sea, a peace-minded Talleyrand returned to the French Foreign Office under a newly formed regime headed by Napoleon Bonaparte, one of whose initial objectives was to make peace with all of France's enemies. An accommodation with the United States fitted smoothly into Bonaparte's over-all plan for a general peace. Meanwhile, in the United States, once Adams had weathered the outcries of the High Federalists, it was becoming apparent that Americans of both parties were generally supportive of the President's decision. In short, the negotiation, once launched, was almost certain to produce a treaty. All that remained was for each delegation in Paris to stake out its position and seek to discover how much of that position the other would agree to.

In essence the French agreed to pay maritime damages, but only if the United States would restore to full effect the old treaties of commerce and alliance which Congress had abrogated in the wake of XYZ. Alternatively, France was willing to consider those abrogations as final, but only if the United States would forego the claims. The American commissioners replied that the old treaties were dead beyond recall and that France must pay for her depredations on American commerce. Between these opposing positions there proved to be ample room for a wide variety of proposals and counter-proposals. In retrospect, it seems reasonable to suppose that the decision ultimately reached—that is, to postpone indefinitely any final determination of the status of old treaties and U.S. indemnity claims—could come only after all possible permutations of proposing had been exhausted. This, after all, is one of the tasks of diplomacy: to discover what cannot be agreed to, as well as what can. It took from March to September of 1800 to complete this process of sifting out unacceptable compromises.

As the delegations moved from one deadlock to another it was Murray and his French counterpart, Pierre Roederer, who emerged as the most active proposers and disposers of various compromises. To say this is not to disparage Oliver Ellsworth's intellectual leadership of the American delegation, nor to denigrate the influence which Talleyrand and Bonaparte imparted to the course of the negotiation. But Murray and Roederer gave the negotiation its internal dynamic, kept it moving, and hastened the setting aside of unworkable compromises so that both delegations could ultimately agree with good conscience that neither the indemnities nor the future of the old treaties could be determined at that time.

If this accomplishment seems wholly negative, the result proved to be salubrious. The Senate's subsequent deletion of the "postponing" article released the United States from its odious alliance with France. The price paid for this release was the amount of spoliation claims which American claimants thereafter sought to extract from Congress. In sum, an alliance that had been contracted "forever" was now set aside; and in return Congress assumed liability for paying off American claimants against France. This was the *quid pro quo* which Murray had strongly recommended midway during the negotiation. Had Murray's advice prevailed, the convention might have been signed in early August instead of at the end of September.

Nor was timing an unimportant consideration. As Murray was all too aware, a demonstrable diplomatic success at Paris would, if it came in time, advance John Adams' bid for reelection. That the convention came too late to serve that purpose sorely troubled him. Still, Murray recognized that the process of proposal and counter-proposal must be played out to the end. No alternative must be left untried, lest the charge later be made that he and his colleagues had failed to press with sufficient ardor for French indemnification. Thus Murray fell in loyally with his colleagues' efforts to revive as little of the old treaties as would win from France a commitment to pay for maritime spoliation. When this effort failed, and both treaties and indemnities were written off for future consideration, the greatest loss was time. Whether or not Murray was correct in believing that this loss contributed to Adams' electoral defeat is a question that cannot be answered, although the likelihood that the Senate would not have been called to act on the convention until after the election tends to lessen its importance. In the end, Murray consoled himself that it was not the tardiness of the convention which figured in Adams' defeat as much as it was the divisions within the Federalist party.

Although the treaty with France produced little political advantage to John Adams, there is no mistaking its service to the nation's vital interest in peace. To the extent that the avoidance of a major war did, in fact, give the United States time to strengthen her national institutions, the convention served well. John Adams recognized his own contribution when he asked that the fact that he had kept the peace with France be inscribed on his tombstone. That William Vans Murray also made a contribution constitutes the *raison d'être* for this study.

Part of Murray's effectiveness as a diplomat lay in his unswerving loyalty to John Adams—loyalty of a caliber too often lacking among the President's subordinates. This devotion made him the willing and sensitive instrument of the presidential peace policy, once he had discerned the direction of that policy, and no hint of disfavor from his fellow Federalists could divert him from the course of action which his loyalty to the President dictated he should take. Another part of Murray's success can be laid to his willingness to lean on the advice of the President's son. He clearly relied on John Quincy Adams for those steady and sobering counsels which the younger Adams could so readily administer. John Quincy's support gave him the boldness to act when action was called for, and lend a reflectiveness to that action which might otherwise have been missing.

Finally, Murray was an effective agent of diplomacy because he had a clear-sighted view of the importance of peace to his country's struggle for nationhood. Peace was the ground which must be held until the nation had fleshed out the bones of national power. Only once, and then only briefly, did he yield to the tempting prospect that his country in concert with Britain might gain more from war than from noninvolvement. The temptation passed quickly. Murray needed only a hint that John Adams would require certain assurances from Paris before sending another mission to set himself the task of securing those assurances. But as a nationalist, he knew that his country could not afford a dishonorable peace. For Adams' sake, but more important for the sake of national unity, France must offer substantial proof that she would not again use her approaches as a cover for a dalliance with American Republicans. By Murray's definition, an honorable peace was one that would not again set American against American. His countrymen had their own destiny to fulfill, and he saw it as one that would be leagued with neither France nor Britain.

Although Murray's attachment to national priorities helps to explain his diplomatic career, his earlier development as an American nationalist should not be overlooked. As a congressman he gave evidence of what it meant to be a thoughtful American groping for a definition of national identity. That groping was partially satisfied by the allegiance which he gave to Alexander Hamilton's financial program. He agreed with the Hamiltonians that a sound public credit was the sturdiest base on which to raise a national government. He agreed, too, that nothing would so gravely endanger the government's revenues (perhaps even the government itself) as a war with England, since the tariff levies on this commerce supplied most of the government's income.

Yet the same Murray who admired Hamilton and who defended Hamilton's treasury operations on the floor of the House, did not fit the stereotype of the merchant-speculator which comprised the core of the Hamiltonian following. Rather, he fitted more accurately the historian

Manning Dauer's depiction of the Agrarian Federalist—coastal farmers who adhered to Hamilton in peace and sound finance, but looked with distrust on Hamiltonian adventurism in foreign policy and sniffed disapprovingly at the interplay between government and speculators.

Murray's outrage at the Randall-Whitney land fraud scheme, his opposition to continuing the 1794 embargo lest it profit speculators in grain futures, his reluctance to accept the Hague post because it would involve tending to the unfamiliar details of servicing the U.S. debt—all these and other fragmentary evidences of distaste for monetary matters seemed to point to a political figure who was as aloof from the politicized commercial community as was John Adams (which was one reason the Hamiltonians distrusted Adams), or as far removed from commercial Federalism as were most of the Eastern Shore gentry whom he represented. And, like other Agrarian Federalists, Murray followed the Hamiltonians in foreign policy only as far as the water's edge where, when the latter embarked on plans for full-scale war, they parted company. Rather than a Hamiltonian, Murray was an "Adams-man," centrist, moderate, mildly agrarian, and intensely nationalistic. He could not be truly identified with the Southern Federalists; his own political circumstance was remote from the "clan" Federalism and opportunism of, for example, South Carolina's Pinckneys and Rutledges. Rather, by his own admission, he felt a closer kinship to the moderate Federalists of New England, men like his House colleague Samuel Dexter of Massachusetts and, of course, the Adamses.

It was also in the nature of Murray's evolving nationalism that he never gave full faith and credit to the leadership of the Federalist party. In every session of Congress he broke one or more times with that leadership, either leapfrogging the avowed intentions of the party or merely taking a course of action dictated by his own reading of what constituted the nation's best interest. A case in point would be his efforts to provide official "protections" to American seamen at a time when British impressments were increasing. The party failed to support him. For this streak of independency, so often recurring, Murray was never quite ostracized from the party, but neither was he accepted into its inner councils.

Although Murray refused to equate every partisan purpose with the national interest, he gave way unreservedly to the symbol of national unity embodied in the person of George Washington. No study of early American nationalism can omit reference to the charismatic and unifying influence of the first President. Murray felt this influence so pervasively that it is difficult to determine at what point his attachment to

Washington left off and a particularized awareness of national interest began. Thus, for example, Murray filled long pages of his diary with painstakingly detailed criticisms of the text of Jay's treaty, only to conclude that he would accept unquestioningly whatever decision the President might make respecting ratification. His Philadelphia acquaintance, Thomas L. Shippen, once wrote: "Murray is loyal to the President as if he were his king." In a nation that had existed only a short time without a king, Shippen's observation spoke as much to the nation's youthful need for personal leadership as it did to Murray's awareness of that need.

Murray's nationalism appeared most strikingly, perhaps, in his concern for the objects of public spending. Few would deny, then or now, that an important measure of national authority is the size of a national government's budget. Republicans saw this correlation between power and spending, and feared it. Federalists, including Murray, welcomed it. Whenever votes were needed for regiments or frigates, shipyards or fortresses, for better postal services or higher federal salaries, Murray was found on the side of the spenders. When Republicans cried out in alarm that the addition of another regiment or two would produce a "standing army" allegedly dangerous to states' rights and individual liberties, Murray was among those who reminded them that there was not a state in the Union that could not call forth a militia more numerous than the entire force of United States regulars.

Murray saw the Army as the vital instrument of frontier defense; he seldom envisioned it as an army of internal suppression. Only once after the days of the Whiskey Rebellion did he suggest (in writing, at least) that the Army might have to be used against his fellow citizens. This occurred at the height of the quasi-war when he wrote John Quincy Adams that some Americans might have to be persuaded by force to support the war against France, should that war reach full-scale proportions. As a member of Congress, however, whenever he spoke for increases in the Army it was in the context of defense of the frontier. And in the same framework, that of national defense, Murray also supported the establishment of a United States Navy. Like John Adams, he understood that a navy was not merely a device to protect American shipping, but that American frigates flying the American colors would also give the outside world the most visible evidence of his country's nationhood.

Any final assessment of William Vans Murray must recognize that the significance of the man's career did not lie in a succession of history-making acts; nor was his the story by which the nation's origins can be told. As a party Federalist, Murray was both different from and over-shadowed by such figures as Alexander Hamilton, Rufus King, Oliver Ellsworth, and Timothy Pickering. As a practicing diplomatist he yielded in stature to John Jay, Gouverneur Morris, the Adamses, and the Pinck-neys. He was, in short, a national figure of the second rank. Murray himself knew this and accepted it. When in 1801 he learned that Jeffer-son had posted Robert Livingston to Paris he wrote in his diary: "It is true I started the negotiation with France . . . helped to get it on, and now shall conclude it alone. Another is placed here—I hear Mr. Livingston—I never considered myself as on the first line of my country-men & on that score I can not complain—!"

In retrospect, Murray's most significant act was that he served John Adams' policy of peace at a time when an important segment of the Federalist party was bent on war. He received the French peace over-tures, shaped, certified, and conveyed them to President Adams. And because Adams found it expedient to respond favorably to those over-tures, Murray has found a secure place in the narrative of peacemaking, 1798–1800. That he acted not only out of loyalty to Adams but also from a well-defined sense of American nationhood makes this story at least a partial answer to Jean Crèvecoeur's famous question: "What then is the American, this new man?"

Notes on Sources

Although the author has consciously selected those letters and diary entries which seemed best to illustrate his subject's place in history, he freely admits to not having done justice to the rich, profuse, and often incisive strokes with which Murray painted the persons and events of his era. Murray had a keen eye for nuance; he wrote reflectively and usually with candor. Had he not been so reticent about the details of his personal life, this biographical study could easily have become a full-scale biography. As it is, his letters and diaries will continue to be a rewarding source of insights to the serious student of the Federalist period.

Four diaries and three boxes of letters comprise the major holding of Murray papers at the Library of Congress. Another diary is at the Princeton University Library. The dates which Murray gave to his volumes of "Commonplace" are not to be taken at face value, however. His diary entries often do not follow in unbroken sequence; each volume contains entries which, though dated, may be widely separated in time. As for Murray's letters, the largest single collection is contained in the five letterbook volumes held by the Pierpont Morgan Library in New York. This collection, mostly copies of personal and official correspondence, is particularly useful for Murray's exchanges with Rufus King. The most accessible collection of Murray letters, however, is the series published in the *Annual Report of the American Historical Association for the Year 1912.* Edited by Worthington C. Ford, this collection of Murray's letters to John Quincy Adams during the period 1797 to 1803 runs to 361 pages and has been well indexed. The best source for Murray's early political outlook is, of course, his own *Political Sketches,* published in London in 1787. This ninety-six-page work contains six essays, entitled "Abbé Mably," "Virtue," "Aristocracy," "Extent of Territory," "Balance of Power," and "Religion." Alexander DeConde has published an excellent analysis of these essays in his "William Vans Murray's *Political Sketches:* A Defense of the American Experiment." *The Mississippi Valley Historical Review,* XLI, No. 4 (March 1955). DeConde may, however, have exaggerated the young Murray's advocacy of a stronger executive. The Brown University Library has a copy of the *Sketches*. Besides these major sources, items of Murray correspondence may also be found in collections of the Maryland Historical Society, the Huntington Library, the Eleutherian Mills Historical Library, and the American Philosophical Society.

The microfilming of the Adams Papers has made it easy to piece together John Quincy Adams' replies to Murray's letters during the significant period of their relationship, 1797–1801. With James McHenry, however, the exchanges tend to be fragmentary. The Maryland Historical Society has the most complete holding of McHenry-Murray correspondence, although the Library of Congress also has some items in its McHenry collection. The more important pieces were published in 1907 in Bernard C. Steiner's *Life and Correspondence of James McHenry*. Also useful to this study were the papers of Sylvanus Bourne, Elbridge Gerry, the Shippen Family, and William Loughton Smith, all at the Library of Congress; the papers of Rufus King at the New York Historical Society, and the enormously important Pickering collection at the Massachusetts Historical Society. Murray had an intermittent correspondence with George Washington (fourteen letters dealing almost exclusively with political appointments in Maryland, held by the Library of Congress), and an even more fragmentary correspondence with Alexander Hamilton. His letters to Republican figures were entirely official in nature.

Official documents also constituted an important source. The substance of Murray's diplomatic activity has been derived from the General Records of the Department of State, Record Group 59, at the National Archives. His dispatches from The Hague, as well as those which he wrote from Paris in the summer of 1801, may be found in volumes II, III, and IV of "Despatches from the Netherlands," although a more convenient compilation is the single volume of duplicate despatches which I have cited as "Netherlands Despatches, I." Also helpful were the relevant volumes of consular dispatches from Rotterdam, Amsterdam, and Paris, the Instructions to U.S. Ministers, the Instructions to U.S. Consuls, and Notes to Foreign Missions, all in Record Group 59 at the National Archives. The most important French sources, official in nature, were volumes 49–52 from the *Archives du Ministère des Affaires Etrangères, Correspondance Politique, Etats Unis,* photostatic copies of which were available at the Library of Congress.

A number of recently published secondary works, some of them biographical, testify to the continuing attention which American historians are giving to the Federalist period. Most competent and far-ranging of these is Alexander DeConde's *The Quasi-War* (New York, 1966), which covers a broad spectrum of diplomatic and political events on both sides of the Atlantic throughout the crisis with France. Gerard H. Clarfield, in his *Timothy Pickering and American Diplomacy, 1795–1800* (Columbia, Mo., 1969), has written a solid and much-needed appraisal of Adams' Francophobic Secretary of State; a work which clearly shows that Pickering was more than willing to abandon the policy of neutrality in favor of full-scale war with France, in alliance with Britain. Marvin R. Zahniser's *Charles Cotesworth Pinckney: Founding Father* (Chapel Hill, N.C., 1967) contains a detailed but readable account of the Pinckney-Marshall-Gerry encounter with Talleyrand and his agents in 1797–98. Robert Ernst's biography *Rufus King: American Federalist* (Chapel Hill, N.C., 1968), does full justice to its subject and leaves few questions unanswered about the hardworking and well-respected New York statesman who served at the American legation in London during this period. George C. Rogers, Jr., has written what must be considered the definitive biography of William Loughton Smith. His *Evolution of a Federalist* (Columbia, S.C., 1962) says more about the South Carolina politics, however, than about Smith's rather unimportant mission to Lisbon.

Older biographies of Murray's contemporaries have been only marginally useful. James T. Austin's *Life of Elbridge Gerry* (Boston, 1828–1829), worthless except for the Gerry letters which it includes, is due to be superseded. William Garrott Brown's *Life of Oliver Ellsworth* (New York, 1905) suffers from a paucity of sources which may not be remediable. Blackwell P. Robinson's *William R. Davie* (Chapel Hill, N.C., 1957) does little to clarify Governor Davie's role during the negotiation of the Franco-American convention.

Of the more general works on the Federalist period, Stephen G. Kurtz's *The Presidency of John Adams* (Philadelphia, 1957) continues to stand forth as a first-rate analysis of party politics and of the issues which contributed to the collapse of the Federalist party in 1800. Page Smith has thoroughly mined the Adams papers to produce a sound and vivaciously written two-volume biography, *John Adams* (Garden City, N.Y., 1962). It is from Manning J. Dauer, however, that I have borrowed most heavily for the insights contained in *The Adams Federalists* (Baltimore, 1953). Dauer analyzes the political and economic ideas of the "Adams-men" which differentiated them from the Hamiltonian and Jeffersonian groups. He finds that Adams relied for political support on moderate Federalists, the most important of whom were export-dependent agrarians. Dauer concludes that Adams was unable or perhaps unwilling to organize a party of moderates in the aftermath of the High Federalist schism, and that Jefferson was the inevitable beneficiary of that failure.

Three scholarly articles have a particular bearing on this study. One is E. Wilson Lyon's "The Franco-American Convention of 1800," *Journal of Modern History,* XII (September 1940), 305–33, which is solidly based on French archival sources but lacking in perspective because of Lyon's failure to make use of the Murray diaries. More recent is Alexander DeConde's "William Vans Murray and the Diplomacy of Peace, 1797–1800," *The Maryland Historical Magazine,* XLVIII (March 1953), 1–26. An elaboration of the DeConde article entitled "The Role of William Vans Murray in the Peace Negotiations between France and the United States, 1800," appeared the previous year in *The Huntington Library Quarterly*. This article established that Murray's diplomacy made it possible for John Adams to confound the Federalist war hawks. Most recent of all is Stephen G. Kurtz's article, "The French Mission of 1799–1800: Concluding Chapter in the Statecraft of John Adams," *Political Science Quarterly*, LXXX (December 1965), 543–57. Kurtz suggests that John Adams' fear of domestic unrest was the principal reason for his appointment of Murray in February 1799. Further, the author finds that Adams delayed the sending of Ellsworth and Davie to Paris not because the High Federalists obstructed him, but rather because Adams was content not to hasten the negotiation until the three new American frigates had put to sea.

To these scholars, and the many others who will see their books and scholarly articles footnoted throughout this work, I extend the sincere hope that they will not find that I have misconstrued either their findings or their conclusions. Except for these "Notes on Sources," the footnotes themselves comprise the working bibliography. Readers will find that the first entry of every source and secondary work has been cited by the name of the author or editor, the full title of the work, and the facts of publication. Whenever possible, individual letters have been cited in the published sources rather than the manuscript collection.

Index